QUANTUM INVESTING

Quantum Physics, Nanotechnology, and the Future of the Stock Market

STEPHEN R. WAITE

Foreword by
Michael J. Mauboussin

Australia · Canada · Mexico · Singapore · Spain · United Kingdom · United States

Quantum Investing:
Quantum Physics, Nanotechnology,
and the Future of the Stock Market
Stephen R. Waite

Co-author of *Boomernomics*

In loving memory of my father,
Barry F. Waite, M.D.

There is a tide in the affairs of men
Which taken at the flood, leads on to fortune;
Omitted, all the voyage of their life
Is bound in shallows and in miseries.

William Shakespeare

CONTENTS

by Michael J. Mauboussin

In the past 50,000 years, a combination of genetic and cultural evolution has shaped what is today the human condition. Remarkably, our genetic makeup remains largely unchanged, and it still plays a significant role in our emotions and perceptions. Now, however, we have the inescapable sense that we're hurtling down a path of extraordinary change in our cultural evolution. This is not steady progress—in fact, if anything, the rate of change is *accelerating*.

Ideas are to cultural evolution what genes are to genetic evolution. Over the centuries, humans have developed and put to work many useful ideas. And these ideas, like genes, don't die. Like genetic evolution, cultural evolution draws on the accumulation of ideas passed from person to person and from generation to generation. Today, humans still have access to nearly all "fit" ideas from the past and the present.

Cultural evolution and change are inextricably linked. Innovation is rarely the result of a unique and isolated idea, but rather the product of existing ideas being combined in new ways.

The more attempts that are made to solve problems, the greater are the chances in finding solutions. In turn, today's solutions are tomorrow's building blocks.

Here's a simple example: Assume you have four building blocks (possible solutions). The number of combinations is 4 x 3 x 2 x 1, or 24. If you increase the number of blocks from four to six, the amount of possible combinations—6 x 5 x 4 x 3 x 2 x 1, or 720—is 30 times higher! As we mix and match a greater number of blocks, we see an increasing, or nonlinear rate of change.

Stephen Waite is one of the very few investors who thoroughly understands this process. Fortunately for the rest of us, *Quantum Investing* explores this engine of change in a lucid and informed way. Waite shows us how yesterday's building blocks have led us to the advances we enjoy today and gives us a captivating glimpse of the types of new structures we can expect in the future. He makes a convincing case that discoveries in emerging technologies—nanotechnology, biotechnology, and quantum computing—will change our lives more in the next few generations than all of the technological breakthroughs of the past century combined. This look into the future alone makes *Quantum Investing* an important book. Waite's message comes through with a serious tone but also with an infectious enthusiasm and appropriate sense of wonder.

Even though investors may find innovation fascinating, they are more interested in making money and betting on stocks. Capitalism is a process that effectively, and sometimes ruthlessly, allocates resources. In a well-functioning capitalist system, capital freely flows to the businesses and stocks that promise high returns and flees those not likely to deliver appropriate profits. The system is not perfect, but it is efficient at facilitating wealth creation.

Financial asset prices, stock prices in particular, reflect investors' expectations for future financial performance. The key to successful investing is to know what level of future financial performance is embedded in today's stock price and to be able to revise one's expectations. What's going on today is not as important as what will happen in the future. Investors must constantly peer into an uncertain future and anticipate change.

How should an investor approach this Delphic task? Berkshire Hathaway's Charlie Munger, one of the most successful and intelligent investors ever, advocates the use of "mental models." Munger argues that investors should build a latticework of mental models—frameworks that reflect reality—in order to effectively anticipate changes in stock prices. Investors with too few models, or improper models, will fail. Munger notes investors' models must be interdisciplinary—solely understanding and applying finance and accounting principles is insufficient. Investors need to get out and explore the world.

Quantum Investing advocates the mental models approach and presents some of the most significant models for today's informed and thoughtful investors. One example is the rising significance of intangible assets. Business has always combined capital—both physical and human—and ideas. Capital drove wealth creation in the past, but ideas have the upper hand today. Since idea-oriented assets have properties and characteristics that are distinct from physical assets, investors need a mental model that captures this pendulum swing. In providing a framework and insights on this important topic, Waite expertly guides investors through discussions of diverse ideas, including complexity theory, bounded rationality, and swarm intelligence.

A discussion of *Quantum Investing* would be incomplete without pointing out two significant ironies: First, Waite stresses throughout the book that the edifice of economics remains deficient in explaining the basic process of change and the workings of markets. Investors who uncritically imbibe economic dogma will be ill-prepared for the future. Second is the irony that the astonishing technological change we see—the source of wealth creation and destruction—has noxious byproducts, including a torrent of information and shortened investor attention spans. Both of these points are antithetical to successful long-term investing.

Thoughtful investors must turn down the volume on the financial TV show and pay limited attention to business periodicals so that they can allocate their time and attention to creating and fortifying their mental models. *Quantum Investing* is a terrific place to start.

Tempus fugit. It's been nearly two years since the hardcover version of *Quantum Investing* was published and much has transpired over that period. As good fortune would have it, there appears to be a renewed appetite for books on technology and investing. Much to my delight, the timing of the hardcover edition coincided with the bottom of the 2000–2002 bear market in U.S. stocks. Contrary to the conventional wisdom of just a couple of years ago, the Fifth Wave is alive and well.

The publication of this paperback edition of *Quantum Investing* has coincided with heightened interest in nanotechnology from investors and companies all around the world. I have long thought that nanotechnology could become "the mother of all quantum revolutions in technology"—a revolution so powerful that it could dwarf the first Industrial Revolution in terms of its economic impact. The nanotech revolution is still in its infancy, and it will be decades before the full fruits of the revolution are harvested. Many of the world's largest corporations, including DuPont, General Electric, General Motors, Hewlett-Packard, IBM and Intel are currently engaged in basic nanotech research and product development and there are thousands of small and medium size companies working around the world to commercialize nanotech in a diverse range of industries. With competition heating up, we can expect to see some dazzling nanotech products hit the market in coming months and years.

Nanotech has become the buzzword du jour in global financial markets and is receiving a great deal of attention from the mainstream media. My friends at Lux Capital, one of the world's premier nanotech venture capital firms and publishers of *The Forbes/Wolfe Nanotech Report*, conducted a search last year through nearly six thousand publications over the past seven years to get an indication of how hyped nanotech had become. They found the number of mentions of the word "nanotech" had increased by some 3,000% from approximately 200 in 1995 to more than 6,000 in 2003. By way of comparison and inference, in 1991 and 1992 there were on average 500 articles with the word "internet." In 1993, 2,713 articles and in 1994 and 1995, 16,912 and 70,951 articles respectively, from a Dow Jones publication search. Based on this, Lux Capital infers that we are at the point in the nanotechnology "hype-line" that equates to 1993, just prior to the Internet boom.

The nanotech revolution is getting increasing attention on Wall Street. Last Spring, Steven Milunovich and his forward-looking technology colleagues at Merrill Lynch launched the *Merrill Lynch Nanotech Index* (the stock market ticker is 'NNZ'). At the time of this writing, there are 22 nanotech companies in the Merrill Lynch Nanotech Index. That may not seem like a large number of companies but remember that the Dow Jones Industrial Average began with 12 companies back in 1896. Of the 30 companies listed in the index today we are likely to witness a great deal of turnover in the index as the Nanotech revolution evolves. To be included in the Nanotech index companies must indicate in public documents that nanotechnology initiatives represent a significant component of their future business strategy. Merrill Lynch designed the index so that investors could more easily track the stock performance of nanotech companies. The fact that a large, global financial services company such as Merrill Lynch is getting involved in Nanotech suggests that investors will be hearing a lot more about nanotechnology in the future.

Many folks may not be aware that even the great "value" investors Warren Buffett and Charlie Munger—self-proclaimed technophobes—expressed an interest in nanotech last year when they bid for Burlington Industries. Burlington is a textile conglomerate that owns a 51% stake in Nano-Tex. Nano-Tex is a company that is creating some of the most revolutionary innovations in the textile market in over half a century. Nano-Tex is utilizing the principles of nanotechnology to create exceptional performance in everyday items: apparel, home furnishings, commercial interiors, and industrial fabrics. Nano-Tex produces polymers that attach to or wrap around fibers to make fabric stain-proof, wrinkle-free and absorbent. Nano-Tex's stain-resistance technology is being incorporated into Gap, Old Navy and Brooks Brothers clothing lines. Nike Inc. is using Nano-Tex's sweat-repellant technology for Tiger Woods golf pants. Buffett and Munger are no strangers to the textile industry. Berkshire Hathaway was a textile company acquired by Buffett decades ago. Berkshire's bid for Burlington and Nano-Tex was not successful. However, the fact that Buffett and Munger wanted to acquire an interest in Burlington was intriguing—especially given their general reluctance to invest in technology companies.

By the time this book is published, the first significant nanotech initial public offering (IPO) in the United States should be in the history books. More nanotech companies will surely follow, although I suspect this wave of IPOs will pale in comparison to what we saw in the 1990s with the dot coms—both in magnitude and in duration. If anything, the nanotech IPO cycle is likely to be similar to what we witnessed with biotechnology stocks in the late 1970s—a flurry of activity in financial markets followed by a winnowing out process and recovery by a select few companies that have built sustainable competitive advantages. As the nanotech sector evolves, there will be many companies who will be what I call "Nano Pretenders" and a select few companies that will be legitimate "Nano Contenders." This is a typical pattern we see throughout business and financial history. The sciences of complexity, which I discuss at length in Chapters 6 and 7, tell us that this pattern of speciation and extinction in business and financial markets is a reoccurring pattern found throughout nature. We should not be at all surprised if, nanotechnology evolves in a similar way.

The future of the stock market and Joseph Schumpeter's process *creative destruction* are discussed at length in my book. Since the publication of the hardcover, there's been no shortage of creative destruction in the business world and financial markets. Earlier this year, three companies—AT&T, Kodak and International Paper—were dropped from the Dow Jones Industrial Average (DJIA). AT&T (a.k.a. "Ma Bell") had been a consistent Dow component since 1939. International Paper had been included in the index since 1956, while Kodak had been part of the Dow since 1930. AIG, Pfizer and Verizon replaced these former blue chip companies in the DJIA.

In my view, recent changes to the Dow Jones Industrial Average— one of the most widely recognized and quoted stock market indexes in the world—are just the tip of the iceberg. I'm anticipating a lot more turnover in the DJIA in coming years. Given my expectation of accelerating technology change, I wouldn't be surprised if half of the stocks currently in the DJIA were replaced by 2010.

If there has been reluctance by the general public to read my book it probably owes to the somewhat intimidating title. In my travels, I have heard over and over again that the word "quantum" scares people. If you want to watch a dinner party conversation come to an abrupt end just mention the word "quantum." I guarantee that people will head for the bar faster than a New York minute. But whether we like it or not, quantum is here to stay. Quantum technology is seeping into the foundation of the global economy at an accelerating pace. It accounts for over one-third of U.S. GDP today and one-quarter of global GDP and that share is destined to rise rapidly.

Consider this list of headlines I pulled from various sources off the World Wide Web in the first half of 2004:

"Quantum Computers Are A Quantum Leap Closer"
(Source: Purdue University)

"IBM Finds Ally For Supercomputer-On-A-Chip" (CNET News.com)

"High Speed Nanotube Transistors Could Lead To Better Cell Phones, Faster Computers" (Source: American Chemical Society)

"Diagnostic Method Based on Nanoscience Could Rival PCR" (Source: Northwestern University)

"Optical Quantum Memory Designed" (Technology Review)

"Could Nanomachines Be Tomorrow's Doctors?" (Nature)

"DNA Self-Assembles Carbon Nanotube Transistor"
(Source: Nanotechweb.org)

"Light-Storing Chip Charted" (Source: Technology Review)

"Nanowire Sensors to Allow Instant Medical Tests" (Source: American Chemical Society)

"Quantum Encryption Inches Closer To Reality" (CNET News.com)

"IBM Exploits Self-Assembly To Make Nanocrystal Memory" (Source: Nanotechweb.org)

A modern day Rip Van Winkle waking up and reading these headlines would no doubt have a very difficult time comprehending the pace of technology change today. Heck, I've been wide-awake for the past couple decades and even I am finding it difficult to keep pace with the accelerating pace of technological change.

Scientist Vernor Vinge envisions a time not too far off in the future when it becomes impossible for humans to keep up with the pace of technological change. I discuss Vinge's vision of the future—dubbed "The Singularity"—in the conclusion of *Quantum Investing*. And while we are not quite there yet, the time when technological change accelerates to a rate beyond our comprehension appears to be on the horizon. When that day arrives is anybody's guess. Vinge believes that it will be within the next 25 years. Some scientists believe it may come sooner, while others say the event is unlikely in our lifetime. Once the Singularity is reached, Vinge believes our old models will have to be discarded because of the emergence of a new reality. On this point, there seems to be little disagreement among scientists.

Many analysts and investors continue to cling to the notion that there isn't anything new under the sun—that the old ways of doing their jobs and looking at the world are sufficient to be successful in financial markets. I think this is a dangerous perspective to have today. Quantum science wasn't around before 1900. It has taken over a century for the nanotechnology revolution to get revved up. Despite the fact that quantum physics may be the most successful science in the history of civilization, scientists' understanding of the quantum world is still primitive. Quantum entanglement is still a mystery as is the phenomena of superconducting. Interestingly, the challenge of quantum computing—that is, harnessing the power of entangled "qubits" to compute—is a driving force today behind efforts to understand the most philosophical and abstract scientific underpinnings of quantum mechanics.

New quantum-based technologies are providing scientists with ever-more powerful microscopy tools that allow them to peer into the Nanoworld. Earlier this year, a major manufacturer of nanotech tools announced that the company's scientists broke the one-Angstrom image resolution barrier with a 200kV transmission electron microscope. This breakthrough allows images to be viewed directly with a resolution of one-tenth of a nanometer in size. A nanometer is one billionth of a meter and one Angstrom is approximately one-third the size of a carbon atom and is a key dimension for atomic level research. With the ability to attain direct, artifact-free images of atoms, the path has been paved for nanotechnology researchers to explore materials at the highest resolution in history.

Like Galileo before them, scientists today have the ability to see things that people only once dreamed of seeing. What they discover in the years ahead using powerful Atomic Force, Scanning Tunneling and Transmission Electron microscopes and other advanced nano metrology tools will in all likelihood have as powerful impact on our understanding of the quantum world as Galileo's telescope had on our understanding of the heavens above.

Speaking of heaven, it's been over three years since my father passed away. There isn't a day that goes by that I don't think of him. Nobody has, or will ever have, a greater positive influence on my life. His love, guidance, encouragement and support were the greatest gifts a son could ever receive. This book is dedicated to him. My mother and my brothers, Lowell and Brad, have been with me through thick and thin. For their unending love and enduring support, I am forever grateful. I would like to send extra special heart-felt thanks to my two beautiful daughters, Madeleine and Kensington—I love you more than words can express.

I owe a big debt of gratitude to my publisher, Myles Thompson, for sticking his neck out at a time when technology was a dirty word in the stock market and for publishing this edition of my book. My former editor Victoria Larson deserves a warm thank you, as does Michael Mauboussin for his Foreword. Thanks also goes out to my nano friends at Lux Capital, Josh Wolfe, Peter Hebert and Rob Paull, as well as to Susan Ballatti and her colleagues at the Santa Fe Institute. Appreciation also goes out to my partners at TheInfoPro. Inc, Dean Mark Thompson of the Quinnipiac Business School, Keith Blakely, Allan and Norman Rothstein of NanoDynamics, Christopher Meyer, Harris Collingwood, Seth Godin, Mark Anderson, Stuart Kauffman, Baruch Lev, Steve Milunovich, Jonathan Rothberg, Michael Rothschild, Gerry Scanlon and Robin Griffiths. Thanks to Scott Schramke and Tomas Stuardo for excellent IT support. Last but not least, I would like to thank my quantum-entangled musical friends Paul Avgerinos, Jeff Epstein, Gene Foley, Tim Godwin and especially Christine Yandell for sharing their extraordinary talents with me.

For those who would like to stay informed of the quantum revolution in technology and its implications for financial markets and investing, check out my website www.quantuminvesting.net. While visiting the website, please sign up to receive a free subscription to *Vitamin B*, your weekly informational supplement of all important things associated with quantum investing.

Stephen Waite
Shelton, Connecticut

An Investor's Lament:
Uncertainty and Opportunity

> The fundamental law of investing is the uncertainty of
> the future.
>
> —Peter Bernstein

The Dow Jones Industrial Average is the best known and most frequently quoted stock market index in the world. Turn on the TV and you hear commentators talking about the Dow rising or falling by *some* number of points during the day. To say how the U.S. stock market did on any given day, people often refer to the performance of the Dow Jones industrials, and not to the many other indexes monitored by investors. To many people, the Dow is the stock market.

What few people realize is how the market has evolved. The market that investors and commentators analyze today is a far cry from the market that existed a century ago. Back in 1896, when it was created, the Dow Jones Industrial Average comprised twelve companies.

The Dow Twelve were the bluest of blue chips, and if you were an investor, you had to consider owning many, if not all, of these stocks. The daily, weekly, monthly, and yearly performance of this small group of blue chip industrials gauged the health and vibrancy of the U.S. economy. If Tennessee Coal and Iron, Chicago Gas, and the other Dow industrials were on the rise, so was the U.S. economy.

The Dow Jones Industrial Average then . . .

American Cotton Oil	American Sugar
American Tobacco	Chicago Gas
Distilling and Cattle Feeding	General Electric
Laclede Gas	National Lead
North American Electric	Tennessee Coal and Iron
U.S. Rubber	U.S. Leather

To even the most casual observers, there are striking features of the original Dow Twelve. First, many of the companies were manufacturers and distributors of basic commodities and natural resources. Second, the index was well represented by energy and utilities. Third, eleven of the twelve original Dow stocks are not in the index today. The only survivor is General Electric.

. . . and the Dow now

Alcoa	American Express	AT&T
Boeing	Caterpillar	Citigroup
Coca-Cola	DuPont	Eastman Kodak
Exxon Mobil	General Electric	General Motors
Hewlett-Packard	Home Depot	Honeywell
IBM	Intel	International Paper
Johnson & Johnson	JP Morgan	McDonald's
Merck	Microsoft	Minnesota Mining (3M)
Philip Morris	Procter & Gamble	SBC Communications
United Technologies	Wal-Mart	Walt Disney

What a difference a century makes. Comparing the Dow of 1896 to the Dow of 2001, one can't help but be amazed by the turnover in the market. It's also remarkable how much more diverse the industrials index is today versus one hundred years ago. Resource, energy, and utility stocks are now a much smaller share of the overall market. Over the years, the Dow has evolved to include transportation, financial services, consumer products, IT, pharmaceuticals, and media and entertainment.

Today's Dow is far more complex than the Dow our great-grandparents and grandparents monitored. Industries that didn't exist or were fledgling a century ago are now key constituents of the stock market. What happened? Why is the stock market so different today? The chief underlying cause is related to advances in science and technological invention and innovation.

SOURCES OF CHANGE

Commenting on the evolution of the global economy at the dawn of the new millennium, the physicist Stephen Hawking noted in "A Brief History of Relativity,"

> The world has changed far more in the past 100 years than in any other century in history. The reason is not political or economic, but technological—technologies that flowed directly from advances in basic science.

Hawking's brilliant insight goes a long way toward explaining why we have seen a seismic shift in the industry composition of the stock market in the past century. Intel and Microsoft, for example, would not be in the Dow index were it not for the development of quantum theory (hereafter used interchangeably with quantum mechanics or quantum physics). Quantum theory is the branch of science that deals with the behavior of matter and light and all things in nature at the atomic and subatomic levels.

In the past several decades, quantum-based technologies have become a significant part of the products and services of nearly half the companies in the Dow Jones Industrial Average. These include General Electric, Hewlett-Packard, IBM, United Technologies, Boeing, 3M, DuPont, Honeywell, SBC Communications, AT&T, Merck, Johnson & Johnson, and Eastman Kodak.

Scientific and technological advances have played a major role in the economy for centuries. Economic historians trace the beginnings of the industrial revolution to the discoveries of Sir Isaac Newton, the English physicist. Newton and his fellow scientists provided the foundation for a number of revolutionary technologies that profoundly altered the economic landscape in the eighteenth and nineteenth centuries.

Newton's physics, still taught to high school students all over the world, continues to exert a powerful influence on the economy. However, advances in the new science of quantum mechanics are fueling another technology revolution that will have economic and social impacts even greater than Newton's.

Scientists began to apply their knowledge of the quantum world more than sixty years ago. The fruits of their efforts produced an explosion of new inventions, including the transistor, the microprocessor, the laser, and superconductors. These inventions, in turn, led to the development of personal computers, cellular phones, optical-based communication networks, CD and DVD players, digital cameras, and magnetic resonance imaging machines, as well as many other products and services.

You don't need a Ph.D. in physics or mathematics to appreciate the astonishing inventions and innovations that have been driven by advances in quantum mechanics. These myriad technologies are meshed with the daily lives of consumers and businesses all over the world. Physicists John Archibald Wheeler and Max Tegmark in "100 Years of Quantum Mysteries" estimate that nearly one third of the U.S. gross national product, or $3 trillion, is now based on inventions made possible by quantum mechanics. Moreover, the lion's share of the growth in the U.S. economy in the 1990s can be traced to inventions and innovations based on quantum physics.

SMALL IS BIG

Scientists tell us that the quantum revolution in technology is just beginning. Just over the horizon is an abundance of products that people think border on science fiction. The mother of all quantum revolutions—the nanotechnology revolution—has the potential to be to the twenty-first century what microelectronics was to the twentieth century.

Nobel Prize-winning scientist Richard Smalley recently observed that even though our twentieth-century technology is fantastic, it pales compared to what will be possible when we learn to build things at the ultimate level of control: one atom at a time. Scientists' ability to construct new technologies from the atomic level up is at a primitive stage today. Yet the commercialization of new quantum-based nanotechnologies could arrive faster than many people think.

In the twenty-first century, small will be big—very big. The convergence of quantum-based technologies will usher in major changes in medicine and health care. The mapping of the human genome in 2000—made possible by the advent of high-speed computing—was a seminal event in the history of civilization. Scientists can only speculate what kind of impact advances in innovative medical technologies will have on industry, businesses, and households in the future.

William Haseltine, chairman and CEO of Human Genome Sciences, believes that in ten to twenty years, more than half of new medicines, if not more, will be gene-based medicines that repair, restore, and restructure our bodies. Francis Collins, director of the National Human Genome Research Institute, believes that by 2010, gene variants for common diseases will be known. Predictive tests will be available for dozens of disorders, with intervention available for most of these conditions. By the end of the decade, Collins believes, primary care providers will practice genetic medicine, and he foresees gene-based designer drugs marketed for several diseases. Cancer therapy will target the molecular fingerprint of each tumor type, and cancer is likely to become a manageable disease, as diabetes is today. Drug susceptibility will be evaluated before prescriptions are written. Diagnosis of mental illness will improve, and new therapies will be developed.

Nanotechnology and biotechnology are just two of the revolutions being fueled by advances in quantum physics. Superconductors, quantum computing, all-optical communications networks, and synthetic quantum-based materials promise to send shock waves through many industries and sectors of the economy in the twenty-first century.

As was the case during the industrial revolution, the upheaval and dislocations caused by the quantum revolution will be painful. But the hardships caused by the wrenching change will be overshadowed by the significant rise in living standards. Abundance will overwhelm scarcity. Economists will learn that in the quantum economy, there are no limits to growth, only limits to our imagination.

THROUGH THE LOOKING GLASS

On the eve of potentially the biggest technology revolution in history, one can't help but wonder what the stock market is going to look like in twenty-five years. How many companies in the Dow Jones Industrial Average today will still be part of the index in 2025? How many companies will be in the Dow index? If the twentieth century is any guide, about twenty-seven of the thirty stocks currently in the Dow will not be part of the index in the future.

Nobody knows for sure which companies will survive the twenty-first century. It's a safe bet, however, that the companies that are dropped from the index will look as antiquated to investors then as many of the original Dow Twelve look today. *Holding stocks in companies that embrace and harness the awesome power of quantum physics will be a very profitable investment strategy in the years ahead.*

Although professional investors are judged year in and year out on how they perform relative to an index, such as the Dow, they rarely outperform the market. It is well known on Wall Street that three-fourths of active investment managers consistently do not beat the market. So investors who don't make a living at investing shouldn't feel too bad. Even the pros find the stock market rough sledding.

What makes it so difficult to beat an index like the Dow? People on Wall Street give many rationales, most related to the conventional view that financial markets are highly efficient in processing information and it is difficult for any individual to consistently outperform the collective wisdom of thousands of investors. There is much truth to this rationale, but it is not the whole story.

The stock market is a complex adaptive system made up of interactions among diverse individuals. It is unconventional to think of the stock market in this way. In financial text books, the conventional image of the stock market is one populated with investors who have perfect foresight and complete knowledge of the underlying structure of the economy. In the textbook world of efficient markets, prices adjust instantaneously to new information because it is assumed that variations in expectations cannot exist. Crashes and bubbles are alien to the textbook world, and technological invention and innovation are determined outside the economic system. In short, the textbook world of the stock market is almost always in equilibrium and consists only of omniscient, homogenous investors.

It's difficult for some investors (including me) to reconcile this world with the real world. Anybody who has spent even a little time on Wall Street knows that the textbook world many of us were taught in school does not exist, and, more importantly, cannot exist. Expectations are diverse among investors—some have short time horizons, others much longer time horizons. Prices adjust with varying speeds, depending on the characteristics of the market and individual securities. Crashes and bubbles occur periodically. Fat-tail events (i.e., events with low probabilities) are common. Technological change is endogenous to the economic system; that is, it is determined within the economic system. Disequilibrium, not equilibrium, is the norm in the real world.

It's absurd to assume that a species with our brain structures could understand the underlying structure of the global economy. As evolutionary psychologists know well, the neocortex is a fine piece of machinery, but it is not capable of comprehending the complexity in the marketplace. Investors don't have perfect foresight and can never have complete knowledge of the structure of the economy. Indeed, one of the greatest investors of all time, Warren Buffett, has repeatedly told shareholders of Berkshire Hathaway stock that he is not fond of investing in technology stocks, because he does not fully understand technology.

Longtime investment counselor and market practitioner Peter Bernstein says the fundamental law of investing is the uncertainty of the future. Certainty has no place in the real world of investing. It is clear to many seasoned Wall Street money managers that there is a huge chasm between the textbook world of financial markets and the real world. What may not be clear is that the chasm is even wider as we enter the twenty-first century. Many investors already suffer from an acute case of what Alvin Toffler calls "future shock." This malady may help explain the Icaruslike behavior of dotcom stocks in the past several years.

Beating the market will continue to be a difficult task for most analysts and investors. First, many professional investors were taught they can't beat the market. Second, the stock market of the twenty-first century will not resemble the economy of the last century, because advances in quantum physics and other sciences are changing the global economic and business landscape. Analysts and investors who comprehend the underpinnings of the technology will have an edge on those who cling to the past.

The models, mind-sets, and metrics that investors use to analyze companies must be updated for the twenty-first century. The life science companies of tomorrow are not identical in corporate and organizational structure to the Distilling and Cattle Feedings of yesteryear. The communication companies of the twenty-first century will not resemble Ma Bell. Tangible, natural resource-based assets will no longer be the preeminent source of value and wealth creation in the global economy.

At the dawn of the third millennium, intangible assets, products of quantum physics-based technologies, are the dominant asset and source of growth and wealth. These technologies leverage the human mind in the same manner that Newtonian physics-based technologies leveraged human muscle. Investors' expectations in financial markets will shift dramatically as what economist Joseph Schumpeter calls a gale of *creative destruction* ebbs and flows, disposing of obsolete products and services.

PEERING INTO THE QUANTUM FUTURE

As we will see in the chapters to come, quantum-based technologies are unique in several key respects:

1. They produce waves of economic activity.

2. They leverage the human mind.

3. They grow exponentially or even superexponentially in power.

4. They generate complexity.

• • •

By their very nature, quantum-based technological invention and innovation are wavelike. Advances in quantum theory have spawned new products that have altered the economy and they will continue to do so. Chapter 1 explains quantum physics and how it contributes to the development of new goods and services that are permanently changing our society.

Several of the revolutionary technologies based on quantum physics can be classified as general-purpose technologies (GPTs) that have a widespread impact on the economy. The digital computer is a GPT, as were the steam engine and the automobile. Conventional economic business cycle analysis cannot explain the dynamics of growth associated with technology. In Chapter 2, we turn to the economics of Joseph Schumpeter, who asserted that technological change is the driving force of economic development. Chapter 3 explores the convergence of quantum-based innovations and how they will change the business and economic landscape.

The power of quantum technologies rises exponentially, that is, in a multiplicative fashion rather than arithmetically. Exponential growth is a feature of any evolutionary process, of which quantum technology is a primary example. Some scientists believe that the global economy could experience the same amount of technical change in the next twenty-five years that it experienced during the entire twentieth century. In the likely event that the pace of quantum-based technological change accelerates in coming years, the "clockspeed" of business will rise. Clockspeed refers to the rate at which companies introduce new products, processes, structures, and organization. Chapter 4 discusses the implications of accelerating technological change for the global economy, financial markets, firms, analysts, and investors.

In the quantum economy, wealth migrates from tangible assets (buildings, plant, and equipment) to intangible assets (human capital, design, brands, and business processes). The transition from tangible to intangible is well underway in the United States and global economies. As the quantum economy evolves, intangible assets will dwarf tangible ones. Traditional accounting concepts, such as book value, will need to be redefined to include a measure of intangible assets. Going forward, the costs of human capital and R&D will have to be viewed as an investment, instead of as an expense, as they are today. Chapter 5 sheds light on the intangible nature of the quantum economy.

Quantum theory has produced a host of innovations that have made our economy more complex. This increasing complexity is due, in part, to convergence and feedback effects. Many quantum-based technologies are complementary—they empower other devices and networks. Just as the development of quantum theory has required scientists to think differently, understanding the quantum economy requires new mental models. The science of complexity, which emphasizes multidisciplinary methods of inquiry, investigation, and analysis, will rise in importance in coming years. Chapters 6 and 7 explore complexity theory and what it means for analysts and investors.

At the dawn of the third millennium, quantum physics is poised to unleash a burst of technological inventions and innovations that will radically reshape the financial markets and drive wealth and prosperity in the years ahead. In addition, the science of complexity will shed much light on the coming revolutions in the life sciences and nanotechnology.

It is fitting that the fundamental law of investing, Uncertainty, lies at the heart of quantum theory. As unsettling as this law is to investors and scientists alike, we nevertheless must cope and adapt. After exhaustively studying the evolution of a wide variety of species, Charles Darwin concluded that the best chance of survival was had by the species that were most adaptable to changes in their habitat—not the species that were the strongest or the smartest. In the quantum future, Darwin's observation will undoubtedly prove true.

Key Takeaways

- Technologies that flowed directly from advances in basic science have been a major source of economic change during the past century and will continue to be a major source of change in coming years.

- Quantum science is the basis for a number of revolutionary technologies, including the transistor, microprocessor, and magnetic resonance imaging machine. Going forward, wealth creation in the stock market is most likely to come from new technologies with which we are not yet familiar.

- Holding stocks in companies that embrace and harness the power of quantum physics will be a very profitable investment strategy in the years ahead.

- Investors must become familiar with the science underlying new technologies so that they can understand whether a company's product will be successful as an investment.

- The source of wealth-creation in the next twenty years will not come from companies with predominantly natural resource-based assets.

- The turnover of companies in the S&P 500 and other stock indexes around the world is rising. By 2025, at least half of the companies in the Dow today will no longer be part of the index.

- The fundamental law of investing is uncertainty and those investors seeking certainty in financial markets will be frustrated by unforeseen quantum-based technologies. Investors would be wise to incorporate a margin of safety into their discounted cash flow valuation models to take this pervasive uncertainty into account.

The Ascending
Quantum Economy

These quantum curiosities, defying logic and common sense, have received little attention from the public, but they will.

—Michael Crichton

On the eve of the twentieth century, the commissioner of the U.S. Patent Office, Charles Duell, reportedly stated that everything that could be invented had been invented. As bizarre as Duell's remark sounds in retrospect, it was a sign of the times. In 1900, America was perched on the highest of plateaus. Humans had conquered nature and knew all there was to know. Over the previous thirty years, Duell and his contemporaries had experienced one of the most remarkable epochs in economic history.

From 1870 to 1900, the fruits of the industrial revolution were harvested. Much to the surprise of the dismal scientists, food supply was plentiful. A tsunami of technological inventions engulfed the global economy, from the telephone, automobile, and incandescent lightbulb, to the radio, phonograph, and electric dynamo. Enterprising individuals amassed great wealth. It was an age of miracle and wonder.

At the time Duell reputedly made his infamous remark, scientists were confident of their understanding of nature and the universe. Classical Newtonian physics reigned supreme. In his inaugural lecture at the University of Cambridge in 1871, the eminent Scottish scientist James Clerk Maxwell boldly proclaimed, "In a few years, all the great physical constants will have been approximately estimated, and the only occupation which will then be left to the men of science will be to carry these measurements to another place of decimals." And, at Oxford University, only 4 of 144 scholarships went to science students.

Little did Duell or the preeminent scientists of the nineteenth century know that their understanding of the world was about to be turned upside down and inside out by the arrival of new scientific theories that would confound some of the brightest minds on the planet. In the following years, scientists found themselves furiously debating how nature behaves at its most fundamental level; whether light manifests itself as a wave or a particle; whether time travels backward as well as forward; whether the universe is deterministic or random; and whether something can be in two places at the same time.

Over the course of the twentieth century, scientific advances would call into question much of what earlier scientists thought they knew about the nature of our world and the universe. The construction of rigorous theoretical mathematical apparatuses, experimentation, as well as many heated debates would, in time, create the most remarkable science ever known. Quantum mechanics would unleash a torrent of technologies that would forever change how people live, work, and play.

A THEORY MULDER COULD LOVE

Quantum theory has been heralded as the greatest scientific achievement in history, yet it is not exactly a household word. You are not likely to hear Homer Simpson and his buddies discussing quantum theory over beers at the local bar. Rather, quantum mechanics is the kind of science Agent Fox Mulder on *The X-Files* would be fully versed in.

Webster's defines *quantum* as "one of the very small increments or parcels into which many forms of energy are subdivided." It defines *quantum theory* as "a branch of physical theory based on the concept of the subdivision of radiant energy into finite quanta and applied to numerous processes involving transference or transformation of energy in an atomic or molecular scale."

With all due respect to *Webster's*, these definitions shed little light on the science of quantum physics. Rather, they seem to induce drowsiness. A clearer and more understandable description of quantum mechanics comes from the Nobel Prize-winning physicist Richard Feynman. In *Lectures on Physics* Feynman defined quantum mechanics as:

> The description of the behavior of matter and light in all its details and, in particular, of the happenings on an atomic scale.

Feynman believed that the principal purpose of quantum mechanics is to uncover the mysterious laws of nature at the atomic level. Matter and light may sound trivial, but they are the two most fundamental things in the universe. Atoms, which make up matter, are the building blocks of life. Light is a supreme force without which we would not exist.

Plato believed that no one could ever understand the universe until the smallest components of matter were known. As a philosopher, Plato thought deeply about all things quantum, but he was unable to grasp the invisibility that shrouds the atomic world. He thought atoms were little cubes and pyramids. Of course, Plato did not have the luxury of the magnifying instruments and other tools that scientists in the twentieth century had at their disposal.

Many scientists today believe that atoms (derived from the Greek word for "undivided,") are not little cubes and pyramids but extremely tiny particles. Atoms are more than 99.9 percent empty space. A typical hydrogen atom, the most abundant element in the universe, weighs one-millionth of a billion-billionth of a gram. Nevertheless, it contains a nucleus and an electron. The nucleus consists of a positively charged proton and an uncharged neutron. Neutrons and protons are made of even smaller particles, called *quarks*. The electron of a hydrogen atom is much smaller than the atom itself. The radius of an electron is incredibly tiny—less than .000000000000000001 inches or, scientifically speaking, 10^{-18} centimeters.

Since Plato's time, scientists have learned much about the behavior of matter. The quantum theory of the atom launched a massive scientific expedition to probe the atom's core, the nucleus. Along the way, scientists discovered that a *strong force* held the nucleus of the atom together. The study of the properties of atomic nuclei and nuclear forces had a profound impact on science and life in the twentieth century. Radioactivity, atomic energy, and nuclear medicine are all by-products of the quantum theory of the atom.

In 1897, the English scientist J. J. Thomson threw cold water on the notion that atoms are indivisible. In experiments, Thomson proved that tiny negatively charged particles (electrons) could be extracted from atoms, leaving behind positively charged residues (ions). Thomson's discovery of electrons showed that atoms were rather complex systems formed by positively and negatively charged parts.

Even though electrons are approximately eighteen hundred times lighter, they still serve as the bodyguards of atomic nuclei (protons and neutrons). Small systems, such as molecules, can by their very nature possess only certain discrete amounts of energy. The transition from one state to another is a rather mysterious event, usually called a "quantum jump." Molecules by necessity have an amount of stability. The configuration of a molecule cannot change, unless the energy difference necessary to "lift" it to the next higher level is supplied from outside. This energy-level difference is the well-defined quantity that determines the degree of stability of a molecule.

On their fantastic voyage into the quantum world, scientists discovered that electrons behave in a counterintuitive manner. Firing a beam of electrons from a conventional cathode-ray tube at a shield plate that contains two small, closely spaced holes through which the electrons can pass doesn't reveal two spots, as one would intuitively expect. Instead, the pattern that shows up on the plate is wavelike. Specifically, it looks like two waves crashing into each other, just as we see on a lake on a windy day. Scientists refer to this as an *interference pattern*. Interestingly, a similar double-slit experiment with a beam of light produces essentially the same pattern.

Scientists had been aware of the wavelike behavior of nature well before the development of quantum theory. In the 1860s, James Clerk

Maxwell showed that light waves are composed of electric and magnetic fields, and that light is electromagnetic radiation. Maxwell showed that a crucial parameter in light is the distance between wave crests—what he called the *wavelength*. He demonstrated that the wavelength of light determines the various colors we see when light is shone through a prism. The colors of visible light range from deep red to deep violet. The lovely rainbow we see when the sun's rays peek through the sky on a rainy day is the result of the interference of light waves.

Curiously, as brilliant as Maxwell's theory of light is, it could not explain why light that strikes the surface of an ordinary piece of metal knocks electrons out of the metal atoms—the *photoelectric effect*. In 1905, Albert Einstein developed a quantum theory of light to explain the photoelectric effect. He theorized that light was concentrated into little packets of energy, later dubbed *photons*.

Photons act more like particles than waves. Each photon of light carries enough energy to collide with an electron and knocks it out of the metal. Einstein assumed that each photon had only one frequency. Viewed in this manner, ultraviolet photons had twice the energy of red photons because they had twice the frequency. Low-frequency red photons did not have enough energy to free up any electrons in metal.

Einstein's quantum theory of light, which was experimentally proven correct in 1923 by the physicist Arthur Compton, stated that increasing the brightness of the light increases the number, but not the energy of the photons. Bright red light consists of many low-energy photons, none of which is capable of ejecting electrons out of metal. The idea that light was composed of photons was revolutionary. As the great quantum physicist Erwin Schrödinger observed years later, the profound revelation of quantum theory was that features of discreteness were discovered in nature.

The duality of light and electrons—the fact that they act at times like waves and at other times like particles—lies at the heart of the mystery of quantum theory. Scientists still puzzle over this oddity today. How can something be both a wave and a particle? It just doesn't make sense. As it turns out, the dual nature of light, and of electromagnetic radiation generally, is a characteristic of all quantum phenomena, including protons and other subatomic particles. They all have a wave nature as well as a particle nature. All matter and energy in the quantum world are dualistic in this way.

In their quest to comprehend what classical physicists could not explain, some of the greatest scientists in history proposed ways of looking at the atomic world that, although counterintuitive, explain what we observe in nature. In Appendix A, the discoveries that produced the science of quantum mechanics are listed in chronological order, beginning with Max Planck's seminal work.

QUANTUM WEIRDNESS

One of the biggest obstacles in trying to come to grips with the strange quantum world is that it is extremely different from the macroscopic world we see. Newton's physics were revolutionary because they brought order to the visible world of ordinary objects, such as falling apples and the motion of planets. He unraveled the ancient mystery of the motion of heavenly bodies. The universe, it seemed, behaved much like a giant clock. Determinism and objectivity ruled, and Newton's mechanics allowed scientists to explain and predict with great accuracy the motion and behavior of visible objects.

Quantum theory flies in the face of classical physics. Scientists refer to differences between the Newtonian world and the quantum atomic world as "quantum weirdness." At the atomic level, determinism and objectivity are elusive.

Scientists tell us that the quantum world is rationally comprehensible, but it cannot be visualized like the Newtonian world. This is not just because the quantum world is invisible to the naked eye, but also because the visual conventions we adopt from the world of objects that we can see do not apply to objects at the atomic level. This is not just scientific smoke and mirrors. Physicists and mathematicians have shown that thinking about quantum particles as ordinary objects conflicts directly with experiments.

Most people grasp Newtonian physics. It's easier to understand things that are deterministic and predictable, neat and orderly. When scientists look at things at the atomic and subatomic levels, however, they see randomness and disorder. Newton's laws tell scientists when Mars will appear in a certain part of the evening sky, but there are no physical laws yet that will tell physicists when an electron is going to jump to a different state. The best scientists can do today is give the probability, or the likelihood, of a jump. At the quantum level, uncertainty is pervasive.

In 1927, Heisenberg put forth his "uncertainty principle" which states that we cannot attempt to measure the position and motion of a quantum object simultaneously. Scientists trying to locate the position of an electron must forgo information about its momentum. Despite the fact that uncertainty is woven into its very fabric, quantum theory churns out predictions that are accurate to eleven decimal places.

SHOCKING SCIENCE

The Danish physicist Neils Bohr, one of the pioneers of quantum theory, once remarked that anybody who is not shocked by quantum theory does not understand it. Several decades later, Richard Feynman stated that nobody understands quantum theory. Scientists' lack of understanding may explain why quantum physics hasn't received more attention from analysts and the media. Imagine Katie Couric of *The Today Show* or some other popular media commentator probing quantum curiosities and their impact on technology and the economy with some well-known quantum physicist. Undoubtedly, the host and many viewers would come away from the interview frustrated, puzzled, or even baffled. It is not exactly the type of interview that would boost viewer ratings.

On the surface, the quantum world appears to be similar to the looking-glass world Alice stumbled into—a world where "everything is nonsense, where nothing would be what it is because everything would be what it isn't; and contrariwise, what it is, it wouldn't be, and what it wouldn't be, it would."

In *Lectures on Physics,* Feynman summed up the weirdness of the quantum world,

> Things on a very small (i.e., quantum) scale behave like nothing
> that you have any direct experience about. They do not behave

like waves and they do not behave like particles. Nor do they behave like clouds in the sky, billiard balls on a pool table, weights or springs. In short, things at the quantum level don't behave like anything that you have ever seen.

Despite its mysterious nature, quantum theory is a force to be reckoned with. As the theoretical physicist John Wheeler observes in *Geons, Black Holes & Quantum Foam*, quantum theory is unshakeable, unchallengeable, and undefeatable—it's battle tested. He likens the strength of quantum theory to that of the second law of thermodynamics, which tells us that heat flows from hot to cold. Wheeler points out that even the great Albert Einstein, who opposed quantum theory in so many ways, said that it would turn out to be as irrefutable as thermodynamics.

Scientists tell us that despite its mysterious, counterintuitive nature, quantum theory works. It works in atoms. It works in molecules. It works in complex solids, metals, insulators, semiconductors, superconductors, and anywhere it has been applied. Shockingly, no known experiment has contradicted the predictions of quantum mechanics in the last fifty years. Its consistent triumphs make quantum mechanics truly remarkable. It is a theory that correctly describes the world to a level of precision and detail unprecedented in science.

Max Planck, the inventor of quantum theory, was greatly disturbed by his own theory. He simply didn't want to see classical physics destroyed. Planck knew his theory was revolutionary and would eventually change the world. As he put it, "We have to live with quantum theory and believe me, it will expand. It will not be only in optics. It will go in all fields." (As we will soon see, Planck's intuition about quantum theory was right on the money.)

THE QUANTUM BOUNTY

Since its unexpected beginnings at the turn of the twentieth century, quantum theory has become a powerful force in the global economy. Now our entire global technological superstructure is based on all things quantum—the electron, photons, and other atomic and sub-atomic entities.

Commenting on the real-world impact of quantum theory, the physicist Heinz Pagels observed in *The Cosmic Code*,

> No single set of ideas has ever had a greater impact on technology—the transistor, the microprocessor, the laser and cryogenic technology have spawned entire industries—and the practical implications of quantum physics will continue to shape the social and political destiny of our civilization.

In their tribute to the centennial anniversary of quantum theory, "100 Years of Quantum Mysteries," scientists Max Tegmark and John Wheeler noted that 30 percent of the U.S. gross national product is based on inventions made possible by quantum mechanics. The Nobel Prize-winning physicist Leon Lederman estimates that quantum theory accounts for more than one-fourth of the developed world's gross national product today. If you are looking for the foundations of the so-called New Economy, quantum theory is the place to start.

It's curious that a science that not even the brightest minds on the planet fully understand accounts for a significant and rapidly growing share of the world's output of goods and services. Indeed, quantum-based technologies are inextricably woven into the fabric of our lives. They are such an ascending force in the global economy that it's difficult to imagine living without them.

EXHIBIT 1: Revolutionary Quantum-Based Technological Inventions

Transistor
Integrated circuit
Laser
Microprocessor
Magnetic resonance imaging machine
High-temperature superconductor
Carbon nanotube

Source: The Timetables of Science, 1991.

•   •   •

Quantum mechanics revolutionized the materials sciences in the twentieth century and gave scientists almost Godlike power to turn three of the most abundant elements on the planet—sand, oxygen, and aluminum—into magnificent fields of gold. Armed with quantum theory, scientists learned to harness and control the properties of metals, insulators, superconductors, and semiconductors.

The preeminent quantum-based technology is the microprocessor, which is essentially a computer on a chip. It is the brains of the modern computer. Without it, there would be no personal computers, no revolution in communications or the life sciences. As Michael Malone observes in *The Microprocessor: A Biography*, the microprocessor, more than any other product, decodes and defines modern life.

The first big quantum-based technological breakthrough came in 1947, when three scientists at Bell Laboratories—William Shockley, Walter Brattain, and John Bardeen—announced the invention of the transistor. The transistor was a competing technology to the vacuum tube, which up to that point had been the technology of choice for computing and other applications.

In its amplification and switching capabilities, the transistor represented a quantum leap over vacuum tubes. Unlike vacuum tubes, the transistor was based on the physics of semiconductors, which was grounded in the science of quantum mechanics. Almost as if by magic, transistors moved electrical charges along controlled paths inside a solid block of semiconductor material. By the mid-1950s, transistors became the most popular technology for radios, amplifiers, hearing aids, and a wide array of other electronic products. The transistor radio, launched during the holiday shopping season in 1954, was the most sought-after new product in retail history.

Today, scientists pack more than 40 million transistors on a conventional microprocessor. This amazing feat is difficult to comprehend for those not acquainted with quantum theory. Although a microprocessor's quantum-based architecture is invisible to the human eye, its beauty and majesty tower over that of the greatest pyramids and cathedrals.

Although the invention of the quantum-based transistor didn't make the front page of *The New York Times*, it laid the foundation for the revolution in computing and microelectronics with which we are familiar. Today, fifty years later, more than 50 thousand trillion transistors are churned out of wafer fabrication facilities around the world for every conceivable application: automobiles, computers, personal digital assistants (PDAs), cellular phones, CD and DVD players, children's toys, musical instruments, washing machines and more.

Another technological gift of quantum physics is the laser, which is shorthand for "light amplification by stimulated emission of radiation." The laser is a complete quantum system. Lasers create beams of coherent light—that is, light beams that vibrate in exact synchronization with each other. This form of light is made possible by manipulating the electrons making "quantum jumps" within atoms.

Invented and developed by Arthur Schawlow and Charles Townes of Bell Labs during the late 1950s and 1960s, the laser launched a new scientific field, revolutionized a number of industries, and opened the door to a multibillion-dollar industry. Today, lasers are used in a wide range of applications in communications, medicine, manufacturing, the construction industry, surveying, consumer electronics, scientific instrumentation, and military systems. Literally billions of lasers are at work around the world in CD and DVD players, at the scanner in the local grocery store, or in the office of your eye doctor. They range in size from tiny semiconductor devices no bigger than a grain of salt to high-power instruments as large as an average living room.

Lasers also are fundamentally altering how information travels in the global economy. Today, incredibly narrow pulses of light a million times brighter than the sun send billions of bits of information per second through strands of glass fibers no thicker than one ordinary human hair. Scientists believe that lasers will become the main medium for the Internet because far more information can be carried on laser beams than on conventional copper wires.

George Gilder, poet laureate of the quantum revolution in economics and technology, notes that innovative optical technologies are turning the entire world of communications networks upside down. In *Telecosm*, he writes that optical communication networks are becoming the medium of choice for telecommunications companies to transmit voice, data, and video.

Today, a state-of-the-art laser-powered fiber-optics communications network can send the entire contents of the Library of Congress from New York to Los Angeles in less than one second. This technology, known as wavelength division multiplexing (WDM), involves lasers and the color spectrum of light to transmit information, and may usher in an era of abundant bandwidth. As the amount of data that can be transmitted grows exponentially, the communications industry will undergo as great a change as the computer industry did in the twentieth century.

In the fields of medicine and health care, lasers allow surgeons around the world to perform highly intricate surgery using photons, rather than scalpels, to operate on and cauterize wounds. Incredibly, lasers today can be inserted inside the body to perform with minimal risk and discomfort operations, that a few years ago were almost impossible. Lasers with shorter wavelengths—green lasers—are being used by optometrists to repair detached retinas. More and more, optometrists are also using lasers to correct faulty vision, which could have a significant impact on the eyeglass industry in the future.

Quantum theory put chemistry on a firm scientific base in 1925 when the path-breaking work of physicist Wolfgang Pauli gave scientists a rule for how the chemical elements change their electronic structure. Pauli's quantum theory accounts for the chemical properties of inert gas and solids, such as metals, by tying them to the numbers and states of the electrons.

As if by magic, Pauli's theory explains the order of the elements in the periodic table most of us are familiar with from our high school chemistry class. Recall that the number in each square of the table gives the atomic number of the element—the number of protons (and, by inference, the number of electrons) in the nucleus. Quantum theory has proved to be enormously useful in chemistry in the past century. Organic, inorganic, and analytical chemists, as well as biochemists now use quantum theory to calculate thermodynamic properties, interpret spectra, and determine molecular properties, such as bond lengths and angles.

Thanks in part to Pauli's herculean efforts back in the 1920s, quantum chemistry is a burgeoning field in the twenty-first century. The development of quantum chemistry has given birth to several new disciplines that

24

are fueling growth in fields such as molecular biology, genetic engineering, and molecular medicine.

Once a backwater of theoretical science, biology has been revolutionized by quantum theory. Molecular biology is the branch of quantum physics dealing with a cell's structure, or the nature of life. Erwin Schrödinger's beautifully written book *What Is Life?* introduced molecular biology in 1944 and was a source of inspiration to a whole generation of physicists in the latter half of the twentieth century. A quantum physicist, Schrödinger posed this question: How can the events in space and time, which take place within the spatial boundary of a living organism, be accounted for by physics and chemistry? His search for an answer gave birth to what we know today as the science of molecular biology.

After the publication of Schrödinger's book, many scientists focused on the possibility of tackling biological problems from a physics standpoint. The ideas in the book had a huge impact on researchers, including the two men who would go on to discover the code of life, Francis Crick and James Watson.

Schrödinger observed that the mechanism of heredity is founded on the very basis of quantum theory. Crick and Watson built and shaped their famous double-helix model to represent the quantum mechanically correct versions of the deoxyribonucleic acid (DNA) molecules. It was discovered that the nucleotide pairs form a simple code that can be read off by a child. Watson and Crick's brilliant insight was rooted in quantum mechanics. It depended on the actual shapes of the bases attached to the sugar-phosphate back-bond of a DNA molecule.

When Watson and Crick built the correct shape of the DNA molecule in to their double-helix model, the links between the nucleic acids adenine (A) and thymine (T), and between cytosine (C) and guanine (G), turned out to be hydrogen bonds, which are features of the quantum behavior of matter. Hydrogen bonds provide the force that keeps the two strands of the DNA double-helix together. Watson and Crick discovered that the components that form the chemical bonds and hold the two strands of a DNA molecule together, have distinctive shapes. These shapes allow only matching pairs of molecules to join. This process is like the fit of a key in a lock.

Some scientists believe that biology will reign supreme in the twenty-first century. Today, sixty years after Crick and Watson's discovery of DNA, researchers are using high-speed computers and bioinformatics to locate and identify all the genes in the body. Dr. Craig Venter, co-founder of Celera Genomics, one of the companies that helped map the human genome, believes that advances in quantum-based technology are the turning points in the history of biology and medicine. Gene-based drug discoveries are now going to move forward at an exponential pace.

Armed with genetic information that doctors could have only dreamed of at the time of Crick and Watson's discovery, researchers note that the number of new drug targets will skyrocket from a few hundred to the tens of thousands in coming years. They believe that the twenty-first century will be an age of personalized medicine with drugs and therapies tailored to people's specific genetic makeup. Moreover, such drugs will work with few, or no, side effects.

It wouldn't be at all surprising to see the biopharmaceutical and health care sectors evolve in the same way the computer industry evolved in the past century—from giant mainframes, to microcomputers, to personal computers and PDAs. The computing industry has shown us that quantum-based technologies, unlike Newtonian technologies, get smaller and more powerful over time. As the quantum revolution in biology evolves, this peculiar characteristic should manifest itself in the biopharmaceutical and health care sectors.

Biology-based quantum computation devices will one day conceivably supplant or supplement conventional electronic devices. Michio Kaku, a theoretical physicist at the City College of New York, observed that new advances in DNA research are making possible an innovative type of computer architecture that actually computes on organic molecules. In 2001, a group of scientists in Israel, led by Ehud Shapiro, professor at the Weizman Institute of Science, using 1 trillion living cells, developed a computing device so small it could fit in a drop of water. Dubbed a "finite automaton," this biological nanocomputer uses enzymes as hardware. The enzymes manipulate DNA molecules as software, creating what effectively is a single mathematical computing machine.

Another bounty from quantum theory is magnetic resonance imaging

(MRI) technology, which has revolutionized medicine in the past twenty-five years. MRIs derive their incredible power from the behavior of atoms: they make use of the fact that the nucleus of the atom spins like a top. When placed in a powerful magnetic field, spinning nuclei become aligned with the field. By applying an external high-frequency signal, scientists can flip the nuclei upside down. When the nuclei revert to their original configuration, they emit a small burst of energy that can be detected. Because different nuclei emit different signals, researchers can differentiate between various atoms found in the body.

As amazing and useful as modern-day MRI machines are, they are a primitive quantum tool compared to what physicians will be using. Now, scientists are discussing new types of MRI machines that will increase imaging speeds to one thousand times or more faster than those used by practitioners today. Farther down the road, researchers believe they can increase the resolution of a brain scan by 1 quadrillion times, which could have significant implications for our understanding of how the brain operates.

Quantum science also gave birth to superconductivity, a state in which a material's resistance to electrical conduction drops to zero. The concept of superconductivity has intrigued researchers since its discovery in 1911, but it took almost fifty years before a theory, based on the interaction between electrons and a crystal lattice, was discovered to explain the phenomenon. For real materials, however, calculations are so complex that theory alone cannot guide the search for new superconductors.

Today, superconductors are found by a combination of luck and intuition. Two main classes of practical superconductors are known: those that exhibit their superconducting properties at very low temperatures (below 23° Kelvin; 0° Kelvin corresponds to absolute zero or minus 273° Celsius) and those that will superconduct at higher temperatures (30° to 164° Kelvin). Currently, applications of superconductors in the economy range from the most sensitive detectors of magnetic fields ever made to large superconducting magnets used in body scanners, levitated trains, and electrical transmission equipment.

A team of scientists and engineers from Pirelli Cables, Detroit Edison, and American Superconductor is working on a new substation in Detroit, Michigan. If all goes as planned, electricity in thirty thousand homes in the city will pass through three superconducting cables that are superior to the conventional copper transmission lines. They lose only one two-hundredth as much power as equivalent copper conductors. Furthermore, one superconducting cable provides three times the capacity of a copper cable of the same size.

According to researchers at the Electric Power Research Institute, the current-carrying capability of superconducting cable has improved so fast that it now far exceeds the capacities they envisaged when they started drawing up the plans for the Detroit substation. Denmark now also sends power through superconducting cables to one hundred and fifty thousand homes in Copenhagen and tests are under way in Tokyo. Some scientists believed that 2001, the year when superconducting cables began lighting up homes in Detroit, would mark the year the electricity industry changed forever.

THE ASCENDING QUANTUM ECONOMY

During the twentieth century, the development of quantum theory profoundly changed the way scientists look at the world. It sparked a revolution in technology that altered the global economic landscape. Nearly one-third of the value of all goods and services produced today in America owe their existence to advances in quantum physics, up from zero a century ago.

Now that we have surveyed the historical development of quantum theory and discussed its major innovations, we can better appreciate "A Brief History of Relativity," in which Stephen Hawking noted, "the world has changed far more in the past one hundred years than in any other century in history due to technologies that flowed directly from advances in basic science."

Economists tell us that more wealth was created in the twentieth century than in all previous centuries combined. And Stephen Moore and Julian Simon note in *It's Getting Better All the Time* that there has been more improvement in the human condition in the past one hundred years than in all previous centuries combined. In fact, the long-term trend of improving living standards for all of humanity, and particularly for Americans, has no precedent.

From 1900 to 1999, the total amount of goods and services produced annually in the United States rose from $500 billion to nearly $9 trillion (in constant 1996 dollar terms). In that same period, the U.S. standard of living rocketed upward at least sixfold. Real U.S. gross domestic product (GDP), that is, GDP divided by population, rose from about $4,800 to $32,000. Even the poorest Americans today live far better than the average U.S. citizen did during the nineteenth century. Productivity growth has been nothing short of spectacular in the past century. Indeed, one of the economic hallmarks of the quantum revolution has been to create huge amounts of value-added output with fewer people and other resource inputs.

EXHIBIT 2: Quantum Ascent

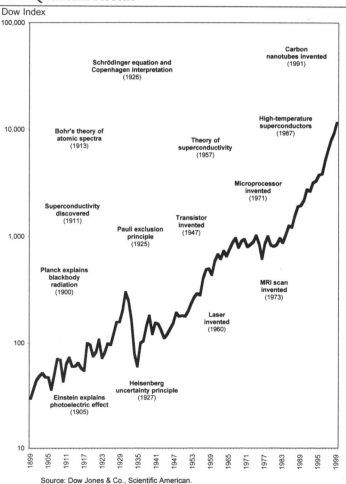

Source: Dow Jones & Co., Scientific American.

The spectacular increase in U.S. living standards and wealth during the twentieth century is reflected in the performance of the Dow Jones Industrial Average. From the time of Max Planck's initial discovery to the end of 1999, the Dow climbed from 44 to 11,497 (see Exhibit 2). A hypothetical investor who would have put $100 in the market in 1900 and held it until 1999 would have seen his or her money grow to be worth more than $1.5 million (assuming dividends were reinvested annually).

The substantial return on investment in U.S. equities during the past century is the result of many economic factors. It also shows the awesome power of the mathematics of compounding. Albert Einstein is well-known in the financial industry for having remarked, man's most important discovery was compound interest.

As powerful as technological advances associated with scientific discoveries have been, the real quantum revolution in technology lies ahead. Tomorrow's technologies will make today's look as primitive as early twentieth-century technologies seem now. On the horizon are carbon nanotube-based computer chips, optical communications devices, hydrogen energy technology, high-temperature superconductors, and quantum computers.

Many of the quantum curiosities that scientists discuss today have received little attention from the public. This is partly because advanced quantum-based technologies look more like science fiction than science fact. Any sufficiently advanced technology, as the eminent futurist Arthur C. Clarke observed, is often indistinguishable from magic.

It is extremely difficult to predict how the quantum technology revolution will evolve, yet all signs point to an acceleration of technical change in the years ahead. As we will see in Chapter 2, the next wave of quantum-based technological invention could unleash a powerful dynamic process that the late, great economist Joseph Schumpeter called *creative destruction.*

The implications of a quantum-based wave of creative destruction for the global economy, financial markets, and lives of consumers and businesses in the twenty-first century will be as profound as those of the industrial revolution. Maybe more profound.

Key Takeaways

- The development of quantum physics over the past century has fundamentally transformed the business and financial market landscape by creating products, such as the transistor, laser, microprocessor, and MRI, with pervasive and widespread consumer value.

- Developments associated with quantum science account for over one-quarter of the developed world's gross national product (GNP) and roughly one-third of the U.S. GNP. It is simply too big today to be ignored by investors.

- As companies have embraced the Internet, most manufacturing companies will have nanotechnology-based processes.

- Many quantum-based technologies have not received much attention from the public, but they will in the years ahead. Investors must become familiar with these products and technologies so they can better understand their investment value.

- Investors are well advised to keep a weather eye on future quantum-based technologies, particularly in the IT, communications, life science, health care, media and entertainment, and energy sectors.

- The convergence of information technology and biology is bringing about a new life-science industry.

- In coming years, investors must be prepared for companies' faster failure rate.

The Fifth Wave

Twentieth-century technology is headed for the junk
heap, or perhaps the recycling bins.
— K. Eric Drexler

In 1989, amid a chorus of doom and gloom from a group of
distinguished economists, Myron Ross, a relatively obscure
academic economist at the University of Pennsylvania, boldly
predicted that the U.S. economy was on the brink of a radical
economic and social transformation. Ross believed that the
American economy and many other developed economies
would experience a *long wave* of economic activity driven
predominately by an accelerating pace of technological change.

Ross argued the radical transformation of the economic
landscape in the next two or three decades would result in rising rates of economic growth and wealth. This "gale of creative destruction," he noted, would produce an abundance of
new innovative technologies and an unimagined increase in
the level of living by the average American.

A little more than a decade has passed since Ross's book, *A
Gale of Creative Destruction*, was published, and much of what
he prophesied is occurring. His predictions have fared far better
than those of many of his distinguished colleagues in academia.

In the late 1980s, the wave of pessimism among the dismal scientists was palpable, and it was fashionable for economists and historians to write books predicting the economic-equivalent of Armageddon: *Day of Reckoning, The Zero-Sum Solution, The Rise and Fall of Great Powers, The Great Depression of 1990.*

The feature of Ross's economic analysis that distinguished it from other views was his focus on technological change and its impact on economic activity. Many economists in the late 1980s were not aware that the United States and other developed countries were building an impressive arsenal of quantum theory–based technological innovations in industries, such as information technology (IT), communications, health care, and consumer electronics.

Ross's insights into the global economy's future emanated from the views of the economist Joseph Schumpeter (1883–1950). Unlike John Maynard Keynes and Milton Friedman, Schumpeter's theories are not widely taught in introductory economics courses. Even though his name has appeared frequently in major world publications over the past few years (see Exhibit 3), and he is receiving far more attention by academic researchers than he did in the last decade of his life, it's safe to say Schumpeterian economics is still not in the mainstream.

EXHIBIT 3

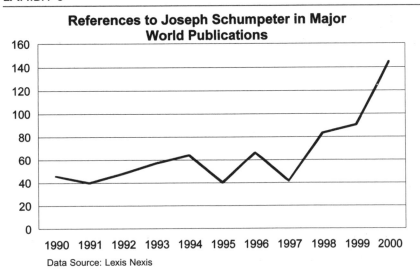

References to Joseph Schumpeter in Major World Publications

Data Source: Lexis Nexis

What is Schumpeterian economics? Why is it important to understand? What might Schumpeter's theories tell us about the evolution of quantum physics–based technology? Most important, what do Schumpeter's theories say about how companies, economies, and the stock market will evolve in the twenty-first century? These questions are addressed in this chapter.

MR. CREATIVE DESTRUCTION

Most people view economics as the study of static, almost mechanistic equilibrium systems, because this is how basic economics is taught at most universities today. If you believe this type of analysis is a useful starting place but of limited use in understanding the world we live in, then you have a lot in common with Joseph Schumpeter.

Schumpeter believed that conventional, static-equilibrium economic analysis was unable to capture the essential features of a dynamic, ever evolving economy like that of the United States. In fact, he argued, it provided only modest insights, because it could not predict the consequences of discontinuous changes in the traditional ways of doing things. It couldn't explain the occurrence of technological revolutions or the phenomena that accompany them. The best that static economic analysis could do, according to Schumpeter, was to investigate the new equilibrium position after changes have occurred.

The study of economics is, according to Schumpeter, simply the study of change over time. Since he saw a market-based capitalist system as constantly changing and evolving, Schumpeter thought that economics should analyze *disequilibrium* as opposed to equilibrium, dynamic processes instead of static ones.

Schumpeter coined the well-known term *creative destruction*. In his classic work, *Capitalism, Socialism and Democracy,* published five years before the transistor was invented, Schumpeter argued that capitalism is a form or method of economic change. By its very nature, it is never stationary.

The fundamental impulse that starts an economy like the United States and keeps it in motion comes from new consumer goods, new methods of production or transportation, new markets, and new forms of industrial organization that the capitalist enterprise creates. Schumpeter wrote,

> The opening up of new markets, foreign or domestic, and the organization development from the craft shop and factory to such concerns as U.S. Steel illustrate the same process of industrial mutation—if I may use that biological term—that incessantly revolutionizes the economic structure from within, incessantly destroying the old one, incessantly creating a new one. This process of Creative Destruction is the essential fact about capitalism. It is what capitalism consists in and what every capitalist concern has got to live in.

Schumpeter argued that whereas most economists and analysts believe that the relevant problem is how capitalism *administers* existing structures, the real problem is how capitalism *creates and destroys* or, alternatively, *transforms* existing structures.

Textbook economies analyzed in school rely on priced-based competition, whereas Schumpeter observed that the success of real-world economies depends on competition from the new commodity, the new technology, the new source of supply, the new type of organization. He believed this type of competition commanded a decisive cost or quality—not price—advantage. This competition strikes not at the companies' profit or output of existing firms but at their very foundations and existence.

UNCHARTED SEA

It is trendy today to view technology and technological innovation as bubblelike, especially following the spectacular rise and fall of the dotcoms. Although these dynamics do exist within the technology sector, the far more dominant dynamic is a long wave or cycle. Bubbles appear, pop, and disappear. Waves, however, ebb and flow over time.

Schumpeter was the most astute economic observer of the wavelike properties of technological change. Unlike other twentieth-century economic luminaries, such as Keynes and Friedman, Schumpeter made technological invention and innovation the focus of his theory. He argued there was no reason to expect a slackening of economic growth through exhaustion of technological possibilities. He pointed out that throughout history, the great bursts of economic activity that spread prosperity were always associated with science- and technology-related capital spending.

Contrary to conventional economic theory, Schumpeter believed that science and technology were endogenous to the economy. In fact, he thought the monetary incentives inherent in capitalism drove the remarkable performances of science and technology. Conventional economic growth theory, on the other hand, assumes that technology is exogenous, or determined outside the economic system.

The neoclassical model of growth, developed by Nobel laureate Robert Solow, is still the mainstream macroeconomic theory of growth. The model states there is a long-run, dynamic, full-employment equilibrium at which planned saving equals planned investment. In the model, the stock of capital in the economy grows at the same rate as income.

Empirical work by academic economists using the neoclassical growth model indicates that as much as 40 to 90 percent of the growth of per capita income (that is, income adjusted for population) is caused by technological change. However, this powerful source of economic growth—technological change—is assumed to be determined outside the economic system. In the neoclassical model, technological change is a given feature, assumed to take place at a steady, constant rate.

The treatment of technological change in the neoclassical growth model perplexes disciples of Schumpeter. They say this unrealistic assumption is designed to avoid modeling a messy, nonlinear process. *In Conversations with Leading Economists,* authors Brian Snowden and Howard Vane report that Solow has stated publicly that the reason he made technology exogenous in his model was simply that he did not understand the causes of technological change.

In the same book, Paul Romer, professor of economics at Stanford University and a pioneer of a competing growth theory to the neoclassical model, points out that Solow should be commended because he brought technology explicitly into the analysis. The real weakness of the neoclassical model, says Romer, is that it treats technology as a public good rather than one subject to private control. Unlike Solow's model of growth, Romer's model assumes that technological change is endogenous.

In the spirit of Schumpeter, Romer's model of endogenous growth captures the fact that private individuals and firms make intentional investments in the production of new technologies. This assumption may sound like common sense to people who run and work in corporations, but it is considered a radical departure from conventional neoclassical economic models of long-term growth. Romer points out that without technological change, growth would come to a grinding halt.

It is easy to understand the frustration among economists when it comes to technical change. Technology is a complex, dynamic process that does not stand still and is never in equilibrium. Moreover, the major source of technological change—scientific discovery—is incredibly difficult to model mathematically and often impossible to predict.

Arthur Clarke observed in *Profiles of the Future,* that although many inventions were anticipated notably by science fiction writers, they missed a number of key inventions. The evolution of the scientific record clearly shows that generations of scientists have been repeatedly surprised by discoveries that were not anticipated and could not have been guessed at. Exhibit 4 shows Clarke's list of the unexpected and expected major inventions in the past few centuries.

Many of the unexpected inventions and discoveries on Clarke's list are related to the development and application of quantum theory. In fact, economic growth and wealth creation would be nowhere near what they are today without these unanticipated technological inventions.

EXHIBIT 4: Expect the Unexpected
(Inventions Not Predicted and Predicted)

Unexpected Inventions	Expected Inventions
X-rays	Telephones
Nuclear Energy	Automobiles
Radio and TV	Flying machines
Electronics	Steam engines
Photography	Submarines
Sound recordings	Spaceships
Quantum mechanics	Robots
Relativity theory	Death-rays
Transistors	Transmutation
Masers and lasers	Artificial life
Superconductors and	Immortality
superfluids	Invisibility
Atomic clocks	Levitation
Neutrinos	Teleportation
Microelectronics	Telepathy

Source: Arthur C. Clarke, *Profiles of the Future.*

The initial breakthrough of the transistor set in motion a vast commitment of scientific resources. Within a decade, the field of solid-state physics, which until then had not even been taught at most universities, became the largest subdiscipline of physics. Nathan Rosenberg, Stanford University professor of economics, pointed out that it was the development of the transistor that changed how science programs at universities were structured, by dramatically upgrading the potential payoff to research in solid-state electronics.

The difficulties with the transistor brought about further research that eventually led to the discovery of the junction transistor and a profound understanding of the science of semiconductors. A similar dynamic occurred with the development of laser technology. Scientists working with lasers in the early 1960s recognized the feasibility of using optical fibers for telephone transmission. The study of optics became a fertile field for researchers at Bell Laboratories and various universities who were interested in commercializing laser technology in telecommunications. Over time, the study of optics changed from a relatively obscure intellectual backwater into a burgeoning field of research with clear economic payoffs.

Schumpeter argued that the advent of the modern corporation had, in effect, endogenized inventive activity. On the basis of the events following the invention of the transistor and the laser, Rosenberg concludes that Schumpeter was indeed correct. The experience of the past fifty or so years suggests that not only does science shape technology but technology shapes science by playing a major role in determining the research agenda of science as well as the volume of resources devoted to specific fields.

WAVES OF CREATIVE DESTRUCTION

In his analysis of the dynamics of economic evolution, Schumpeter noted that there were three dominant waves or cycles of economic activity. These three waves are,

1. Short waves—lasting roughly four years (known also as the "Kitchin" waves)

2. Medium waves—lasting roughly ten years (called the "Juglar" waves)

3. Long waves—lasting roughly 60 years (also called the "Kondratieff" waves)

The short, or Kitchin, wave is the conventional business cycle. Although Kitchin waves receive the bulk of the attention from policy makers, analysts, and the financial media, they are the least interesting of the three waves. The medium and longer-term waves, as Schumpeter demonstrated in his book *Business Cycles*, are powerful sources of economic change. We may think of Kitchin waves as ripples on an economic pond. In contrast, Juglar and Kondratieff waves are tsunamis. The gales of creative destruction that Schumpeter observed were in the longer-term waves of economic activity.

The long waves, Schumpeter noted, tend to last about sixty years—a lifetime for many people back in the early twentieth century and a career for many people today. The heart of the long cycle is the development and diffusion of major technological innovations. World-changing technologies, such as the steam engine, railroads, electricity, and the automobile were observed during long waves of economic activity.

Schumpeter underscored the point that innovations in technology cluster in time, and are the major causes of the long cycle. During long waves, he observed, the economy is out of equilibrium as new products, companies, and industries are born and old ones go out of business. As the science-and-technology-based inventions matured, they set in motion phases of increasing returns whereby industries become larger and more profitable. Technological progress differed from industrial production in that it supported sustained growth and did not obey the laws of diminishing returns.

Only a handful of economists, notably Schumpeter, focused on technology's role in altering the economic landscape. Recently, however, academic economists have begun working on a universal theoretical framework to understand the economic, social, and political effects of major technological innovations.

This theoretical work explores the impact of general-purpose technologies (GPTs) on the entire economic system, as well as political and social structures. GPTs are, by definition, technologies that fundamentally transform the way people live, work, and play. Examples include the steam engine, the internal combustion engine, electricity, the transistor, the laser, the electronic computer, and the Internet. Elhanan Helpman, professor of economics at Harvard University, notes that although the study of GPTs is relatively new and a universal theoretical framework for them does not exist, they are a fertile area of research.

Schumpeter detected a huge shift in the economic landscape in the late eighteenth century, when scientific knowledge was rising rapidly and fueling a growing number of major technological inventions and innovations. For the first time, innovation became a flow, not a series of sporadic, widely spaced events. The process of technical change accelerated further in the nineteenth century, and the great scientist, Alfred North Whitehead, wrote in *Science and the Modern World* that the greatest invention of the nineteenth century was the invention of the method of invention.

Using Schumpeter's analytical framework, Myron Ross identified the ebb and flow of four long waves in U.S. economic history and predicted a fifth wave.

EXHIBIT 5: Long Waves in U.S. Economic History

	Time Period	Up Phase	Down Phase
First Wave:	1790–1851	1790–1817	1818–1851
Second Wave:	1852–1896	1852–1866	1867–1896
Third Wave:	1897–1945	1897–1920	1921–1945
Fourth Wave:	1946–1993	1946–1969	1970–1993
Fifth Wave:	1994–2045(e)	1994–2020(e)	2021–2045(e)

Source: Myron Ross, *Gales of Creative Destruction.*

The first long wave of economic activity in America corresponded with Eli Whitney's invention of the cotton gin in 1793. The late eighteenth century saw a feverish wave of inventions in the manufacturing of cotton, after which the cotton industry grew at a rate never before witnessed in the textile industry. Economic historians regard the cotton industry as the quintessential growth industry of the early stages of the industrial revolution. The steam locomotive and telegraph were other important inventions during the period. It's easy to understate the telegraph's impact on the global economy and society overall. Many historians believe that the telegraph's economic impact was as great as the railroad's. Before the telegraph, information had never traveled faster than people.

The second long wave (1852 to1896) was a golden age of invention characterized by a series of innovations in transportation, agriculture, and manufacturing. Between 1850 and 1860 some 28,000 patents were issued, up from 6,480 in the period 1840 to 1850. Among the key inventions of the second long wave were Bessemer steel, the internal combustion engine, the telephone, the electric dynamo, the lightbulb, wireless telegraphy (Morse code), and the phonograph.

The industrial revolution became firmly established during this time. Railroad building expanded rapidly, as did manufacturing firms, and factories replaced homes as a place of work. After 1850, science became the driving force of technology and the complexity of technological systems increased significantly.

From 1897 to 1945, the third long wave saw a rapid acceleration in the development of new technologies in electronics and media. The radio and television were among the most important inventions, and today there are more than two hundred thousand radio stations across the globe, transmitting news and entertainment to the world's population. The third wave also witnessed the birth of the Model T, stainless steel, and the airplane. These inventions changed the global economy and society in profound ways. Economic historians point out that many of these inventions would have been impossible without the advances in mathematics, chemistry, and physics during the late nineteenth century.

The quantum revolution in technology dawned during the fourth long wave (mid-1940s to early 1990s). The key inventions included the transistor, integrated circuit, microprocessor, laser, magnetic resonance machine, and personal computer. Other notable inventions were the geostationary satellite, the spacecraft, the heart-lung machine, the Internet, and the World Wide Web.

THE FIFTH WAVE

After surveying and analyzing each long wave, Ross concluded that the United States and much of the world would experience a fifth long wave of economic activity. This wave would span most of the 1990s and extend into the first part of the twenty-first century. Drawing on Schumpeter's brilliant economic insights into the dynamic forces of economic evolution, Ross predicted that U.S. per capita GNP—a commonly used gauge of the standard of living—would increase by at least 2.5 percent annually over the next twenty-five or thirty years.

Ross argued that the dominant force behind the higher per capita GNP growth rate would be a surging rate of technological progress. Technological change would accelerate mainly because of the large and growing pool of basic research, which in turn, would significantly increase the range of possible economic applications. In addition, the inevitable internationalization of the world economy would, Ross believed, intensify competition among firms, compelling them to use the latest technology.

In retrospect, Ross's views about the source of accelerating technical change are well founded. As Exhibit 6 shows, patent activity in the United States has skyrocketed since the early 1990s. From a longer-term perspective, Exhibit 6 shows that patent activity has been growing exponentially—that is, the pace of patent activity in America has been accelerating since the late eighteenth century.

EXHIBIT 6: Onward and Upward

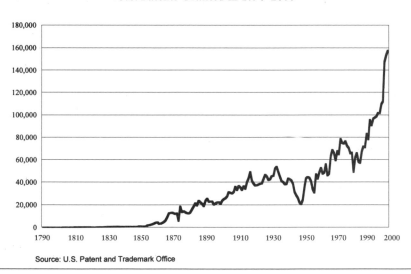

U.S. Patents Granted in 1790–2000

Source: U.S. Patent and Trademark Office

A large share of the growth in patents in the past decade has been in areas related to the fields of IT, communications, and life science. Eight of the top ten companies investing in R&D in 1999 were in the IT and life science industries, and nineteen of the top twenty-five, as well as thirty-five of the top fifty R&D leaders were in these two innovative industries.

Signs that the U.S. economy is experiencing a powerful fifth long wave of economic activity abound. Consider comments by Louis

Gerstner Jr. in his foreword to the *IBM 2000 Annual Report*. Gerstner noted that IBM research was in the midst of what he called "a golden age." He pointed out that the scope and impact of what IBM researchers have invented in just the past eight years is remarkable. From silicon germanium to copper chips, from silicon-on-insulator to WebSphere, from self-managing servers to microdrives—IBM's technology business has become a multibillion-dollar juggernaut. Gerstner went on to say,

> Make no mistake. A world of standard computing technology increases, not decreases, the value and competitive advantage of innovation. And that requires real science. Not just software developers, but also quantum physicists. Not just storage specialists, but computational biologists. Not just people who move data, but people who move atoms—one at a time.

It is evident from Gerstner's comments that researchers at IBM believe a powerful wave of technological innovation is to come—a wave of invention and innovation that has its roots in quantum physics and biology. Astonishingly, IBM filed for nearly three thousand patents in 2000 and today is filing for about ten per business day. As Exhibit 7 shows, IBM leads the pack in the number of patents issued to corporations.

EXHIBIT 7: Top Ten Patent Earners in 1999

	Number of Patents Received
1. International Business Machines	2,789
2. NEC Corporation	1,853
3. Canon, Inc.	1,800
4. Samsung Electronic Company Ltd.	1,544
5. Sony Corporation	1,439
6. Fujitsu Limited	1,231
7. Toshiba Corporation	1,225
8. Motorola, Inc.	1,207
9. Lucent Technologies	1,156
10. Mitsubishi Electric Corporation	1,089

Trends in R&D suggest a new long wave of economic activity is upon us. According to the National Science Foundation, from 1994 to 1999, the total industrial R&D investment in the United States rose a stunning 71 percent, from $97.1 billion to $166 billion (see Exhibit 8). The United States spends more money on R&D activities than do the rest of the G-7 countries—Canada, France, Germany, Italy, Japan, and the United Kingdom—combined. Equally impressive is that direct basic research in U.S. industry, research geared toward future products, processes, or services, has risen more than 80 percent, from $6 billion in 1994 to $11 billion in 1999. Spending on applied research has nearly doubled in the same period.

EXHIBIT 8: Investing in the Future:
Real Nondefense R&D Expenditures

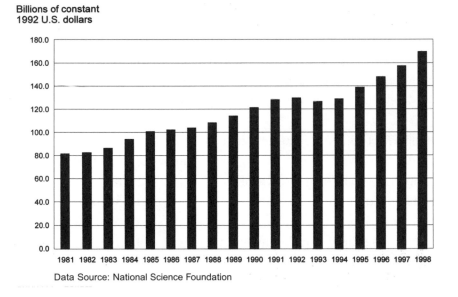

Billions of constant
1992 U.S. dollars

Data Source: National Science Foundation

Ross believed that Schumpeter's economic theories provided a solid foundation from which to assess the impact of technological change on economic growth. Of course, the difficult task for any economist or analyst is predicting what technologies will drive growth in the future. Equally arduous is how to assess their impact on the global economy, industries, companies, and financial markets. As Nobel Laureate Lawrence Klein wisely noted in the foreword to Ross' *A Gale of Creative Destruction*, Schumpeterian innovators have an ample store of new developments that await creative transfer from scientific discovery to commercial exploitation.

What technological inventions and innovations will the second generation of quantum theory bring during the fifth wave, and when will they arrive? Nobody knows for sure. We can, however, attempt to define the boundaries of the coming technology revolution.

DYNAMIC WAVES

In the past few years, there has been a lot of discussion and talk in the media about the "New Economy" and "Old Economy." It's never exactly clear what people mean by these terms. Some folks apparently link the New Economy to the proliferation of dotcoms that appeared after the commercialization of the Internet in 1995. Others use the term New Economy to mean a significant positive change in the economy's overall rate of labor productivity growth from previous periods.

As we saw in Chapter 1, there is definitely something new and different—indeed, radically new and different—about the economy today versus, say, fifty or one hundred years ago. Investment strategist Woody Brock believes that the New Economy does exist and it can be meaningfully addressed in a rigorous manner by drawing from endogenous-growth theory associated with Schumpeter, Romer, and others.

Brock notes that the degree to which an economic regime can be said to be new is a function of two measures: the degree to which new technologies and production platforms enable producers of preexisting goods to significantly lower their cost curves; and, the degree to which these same technologies and platforms bring into being new products and services. Brock argues that by these two measures, the economy of

47

1995 to 2025 has been and will continue to be quite "new." He cites the forthcoming fusion of digital and genetic logic as one of the greatest technological advances in history.

In 2001, *The Economist* made a similar observation supporting the existence of a new long wave of economic activity. The magazine noted that Schumpeter's fifth industrial wave is far from over. In all likelihood, this long wave will run for twenty to twenty-five years. Events like the crash of the Nasdaq in April 2000 and the evaporation of venture capital are nothing more than the first up phase of the long wave coming to an end and the transition to the second phase of the wave.

The evolution of the computer industry has been characterized by new waves of technology, led by new vendors, rapidly overpowering the existing order. There are few better business examples of Schumpeter's creative destruction process. The computer industry's rate of technological advance is unprecedented in business history. An industry that didn't exist in 1950 grew to $50 billion in 1980 and exceeded $500 billion in 1995, with no end in sight.

David Moschella, in *Waves of Power*, writes that the pattern of wavelike evolution witnessed in the computer industry in the past several decades is likely to continue in the years ahead. He points out that as Internet and World Wide Web user populations swell into the hundreds of millions, once again a new computer industry is being born. Just as the IT industry of the 1980s shifted away from mainframes toward personal computers (PCs), the PC era is now giving way to a global network infrastructure. This "network-centric" era has thrust the IT and communications industries on to new and unstable ground.

Moschella believes that the network-centric era will result in a restructuring of the market and supplier. As the computer, telecommunications, consumer electronics, and publishing/media industries converge, the IT industry will once again witness the emergence of new vendors, new business models, and new patterns of global market leadership.

Looking farther down the road, Moschella believes that the

network-centric era is simply another step toward a true information society. On the not too distant horizon lies the "content-centric" era, and the key enabling technology during this wave, which will prevail from 2005 to 2015, will be software. Tremendous advances in software will spawn virtual businesses and a wide variety of individualized services and "intelligent agents."

The first large computer industry wave spanned 1964 to 1981 and produced a $20 billion market. The second wave, what Moschella calls the "PC-centric" era, extended from 1981 to 1994 and produced a $460 billion market. The "network-centric" era is expected to last until 2005, and could produce a $3 trillion market. Moschella believes the fourth wave, the "content-centric" era, could produce enormous wealth during the period 2005 to 2015—perhaps more wealth than the previous three waves combined.

Schumpeter's wave analytics tell us that the next powerful upswing in technology is at hand. Given the complex dynamics of technological change, timing the upswings in economic activity is always tricky. From Ross's work, we can surmise that the U.S. economy is approaching the midpoint of the up phase of the fifth long wave. It also appears that both the short (Kitchin) and medium (Juglar) waves are in the process of turning up again in late 2002.

A NEW INDUSTRIAL REVOLUTION

Economic historians cite 1760 to 1830 as the beginning and end of the first wave of the industrial revolution. T.S. Aston, a professor of economics at the University of London notes that during those seventy years, the face of England was transformed: Land that for centuries had been cultivated as open fields was hedged or fenced. Hamlets grew into populous towns. Steam power, iron making, and cotton spinning became the driving forces of economic activity. Fresh sources of raw material were exploited, vast new markets were opened, and new methods of trade were devised.

Aston points out that parallel changes took place in the structure of society. The outstanding feature was the rapid growth of population;

after 1760, the number of people in England and Wales more than doubling, from 6.5 million in 1750 to 14 million by 1831. Aston notes that the dramatic rise was due primarily to declining mortality rates. In addition to a rising population, labor became more mobile and higher standards of comfort were offered to those able and willing to move to centers of opportunity.

The industrial revolution gave birth to the first and perhaps greatest long wave in economic history. Since then, the U.S. economy has experienced three new long waves that have wrought dramatic changes in the business landscape. New technological inventions and innovations spawned new industries and companies. During each wave, many industries and companies prospered while others withered. Analysts who believe we are on the cusp of another industrial revolution cite an accelerating pace of technological change today. New ideas and products are exploding onto the market and an increasing number of new fields are being created.

The creative destruction unleashed during the fifth wave has just begun. In coming years, we will see numerous changes in the marketplace, although predicting these changes will be difficult. In 2002, futurists at British Telecom produced a technology timeline that extends well into the twenty-first century. Exhibit 9 lists some of their predictions for the coming decade. You may be surprised at how quickly British Telecom expects these technologies to arrive. It's a safe bet that some of these predictions will not pan out, but many will. There is one thing that we can say with confidence: In the not too distant future, the world will be a very different place.

Schumpeter believed that technological possibilities were an uncharted sea and there was no reason to expect a slackening of economic growth through exhaustion of these possibilities. This view is hard to reconcile with the views expressed by many analysts and the media. Conventional economics views technology as an exogenous force that grows at a constant rate. But the evidence amassed in the past three centuries clearly shows that the rate of technological progress is not constant.

EXHIBIT 9: Fifth Wave Technologies

- Use of molecular computers by 2003.
- Smart pills with a chip dispensing drugs by 2003.
- Virtual retinal displays, glasses based, by 2003.
- Cars powered by hydrogen fuel cells by 2004.
- Real time language translation by 2004.
- Instruction from artificial intelligence in school by 2004.
- Household gadgets controlled by voice by 2005.
- Designer babies by 2005.
- Computers that write most of their own software by 2005.
- Global broadband fiber-optic network by 2005.
- Use of quantum cryptography by 2005.
- Quantum computer and optical neurocomputers by 2007
- Totally automated factories by 2007.
- Cars with automatic steering by 2008.
- DNA storage device by 2010.

Adapted from website, British Telecom Exact Technologies by Pearson and Neild.

Events of the past decade lend a great deal of support to the assertions and predictions of Myron Ross and Joseph Schumpeter. If Ross is correct, the fifth long wave should continue for the next two decades. During this period, quantum-based technologies inventions and innovations will flourish. Many of the products that populate the marketplace today are destined for the junk heap and recycling bins of tomorrow.

The convergence of quantum-based technologies with biology will be the driving force of creative destruction during the fifth wave. David Baltimore, president of Caltech, notes that biology has become an information science in the twenty-first century. However, he observes there is a lot more to biology than just manipulating the information in DNA. Not only are there proteins, which are the workhorses of biology, but also there are cells, which comprise the central organization of biological systems. The biology of the future will be the biology that manipulates DNA, proteins, and cells.

It's not surprising that Gerstner singled out quantum physicists and biologists as key resources for future technological inventions and innovations. The convergence of these two sciences in coming years is likely to lay the foundation for the next gale of creative destruction in the global economy.

Could the fifth wave spawn a new industrial revolution? All indications are that the answer is yes. The life science and nanotechnology revolutions appear capable of unleashing a powerful wave of economic change to rival the industrial revolution.

If the fifth wave contains the seeds of the next industrial revolution, as is suspected, individuals and businesses must be prepared to live in a world of accelerating technical change. This is much easier said than done, of course. The industrial revolution gave birth to a vast number of new industries and companies that thrived for decades. However, it also swept away many companies that could not adapt to the radical shift in the economic landscape. As we will see in Chapters 3 and 4, navigating a world of accelerating technical change will be an extremely daunting task for many businesses and investors in coming years. Hang onto your hats.

Key Takeaways

- Joseph Schumpeter's *creative destruction* process is alive and well today. Companies today are being threatened by the development of new markets, products, technologies, and organizational structures.

- Investors should realize that long waves of technological change have swept across the global economy periodically over the past three hundred years. The process itself is old. However, today it appears to be accelerating.

- The U.S. and global economies are currently in the up phase of the fifth long wave, which is expected to crest around 2020. By that time, we should expect the use of molecular computers, cars powered by hydrogen fuel cells, computers with human level intelligence, household gadgets that speak, DNA storage devices, and an all-optical global broadband network.

- As the fifth wave, which began in the early 1990s rolls on, new quantum-based technological innovations will flourish and change the way we live, work, and play.

- Investors must always expect the unexpected. For example, X-ray machines, nuclear energy, radio, TV, photography, and quantum mechanics, to name a few, were unexpected inventions that radically changed our society.

- A new, fertile field of research is General Purpose Technologies (GPTs) that, by definition, are technologies that impact how people live, work, and play. Investors would be wise to focus on these products with mass consumer appeal. Examples from the past include the steam engine, electricity, and the internal combustion engine.

Convergence Ahead

The dominant language and economic driver of this century is going to be genetics.

—Juan Enriquez

While many analysts and investors were preoccupied with the dotcom sector at the end of the twentieth century, a massive technology revolution was brewing in the biological sciences. James Watson and Francis Crick's quantum physics–inspired discovery of the double-helix DNA molecule in the 1950s had kicked off a revolution in molecular biology that became a force to contend with at the beginning of the twenty-first century. In fact, scientists did what many researchers once thought impossible: They produced a map of the human genome.

The mapping of the human genome is among the most important scientific events in human history. Harvard Business School professors Juan Enriquez and Ray Goldberg wrote in *Transforming Life and Transforming Business: The Life Science Revolution* that the ability to manipulate the genetic codes of living things is likely to set off an unprecedented industrial convergence. What lies ahead is a major transformation in the economic landscape—a gale of creative destruction—driven by inventions and innovations in life science.

As the revolution in biology unfolds, Enriquez and Goldberg argued that farmers, doctors, drug makers, chemical processors, computer and communications companies, energy companies, and many other commercial enterprises will be drawn into the business of life science. The inevitable convergence of these enterprises will result in the largest industry in the world: the life science industry.

Boundaries between many once distinct businesses, from agriculture and chemicals to health care and pharmaceuticals to energy and computing, already are blurring. Consumer goods companies like Procter & Gamble and cosmetics companies like L'Oreal are building new alliances, acquiring and/or merging with genomics, agribusiness, and pharmaceutical firms. And because genetic research involves processing a vast amount of data, information technology (IT) and communications companies are also being drawn into the life science sector.

At the start of the new millennium, IBM set up a life science division to address the computer needs of pharmaceutical and biotechnology companies that require powerful number-crunching machines to carry out their research and development. According to IBM's website in early 2002, Caroline Kovac, the general manager of IBM's life science unit, expects the company to aggressively expand the division in coming months and years. She foresees the unit generating at least $7 billion of new sales—more than double current revenues—to life science customers in three years.

IBM expects to significantly expand its market presence in the life science industry with sales of supercomputers and databases as well as by integrating complex and diverse computer systems and software. IBM also announced that it plans to spend some $100 million to build a supercomputer far faster than any existing machine today. The machine, dubbed "Blue Gene," will push the boundaries of our knowledge of human disease. Supercomputers alone, currently a niche market, are an estimated $2 billion-per-year global market.

IBM's Blue Gene will be capable of more than one quadrillion operations per second. The machine will be one thousand times more powerful than the "Deep Blue," the IBM supercomputer that defeated world chess champion Gary Kasparov in 1997. Such speeds may seem astonishing to the average personal computer user today, but they are necessary given the enormous computational complexity of the human genome.

Researchers in the life science industry will use the new powerful supercomputer to model how proteins in the human body fold. The hope is that if the complex folding activities of proteins are discovered, scientists and doctors will have better insight into life-threatening diseases and how to combat them.

Another approach to facilitating new discoveries in the life science industry is to use distributed-computing architectures. Last year, the National Foundation for Cancer Research (NFCR) launched a distributed-computer project intended to advance research to fight cancer. The original NFCR plan was to enlist up to 6 million PCs to work in concert to help uncover new treatments for leukemia. Participants simply download a screen saver (which can be obtained for free over the Internet) that will allow the NFCR to perform calculations using the PCs when people are not using them.

The NFCR's idea is similar to what the researchers at SETI@home are doing. Scientists at SETI (Search for Extraterrestrial Intelligence) are using a network of PCs to search for signs of extraterrestrial intelligence in the universe. SETI has attracted more than 3.5 million participants and has around (23) teraflops (i.e., megasupercomputing) processing power at its disposal. The NFCR's plan puts at the hands of researchers a computing resource they otherwise would never be able to afford or get access to.

Distributed computing is also being used by the Rothberg Institute for Childhood Diseases, a nonprofit organization whose mission is to help find a cure for children who suffer from benign tumors in multiple organs, including the brain, kidneys, heart, eyes, and lungs. During the first few years, the severity of Tuberculosis Sclerosis Complex (TSC) can range from mild skin abnormalities to seizures, mental retardation or renal failure. The founder of the institute, Jonathan Rothberg, CEO of CuraGen Corporation, believes that genomics and virtual drug screening on distributed-computing networks offer great promise in discovering a cure for TSC. He hopes this approach will serve as a model for finding cures for other orphan diseases.

Researchers note that depending on how many people participate, the time required to develop new drugs could be cut to as little as five years from the current twelve. Using advanced, unproven computing architectures like distributed computing to help fight cancer may seem fanciful to some, but to the unfortunate people suffering the effects of the deadly disease, it's a bright ray of sunshine in otherwise dark and stormy skies.

GOLDEN AGE OF MEDICINE

The convergence of IT and medicine is ushering in a new epoch in the field of medicine and health care. Peter Ringrose, chief scientific officer of Bristol-Myers Squibb, believes we are in "a golden age" of biomolecular medicine.

According to Ringrose, the medicines in use today reach only about 10 to 20 percent of the body's possible drug targets, or about five hundred to one thousand protein receptors and enzymes out of an estimated five thousand. In the next twenty years, as the pace of technological innovation accelerates, he believes we will access virtually all of those targets. Other researchers note that the mapping of the human genome will increase the number of drug targets from five hundred to ten thousand.

The golden age of biomolecular medicine will have a far-reaching impact on the health care industry, says Ringrose. In coming years, medicine will migrate from a "one size fits all" method of treatment to targeting people's specific genetic makeup. In addition, it's likely that physicians will treat and prevent the root causes of cancer, heart disease, and Alzheimer's disease—three of the most debilitating and costly diseases known to humans.

Cancer is one of the most promising areas of medical research today. Cancer research is undergoing a sea change, thanks to the genetics revolution, which has uncovered many of the gene defects responsible for causing the disease. Using the latest molecular biology techniques to home in on cancer's genetic roots, doctors are starting to halt precancerous growths before tumors develop and to target cancers that have already started to grow with a precision unimaginable just a decade ago.

Pfizer's top cancer researcher, Michael Moran, believes that cancer may become a manageable disease, like diabetes, in the not too distant future. The "kill everything that grows" approach to treating cancer, which relies on chemotherapy and radiation, is being replaced by new innovative techniques that involve antigen or site-specific targeting.

The new approach to treating cancer is the result of scientists having a better understanding of the biology behind the causes of cancer. Rising knowledge of the biology of cancer is leading researchers to produce more efficient therapeutic targets that zero in on the specific problem, in contrast to conventional therapies, which don't distinguish between targets and nontargets. The difference between approaches is like night and day.

The emergence of specific targeting in the treatment of cancer has led to the development of several new innovative drugs. Among these are Genentech's Herceptin, which uses an antibody to target breast cancer cells that express the antigen Her 2, IDEC's Rituxan, an antibody to the CD20 antigen for the treatment of B-cell non-Hodgkin's lymphoma, and ImClone's Erbitux, an antibody that binds to the Epidermal Growth Factor (EGF) receptor and inhibits the growth of solid tumors in the body.

Monoclonal antibody drugs, such as Herceptin, Rituxan, and Erbitux are just the tip of the antibody iceberg, accounting for roughly one-fourth of biotechnology drugs in development. In the pipeline, there are dozens more antibody drugs for the treatment of multiple cancer cell lines. It's likely that antibodies will play a more important role in treating cancer in the years ahead.

William Haseltine, chairman and CEO of Human Genome Sciences, notes that U.S. consumers today spend about nine times as much on doctors and medical interventions as they spend on medicines and prevention. As the life science industry evolves and researchers increase their understanding of how viruses, bacteria, and our bodies are programmed, and how they can be reprogrammed, medical treatment will shift from emergency interventions to personalized prevention.

Haseltine thinks that households in the future may end up spending just as much on pharmaceuticals as they do on doctors today. The types of medicines that are likely to appear on the market in coming years will not necessarily be akin to conventional pills or injections, he notes. They may consist of our own human substances, such as proteins.

Proteins build us from a fertilized egg into an adult. Insulin, for example, is a protein made by one gene in the body. They regulate the behavior of each and every cell in our body. They also keep our cells finely tuned, and they allow us to repair injury to our body. These substances are all the products of individual genes—genes that researchers have mapped and stored in databases. Haseltine believes that naturally occurring substances in the body have the potential to be the bulk of future medicines in the twenty-first century.

Other scientists envision "nutriceuticals" or medicines that are contained in foods, soaps, or cosmetics. Campbell's, for example, is selling soups designed for hospital patients with specific diseases. Such innovative products will flourish in the twenty-first century.

Another area that will get a quantum boost in coming years is the already large field of diagnostics. Even with the sophisticated technology physicians have at their disposal today, discovering various types of illnesses before they become life threatening is still more art than science.

One technology particularly well suited to enhancing physicians' ability to diagnose illness is biochips. Similar to conventional microchips, biochips are embedded with DNA molecules rather than electronic circuitry. Researchers believe various types of biochips could help doctors predict a patient's response to drugs or screen patients for thousands of genetic mutations and diseases—all with one simple lab test.

According to a recent study from BioInsights, the worldwide biochip market, consisting of DNA chips, lab chips, and protein chips, will reach nearly $1 billion in sales by 2005. Driven by new products and the formation of new companies, the market for biochips is expected to grow at a compound annual rate of around 30 percent in the next five years. Analysts at BioInsights expect DNA chips to retain the largest share of the biochip market, reaching sales of $725 million in 2005. Lab chips are poised to reach $160 million in sales by 2005. Although there is considerable demand for protein chips, technical limitations will hinder the growth of the market.

Given the tremendous potential for biochips, it's not surprising that many researchers in the field express an ambition to become the Intel of the biochip market. Pharmaceutical companies currently spend billions of dollars testing drugs in clinical trials. In addition, many of the technologies used to detect disease today are extremely costly and time-consuming; often physicians find themselves treating symptoms that pop up, rather than anticipating disease. Biochips will put an end to the current excessive costs, in money and time, of diagnostics.

In coming years, researchers will be able to put thousands of strands of DNA onto a chip that can screen for the genes linked to breast cancer, cystic fibrosis, prostate cancer, and other life-threatening diseases. The highly parallel nature of biotech technology will allow researchers to do thousands or tens of thousands of experiments at once. This will greatly boost the efficiency of diagnostics.

It is too early to say just how big the market for biochips will be in the coming decade and beyond. If the past experience with semiconductors is any guide, biochips will grow exponentially in power. Accelerating processing speeds and rapidly declining prices will push the market for biochips far beyond what analysts can imagine today.

From a demographics perspective, the quantum-based revolution in life science could not have come at a better time. The global population is aging at a rate never seen before. Some eight hundred thousand people reach the age of sixty-five every month. Population aging is fundamentally transforming human society, and many governments and international agencies, as well as demographic researchers, have only recently begun to pay attention to this important trend.

Economists who study global aging tell us that the payoff from innovative types of life-saving drugs and therapies could be astronomical. In *Exceptional Returns,* researchers Kevin Murphy and Robert Topel estimate that eliminating all deaths from heart disease in the United States would increase national wealth by about $48 trillion. Doing the same with cancer would generate another $47 trillion in national wealth. Eliminating deaths associated with both illnesses could raise national wealth by nearly $100 trillion.

To be sure, it's unlikely that the death rate from the two leading causes of death in America will be brought down to zero anytime soon.

Murphy and Topel believe that a realistic value of wealth generated in the United States from reducing the number of deaths from heart disease and cancer in the foreseeable future is around $10 trillion. While well shy of $100 trillion, that's a lot of economic value potential.

From a global perspective, the economic windfall of new forms of medicine could be in the tens of trillions of dollars. With some 400 million people aged sixty-five and older in the world today, and that number expected to double by 2025, it's difficult to imagine a more propitious time to bring medicine into the Golden Age.

In the 1990s, scientists crossed a threshold in biology that will rival the computer revolution. Researchers learned to construct enormously diverse "libraries" of different DNA, ribonucleic acid (RNA), proteins (i.e., strings of amino acids), and other organic molecules. Armed with these libraries, we are in a position to begin to study the properties of complex chemical reaction networks.

Scientists' ability to create libraries with 100 trillion different proteins allows them to study molecular binding and to investigate the collective behaviors of hugely diverse molecular libraries. As scientists better understand the genetic diversity of the human population, they will create molecules with increased efficacy as drugs, vaccines, enzymes, and novel molecular structures.

When the capacity to craft such molecules is married to increased understanding of the genetic and cellular signaling pathways, we will enter an era of "postgenomic" medicine. By learning to control gene regulation and cell signaling, researchers will begin to control cell proliferation, cell differentiation, and tissue regeneration to treat pathologies such as cancer, autoimmune diseases, and degenerative diseases.

The revolution underway in the life science industry has all the hallmarks of the classic Schumpeterian gale of creative destruction. Left unfettered, the life science industry will transform the economic and social fabric of the global economy as well as the stock market and other financial markets in the years ahead.

The life science revolution, however, will not be the only quantum-based revolution to transpire during the fifth wave. There is an equally profound revolution on the horizon that has its foundation in the vision of the legendary physicist Richard Feynman.

LET'S GET SMALL

Giving a talk titled "There's Plenty of Room at the Bottom," to the American Physical Society at Caltech on December 29, 1959, Richard Feynman told his audience that there were no laws of physics preventing scientists from putting the entire contents—all 24 volumes—of the *Encyclopedia Britannica* on the head of a pin. Moreover, Feynman noted that it was physically possible to put all the information humankind has ever recorded in books in the size of an ordinary pamphlet.

In his now famous talk, Feynman stated that the world of what we now call nanotechnology is a "staggeringly small world." He observed an enormous amount of information can be carried around in an exceedingly small space is well appreciated by biologists. Each tiny cell in the human body contains an exact copy of the chain of 3 billion DNA molecules that we know as the instruction code of life.

Feynman told his audience there could be an economic point to the business of making things very small. For example, some problems with computers could be addressed via miniaturization. At the time, computers were so large that they occupied entire rooms, and Feynman wondered why scientists couldn't make computers very small, with wires no more than ten or one hundred atoms in diameter and circuits no more than a few thousand angstroms across. As he put it,

> There is plenty of room to make them smaller. There is nothing that I can see in the physical laws that says the computer elements cannot be made enormously smaller than they are now. In fact, there may be certain advantages.

Feynman stated that when we get to the very, very small world—a world where circuits could consist of only seven atoms—there will be new, exciting opportunities for design. He noted that atoms on a small scale behave like *nothing* on a large scale because they obey the laws of quantum mechanics. At the atomic level, there are new kinds of forces and new kinds of possibilities and effects. As a result, researchers can think about manufacturing things in different ways.

Feynman's visionary talk at Caltech back in 1959 stoked the imaginations of researchers, corporations, governments, and venture capitalists around the world (see Exhibit 10 for one example). Today many scientists and researchers believe nanotechnology is the future.

In a statement made before a committee of the House of Representatives in 1999, Nobel Prize-winning physicist Richard Smalley noted that there is a growing sense in the scientific and technical community that we are about to enter a golden new era. He stated that we are about to be able to build things that work on the smallest possible length scales, atom by atom, with the ultimate level of finesse. These "little nanothings" and the technology that assembles and manipulates them—nanotechnology—will revolutionize our industries and our lives.

EXHIBIT 10: A Glimpse of the Nanoworld

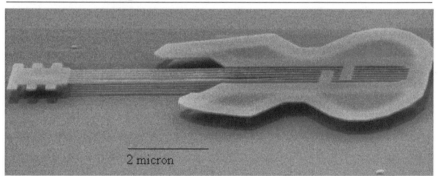

This is an electron-microscope image of the world's smallest guitar, based roughly on the design for the Fender Stratocaster, a popular electric guitar. Its length is 10 millionths of a meter—approximately the size of a red blood cell and about one-twentieth the width of a single human hair. Its strings have a width of about 50 billionths of a meter (the size of approximately one hundred atoms). Plucking the tiny strings would produce a high-pitched sound at the inaudible frequency of approximately 10 megahertz. Made by Cornell University researchers with a single silicon crystal, this tiny guitar is a playful example of nanotechnology, in which scientists are building machines and structures on the scale of billionths of a meter to perform technological functions and study processes at the submicroscopic level.

Source: Dustin W. Carr and Harold G. Craighead, Cornell University.

Smalley went on to say that everything we see around us is made of atoms, the tiny elemental building blocks of matter. From stone to copper, to bronze, iron, steel, and now silicon, the major technological ages of humankind have been defined by what these atoms can do in huge aggregates, trillions upon trillions of atoms at a time, molded, shaped, and refined as macroscopic objects. Smalley pointed out that even our vaunted microelectronics of the late-twentieth-century in our state-of-the-art microprocessor is a mountain compared to the size of a single atom. He noted that as fantastic as the technology of the previous century is, it pales in comparison to what will be possible when we learn to build things at the molecular level, one atom at a time.

Molecular nanotechnology can be defined as the thorough, inexpensive control of the structure of matter based on molecule-by-molecule control of products and by-products. *Nano* is derived from *nanos,* the Greek word for "dwarf." Nanotechnology is the science of fabricating things smaller than 100 nanometers. A nanometer is one-billionth of a meter. Four atoms laid end to end are roughly equivalent to 1 nanometer. To get an idea of the nano scale, if the width of a penny represented 1 nanometer, a foot-long ruler would have to be represented between Richmond, Virginia and Miami, Florida.

Mother Nature has employed this process to build the world around us for billions of years. Every living thing is made of cells that are chock-full of nanomachines, including proteins, DNA, and RNA. Each one of these cells is perfect, right down to the last atom. Their inner workings are so exquisite that changing the location or identity of any one atom would cause damage.

In the past century, scientists have learned much about the workings of cells—which Smalley calls "biological nanomachines." The benefits of this knowledge are beginning to be seen in medicine. In homage to Feynman, Smalley stated that in coming decades scientists will learn to modify and adapt this machinery to extend the quality and length of life. Biotechnology was the first nanotechnology, and it has a long way yet to go.

In fact, Smalley believes, as do many other scientists today, that nanotechnology could lead to a new industrial revolution—a revolution that will produce profound technological breakthroughs in IT, advanced manufacturing, medicine and health, environment and energy, and perhaps even national security. Smalley notes that the impact of nanotechnology on the health, wealth, and lives of people will equal or even surpass the combined influences of microelectronics, medical imaging, computer-aided engineering, and artificial polymers.

K. Eric Drexler, chairman of the Foresight Institute, a nonprofit educational organization formed to help prepare society for anticipated advanced technologies, points out in his book, *Engines of Creation,* that science and technology are advancing toward molecular manufacturing along many fronts, in chemistry, physics, biology, and computer science. We can see this clearly today from the almost daily media dispatches from university and corporate laboratories and research facilities around the world. These dispatches give us a glimpse of the technological boundaries that might define the twenty-first century. From them we can begin to see how the quantum-based revolution in technology contains the seeds for another revolution in industry that could rival or surpass the Newtonian-inspired industrial revolution of the eighteenth century.

SMALLER IS BIGGER

The transition from the microworld to the nanoworld is most evident in the information technology (IT) sector. The first commercial microprocessor, manufactured by Intel in 1971, contained twenty-three hundred transistors. Today, Intel is making Pentium 4 microprocessors that contain over 40 million transistors. By 2007, researchers at Intel tell us they will be manufacturing chips that contain more than 1 billion transistors that will be ten times faster than today's fastest microprocessor. Many scientists believe that nanotechnology holds the key to smaller, faster, and more inexpensive chips in the twenty-first century.

Nobody knows for sure how quickly the transition from the microworld to the nanoworld will occur in the IT sector, but the writing is on the wall. Exhibit 11 shows research in nanotechnology has accelerated sharply in the past decade or so. The graph shows the number of scientific publications with the word nano in the title listed in the ISI Web of Science Citation Index. The ISI Web of Science tracks more than 1.2 million publications in its database. The number of publications with *nano* in the title has risen from 237 in 1987 to nearly ten thousand today.

EXHIBIT 11

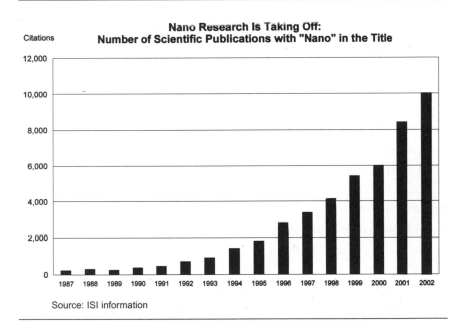

Source: ISI information

In 2001, a team of scientists at Intel unveiled the world's tiniest and fastest transistor. The 20-nanometer transistor is so small that a vertical stack of five thousand of them would equal the thickness of one sheet of paper. The size of each transistor's gate—only three atoms wide—allows it to open and close an astonishing 1.5 trillion times per second (i.e., at 1.5 terahertz).

Intel's transistor technology sounds more like science fiction than science, but it's really just the beginning of another transformation of computing technology. Tom Theis, director of IBM's physical sciences, believes that advances in nanotechnology will allow researchers to build an incredibly powerful computer the size of a sugar cube. Such a feat would require wires and transistors in computer chips to shrink to sizes smaller than dust particles. This may sound fanciful to nonscientists, but as Feynman told us in the late 1950s, there's not just room at the bottom—there is *plenty* of room.

In the twenty-first century, things that are very small have the potential to be very, very big. At the moment, conventional fabrication technology and techniques are not capable of building nanocomputers. However, scientists believe that at some point in the future they will be able to build (or more precisely, *grow)* chip circuitry six atoms wide that assembles itself in controlled chemical reactions.

In 2001, more than 450 companies and 271 leading academic institutions in more than 29 countries were working on nanotechnology. Some of these companies are manufacturing tools that will give researchers the capability to produce nanocomputers, nanoelectronic, and nano-optical devices. Companies involved in nanotechnology today include Arryx, Capsulition Nanoscience, FeRx, Molecular Electronics, NanoGram, NanoOpto, Nanostream, Nanosys, Nantero, and Quantum Dot. Some of the largest technology companies in the world are spending millions on new nanotech facilities, equipment, and talent, including Bell Labs (Lucent), IBM, Intel, Hewlett-Packard, NEC, Mitsubishi, and Motorola.

Perhaps the most promising nanotechnology on the immediate horizon is the carbon nanotube transistor. Carbon nanotubes are very strong elastic cylinders of carbon atoms that bear a striking resemblance to a tube of rolled-up chicken wire. One nanotube is about one hundred-thousandth the thickness of a human hair. Carbon nanotubes have some remarkable properties: They are one hundred times stronger than steel, tougher than diamonds, and have better thermal and electrical conductivity properties than any other material scientists are aware of today.

Last year, researchers at IBM took a quantum jump toward the post-silicon age of computing by creating a computer circuit out of a single strand of carbon. This was the first time that a device made of carbon nanotubes was able to carry out any sort of logic. It also marked the first logic circuit made of a single molecule. At this juncture, it's not clear whether IBM will be able to manufacture a practical computer chip based on carbon nanotubes.

Nanotube chip architecture needs further research, but there is no doubt the physics work. The day is not far off when nanotubes will be used for computer processors that might pack up to ten thousand more transistors in the space currently taken up by one silicon transistor. Since Sumio Iijima of NEC Corporation reported the discovery of carbon nanotubes in 1991, they have been a focus of intense research around the world. Today, carbon nanotubes have potential uses ranging from wiring in integrated circuits to components in nanoscale motors and energy storage.

Nanotubes also have the tantalizing potential to be a new storage system for hydrogen fuel. Hydrogen is viewed by many in the energy business as *the* energy source of the twenty-first century. Unlike fossil fuels such as petroleum, hydrogen is plentiful and clean. Some researchers believe that fuel cells—batteries that combine oxygen and hydrogen to produce electricity—could one day power virtually all cars and buses, pumping out nothing more harmful than warm, clean water. However, for hydrogen to become a practical alternative fuel in the future scientists must first develop a lighter storage system to replace the bulky tanks of liquefied or condensed hydrogen found in many of today's electric vehicles.

Carbon nanotubes appear to have the right qualifications to construct a state-of-the-art storage system for hydrogen. They can be arranged in groups to form ropelike bundles. The diameter of an individual carbon nanotube is typically two or three times that of a hydrogen atom, and researchers believe that hydrogen could be tucked both inside and between the tubes. While there is much more research to be done, carbon nanotubes appear to have a promising future in the energy sector.

Carbon nanotubes may also be the source of future superconductors. In 2001, scientists turned the world's smallest nanotubes into superconductors: A team of scientists from Hong Kong University of Science and Technology demonstrated that the world's smallest nanotubes reach superconductivity at temperatures below 20° Kelvin.

It is thought that superconducting nanotubes could one day be used in nanoscale sensors and nanoelectronic devices. Their lack of electrical resistance could mitigate one of the anticipated problems of nano-electronics: the buildup of heat from tightly packed components. The next challenge for scientists is to find ways to dope, or add other atoms to, the nanotubes. It's possible that doping nanotubes with lithium or potassium could raise the temperature at which they superconduct and make nano-superconductors a valuable part of the nanoelectronic toolbox.

Although it is still early days, nanotechnology has the potential to be to the twenty-first century what microelectronics was to the twentieth century. Researchers see the potential for a number of new markets forming in the years ahead. The market for tools and devices is likely to mushroom as new types of instrumentation become necessary for manufacturing at the nano level. There is also an extensive market opportunity for nanomaterials. In fact, nanotechnology in materials developments is already a significant business.

In early 2002, scientists built atomically thin layers of crystalline silicon called "quantum wells." A quantum well is made of sandwiched layers of electrically insulating material and semiconductive films, each only a few nanometers thick. The electrons packed together in the atomically thin semiconductor layers remain confined by the insulating nanofilms, forcing the electrons to increase one another's energy levels and emit bright light. Quantum wells could prove invaluable in light-based electronics. This type of nanotechnology may one day lead to the development of handheld supercomputers and a far more powerful communications network.

In the life science industry, cancer researchers have developed an ultra-tiny nanoscale device that slips inside cancer cells and releases radioactive isotopes that kill them. The device has proven effective in mice and eventually will be tested on humans. The device consists of a highly potent single radioactive atom entombed inside a molecular cage. The cage is attached to an antibody that serves as a homing device, steering the "nanogenerator" into cancer cells. Once inside the cancer cell, a powerful atom, called actinium-225, breaks down, releasing high-energy alpha particles capable of razing the cell's DNA and proteins. Researchers are testing the nanoscale devices against several types of cancerous cells, including lymphoma, leukemia, ovarian, breast, and prostate.

While research in nanotechnology and life science is heating up in the private sector, it is also receiving a good deal of attention from governments around the world. In the last few years, the U.S. government has provided funding for research in the following areas:

- Nanostructured materials

- Molecular electronics

- Spin electronics

- Lab on a chip (nanocomponents)

- Biosensors and bioinformatics

- Bioengineering

- Quantum computing

- Nanoscale theory, modeling, and simulation

- Nanorobotics

A number of distinguished scientists believe there are a vast number of applications for these technologies. Ralph Merkle of Zyvex, a pioneer in nanotechnology, believes that nanotechnology will eventually replace our entire manufacturing base with a radically more precise, less expensive, and flexible way of making products. This may sound fanciful to some analysts, but scientists well-versed in quantum theory have little doubt about the potential for nanotechnology to completely restructure the global economic landscape.

Steve Jurvetson, a Silicon valley–based venture capitalist, and a man who makes his living putting his money where his mouth is, believes that we will see a powerful convergence of nanotechnology, biotechnology, and information technology in the next twenty years. As he puts it, we are entering a time when matter itself is becoming code—a time when matter is becoming digitized. He believes that this phenomenon is more than just a transition from micro to nano. Rather, the convergence is creating a whole new domain where we can put matter into digital instead of bulk form.

In Jurvetson's view, nanotechnology is, essentially, the digitization of all manufacturing of matter. As a result of the quantum revolution in technology, he believes the pace of disruption in industry is going to accelerate in coming years. He adds that it's not just the the pace of technical change that is accelerating—the pace of acceleration is itself accelerating. In other words, the pace of disruption is growing not exponentially, but rather superexponentially. However difficult to comprehend, exponential growth is an essential feature of technological progress that will impact the business world and, as we will see in Chapter 4, is an unstoppable force.

Key Takeaways

- Investment opportunities in genetics and bioinformatics will be prevalent as researchers network to discover the genetic origin of, and protein-based cures for, many fatal diseases from heart disease to cancer.

- Biochips, another quantum-based technology, are transforming health care diagnostics into a more efficient and productive tool for science.

- Global aging is an inevitable trend that will encourage innovative types of life-saving drugs and therapies. The potential payoff from these new medicines is in the trillions of dollars.

- Investors should be aware of the fusion and convergence of nanotechnology, and genetic and digital technologies that will transform how companies will operate.

- There will be investment opportunities in companies that manufacture the tools that build nanotechnology.

Fast Forward

We'd better not blink. The next couple of years are
going to go by in a flash.
                                        —Louis Gerstner, Jr.

In early 1949, a year before Joseph Schumpeter's death, an article titled "Brains that Click," appeared in *Popular Mechanics*. The author of the article enthused over a state-of-the-art supercomputer called the Eniac that was equipped with eighteen thousand vacuum tubes and weighed thirty tons. He predicted cheerfully that computers in the future might have only one thousand vacuum tubes and perhaps weigh only 1.5 tons. The author was in very good company. Six years prior to the publication of his article, Thomas Watson, chairman of IBM had remarked that he thought there was a world market for *maybe* five computers.

At the time, these predictions seemed reasonable to researchers and scientists. Watson was correct in his assessment of the world market for computers. After all, a computer back then cost a fortune and had to be stored in a room the size of a basketball court. The author of the *Popular Mechanics* article was equally justified in his enthusiasm for computers of the future. Scientists were quickly finding more efficient ways of building computers that weighed a fraction of their predecessors and operated on far fewer vacuum tubes than needed for the Eniac.

Of course, now these pronouncements look as outrageous as Charles Duell's statement about the future of inventions at the end of the nineteenth century. Today, there are more than 500 million computers in use in the global economy, and one of the fastest growing segments of the computer market is in handheld and pocket PCs —computers that weigh less than 7 ounces and contain chips that have over 40 million transistors.

FUTURE SHOCK

If Rip van Future (a distant cousin of Rip van Winkle) were awakened today after sleeping through the last half of the twentieth century, he would be overwhelmed at the speed of technical change in the global economy. He would be in a state of "future shock," Alvin Toffler's term for the dizzying disorientation brought on by the premature arrival of the future. Assuming he recovered from the initial shock of how different the economic landscape looks, he might observe that the pace of technical change is accelerating over time. In fact, he might note that the pace of change of just about everything in the global economy is accelerating. Rip's doctor might console him, relaying that his illness was common among people at this time and that signs of Toffler's future shock are everywhere.

Future historians will mark the start of the twenty-first century as a time when quantum physics became the predominant source of technological change in the global economy; when scientists provided a working draft of the human genome, ushering in a new era in medicine and biology; when new techniques in computer chip production began to exceed the pace of Moore's law (a law that states the number of transistors on a chip doubles every eighteen months); scientists produced a seven-qubit quantum computer, a feat many said could never be accomplished; researchers created from strands of synthetic DNA, a computer that was used to solve relatively complex calculations; advances in optical communications and storage technology accelerated sharply; and distributed-computing architectures fundamentally began to alter the way we think about and use computers.

The beginning of the third millennium will also be remembered as a time when the chairman of Ford Motor Company, William Clay Ford, predicted the end of the hundred year reign of the internal combustion engine and the ascent of fuel cell technology; electronic commerce became a major force in business; data traffic, not voice traffic, became the driving force in the world's communications networks; when cellular phone penetration in Japan and in several Nordic and Latin American countries exceeded fixed-line penetration; and cell phones would soon outnumber fixed telephone lines worldwide.

As if all that were not enough, future historians will identify the twenty-first century as a period when analysts and investors began to contemplate the serious problems with the five-hundred-year-old accounting discipline; the chairman of the Federal Reserve Board stated that the spread of information technology (IT) has revolutionized business conduct and caused rising rates of productivity growth and living standards in America; and a number of "dotcom" companies saw their market caps shrink by 90 percent or more and were either acquired or went out of business.

Some scientists who study the evolution of technical change believe the pace of change in the twenty-first century will be so fast that the equivalent of twenty thousand years of progress (at today's rate of change) will occur in the next one hundred years. If this is correct, we could experience as much technological change in the next twenty-five years as we experienced during the entire twentieth century. Imagine condensing one hundred years of Joseph Schumpeter's *creative destruction* process into twenty-five years. To quote Arthur Clarke, "the future isn't what it used to be!"

In the early 1960s, Clarke observed that biological evolution had given way to a far more rapid process—technological evolution. Today Brian Arthur, former Stanford University economics professor and Citibank Professor at the Santa Fe Institute, says that it is difficult to clock something as ill-defined as the speed of technological evolution. It is reasonable, however, to ask how fast we would have to speed up biological evolution of life to make it roughly match a particular technology's rate of change.

THOUGHT EXPERIMENT

To gauge the speed of technological evolution, Arthur conducts the following thought experiment. First he speeds up biological evolution in history by a factor of 10 million. Instead of life starting around 3,600 million years ago, the first crude blue-green algae would have appeared 360 years ago, about the year 1640. Multicellular organisms would have arisen in Jane Austen's time, about 1810 or so, and the great Cambrian explosion that produced the ancestors of most of today's creatures would have happened in the early 1930s. Dinosaurs would show up in the late 1960s, and rule the planet during the 1970s and 1980s. Birds and mammals would appear in the mid-1970s but would not come fully into their own until the 1990s. The first hominids would emerge only in the past year or two, and Homo sapiens only in the past month.

Arthur then does the same exercise for technology, starting with calculating machinery. He puts technical changes in calculating devices on the same timeline as biological evolution but uses the actual rate of technical change. Early calculating machines—for example, the abacus—extend back into antiquity, but the modern era of mechanical devices starts in the 1640s, when the simple calculating machines of Wilhelm Schickard, Blaise Pascal, and Gottfried Wilhelm Leibniz began to appear. The first successful multicellular devices (i.e., machines that use multiple instructions) are the Jacquard looms of Jane Austen's time. Calculators and difference engines of varying ingenuity arise and vanish throughout the 1800s. Not until the 1930s—the Cambrian time on Arthur's parallel evolutionary scale—is there a true explosion. At that time, calculating machines become electrical, government goes statistical, and accounting becomes mechanical.

The 1960s see the arrival of large mainframe computers, Arthur's parallel to the dinosaurs, and their dominance lasts through the 1970s and 1980s. PCs show up, like birds and mammals, in the mid-1970s, but do not take hold until the late 1980s and early 1990s. The Internet and, more specifically, the World Wide Web, corresponds to the appearance of humankind on Arthur's parallel evolutionary timeline. At its current evolutionary stage, the Web is a primitive but powerful technology.

Crude as it is, Arthur's thought experiment tells us that technology is evolving at roughly 10 million times the speed of biological evolution. As Arthur puts it, that's warp speed.

THE EMPEROR'S FOOLISH WAYS

Given the almost incomprehensible rate of technical change, it's no wonder that many people today suffer from Toffler's future shock. Raymond Kurzweil, scientist, entrepreneur, and author, observed in his precis *The Singularity Is Near* that it is human nature to try to adapt to the changing pace of technology. He points out that many long-range forecasts of technical feasibility—like those of Charles Duell, Thomas Watson, and others—dramatically underestimate the power of future technology because they are based on what he calls the "intuitive linear" view of technological progress, rather than the "historical exponential view."

The intuitive view sees the pace of technical change continuing at the current rate. Kurzweil points out that even for those of us who have lived through a sufficiently long period of technological progress to experience how the pace increases over time, our unexamined intuition nonetheless gives us the impression that progress changes at the rate that we have recently experienced. One reason for this, he believes, is that an exponential curve approximates a straight line when viewed for a brief duration.

Thus, even though the rate of progress in the very recent past is far greater than it was ten years ago, our memories are nonetheless dominated by our very recent experience. You can see this clearly by observing the formation of analysts' earnings expectations on Wall Street. It is typical of even highly trained analysts to extrapolate the current pace of change into the future as a way of forming their expectations.

In *Faster: The Acceleration of Just about Everything*, science writer James Gleick explores the impact of accelerating technical change on the economy and society. Gleick quotes the scientist Greg Blonder:

> Humans endure a more or less confined life, far removed from the hurried pace of exponentials. Forty-five Fahrenheit is cold, eighty-five

Fahrenheit is warm; Five hundred calories a day, you starve; three thousand a day, you're fat as a pig. By contrast, exponentials start slowly and remain disarmingly out of sight. Yet they build strength relentlessly until they've grown too large to ignore. By then, whole industries have changed and whole cultures have fallen.

The clash of the speed of biological versus technological evolution or, alternatively, the intuitive linear view of the world versus the historical exponential view was the proximate cause of Toffler's future shock. We can see now that Clarke was accurate in his observation that biological evolution has given way to a far more rapid process in technological evolution. It's as if biological evolution proceeds on a slightly upward sloping path while technological evolution traces out a hockey stick-like curve that rises rapidly upward into the stratosphere.

There is an ancient tale about the emperor of China who was so taken with the game of chess that he offered its inventor a reward of anything he wanted in the vast kingdom. The inventor said one grain of rice on the first square of the chessboard, two grains of rice on the second square, four grains on the third square, eight grains on the fourth square, and so forth.

As the story goes, the emperor granted the inventor's seemingly humble request only to learn that he had promised him 18 million trillion grains of rice! This much rice would cover the entire surface of the Earth almost twice over.

The emperor's behavior is typical of how humans perceive exponential change. Cognitive psychologists point out that people have difficulty comprehending accelerating rates of change. To see this, consider the implications of the emperor's decision to grant the inventor of chess his wish: one grain of rice on the first square, two grains on the second square, four on the third square, and so on. Exhibit 12 shows the outcome of carrying out this exercise to cover the entire chessboard. As the calculations show, the process of doubling the amount of rice for each square on the chessboard rapidly escalates the farther away one moves from the first square.

EXHIBIT 12: Grains of Rice Granted to Inventor of Chess

1	2	3	4	5	6	7	8
1	2	4	8	16	32	64	128
9	10	11	12	13	14	15	16
256	512	1024	2048	4096	8192	16384	32768
17	18	19	20	21	22	23	24
65536	131072	262144	524288	1048576	2097152	4194304	8388608
25	26	27	28	29	30	31	32
16777216	33554432	67108864	134217728	268435456	536870912	1073741824	2147483648
33	34	35	36	37	38	39	40
4294967296	8589934592	17179869184	34359738368	38719476736	137438953472	274877906944	549755813888
41	42	43	44	45	46	47	48
1099511627776	2199023255552	4389046511104	8796093022208	17592186044416	35184372088832	70368744177664	140737488355328
49	50	51	52	53	54	55	56
281474976710656	562949953421312	1125899906842620	2251799813685250	4503599627370500	9007199254740990	18014398509482000	36028797018964000
57	58	59	60	61	62	63	64
72057594037927900	144115188075856000	288230376151712000	576460752303423000	1152921504606850000	2305843009213690000	4611686018427390000	9223372036854780000

Source: Author's calculation.

By the time we get to the thirty-second square on the chessboard, the emperor has granted the inventor 2,147,483,648 grains of rice—more than two billion grains. It's at the thirty-second square where the process of doubling mushrooms into numbers that are difficult for even the emperor of China to comprehend. Extending the doubling process out to encompass the entire chessboard, we find that the emperor has granted the inventor of chess 18 million trillion grains of rice. At ten grains of rice per square inch, this would require rice fields that span twice the surface area of the entire planet—obviously far more than the emperor could ever hope to repay, let alone produce.

The thirty-second doubling represents an inflection point in the geometric progression, as shown in Exhibit 13. The inflection point in the progression is sometimes referred to as "the knee of the curve." It is the point where the pace of change switches from more or less a horizontal straight line (from the first square to the thirty-second square) to a vertical straight line.

EXHIBIT 13

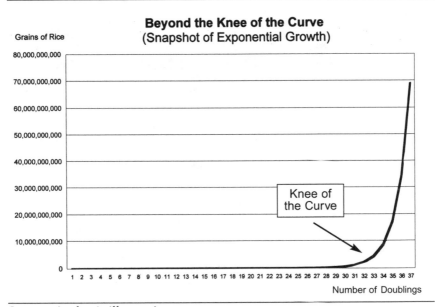

Beyond the Knee of the Curve
(Snapshot of Exponential Growth)

Grains of Rice

Number of Doublings

Source: Author's illustration

Although many people—particularly those born before 1940—have experienced a great deal of technical change in their lifetimes, it's nothing compared to the amount of technical change they will experience in the next decade or two. As Exhibit 13 shows, later doublings in a geometric progression, especially the kind witnessed in the power of computers, are pronounced. Inventor and author of *The Clock of the Long Now*, Stewart Brand says the changes that occur during the vertical ascent on an exponential growth path no longer feel quantitative or qualitative but cataclysmic. Each new doubling after the knee of the curve is a new world.

At the outset of the twenty-first century, we can already detect signs of life in the post–thirty-second square world. Mark Anderson, president of Strategic News Service and an astute commentator on technology and communications, writes in his newsletter that the speed with which decisions are made in the economy today has accelerated greatly since the days when General Motors and other large companies dominated the business landscape. Now many technology firms respond to changes in their end markets within virtual minutes of getting news from their sales force, according to Anderson. This is a dramatic shift from yesteryear, when General Motors and the other big auto manufacturers would have responded not in days, but in months and quarters, or even years.

The way businesses have been managed closely parallels the evolution of IT. Companies have gone from batch processing wherein decisions might take weeks or months to real-time information systems, wherein decisions are made almost instantaneously. The combination of high-speed PCs, powerful communications networks (e.g., broadband Internet), and innovative software has greatly accelerated the speed at which important corporate decisions can be made today, especially for large, multinational firms. Modern technology gives senior executives and other key corporate decision makers instant access to company information so they can make decisions quickly.

Robert Herbold, former Microsoft chief operating officer, notes in "Inside Microsoft" that the company's technology infrastructure has yielded tremendous benefits. For starters, the firm can now close its books in three days instead of twenty-one. Software gives Microsoft's top management team access to all kinds of up-to-the-minute financial information. Within seconds, executives can see any geographical or business unit's operating expenses, stated in dollars and broken down by type of cost, while also having each type measured as a percentage of revenues. These numbers can in turn be compared with historical figures. Without its technology infrastructure, Microsoft would be forced to make decisions in the dark, with outdated information.

Tom Siebel, founder and CEO of Siebel Systems, uses the sales automation software that his company sells to run his business virtually in real time. In a *Forbes* article "The Man Who Sees Around Corners," in 2002, Siebel noted that access to real-time information allowed him to react quickly to the harsh downturn in technology spending in early 2001. Within weeks, Siebel turned a $4 billion company back into a $2.6 billion company. Access to real-time information on products and markets led Cisco Systems CEO John Chambers to make a decision to lay off 20 percent of the company's workforce in early 2001, just weeks after the downturn. Imagine what shape Japan's economy would be in today had policymakers and executives there been able to make swift and dramatic adjustments to changing economic conditions.

New software and business processes are also quickening the pace of business. Analytical dynamic pricing tools are now available that combine and compress a variety of information to quickly give sales representatives a yes or no answer when they are facing a decision about specific product pricing. These tools also give senior management a higher-level view of business efficiency and profit drivers. The main attraction of dynamic pricing lies in the analytics and business rules that automate and report point-of-sale decision making.

Maxager Technology CEO Michael Rothschild and his colleagues have developed a powerful yet practical solution for aligning daily decisions with corporate time-based profitability metrics. Maxager's innovative technology calculates the time-based profitability of every production batch, giving managers a new set of profit-based metrics on which to base their daily decisions. As a result, manufacturers can now sell their capacity for the most profit possible in both traditional sales channels and online e-markets. Maxager Technology's Enterprise Profit Management software helps capital-intensive manufacturers make money faster by revealing how fast every customer, product, process, facility, and asset contributes cash to the business.

RISING CLOCKSPEED

The acceleration in the speed of business is not confined to the technology sector. In "Jack: The Exit Interview," Jack Welch, former CEO of General Electric (GE), notes that the biggest change in the business environment during his tenure at the helm of GE was the speed at which change occurs. Welch would be the first to say that the key to sustaining competitive advantage in the global economy today is to have an organization that can adapt quickly to a rapidly changing business landscape. It's common to hear prominent CEOs of large multinational corporations talking about the need for faster decision making in their organizations.

Charles Fine, professor of management at the Massachusetts Institute of Technology's (MIT's) Sloan School of Management, asserts in his book *Clockspeed* all competitive advantage is temporary in business today. To survive and thrive, companies must be able to anticipate and adapt to change. Interestingly, Fine takes inspiration from the world of biology to analyze the twenty-first-century business landscape. He argues that each industry has its own evolutionary life cycles, or what he calls "clockspeed." The clockspeed of any given industry is measured by the rate at which it introduces new products, processes, and organizational structures.

Exhibit 14, which Fine developed, provides some quantitative measures of clockspeed for various industries. Fine breaks down clockspeed into three broad categories—fast, medium, and slow—and then shows the clockspeeds for each industry's product technology, organization, and process technology. He notes that although the quantitative measurement of industry clockspeeds is in its infancy, quantum technology-intensive industries are significantly faster than traditional industries, such as agriculture, machine tools, steel, paper, and petrochemicals.

To measure clockspeed in a manufacturing company, for example, one needs to look only at metrics, such as capital equipment obsolescence rates. Intel's state-of-the-art, billion-dollar-plus wafer fabrication facility will be out of date in four years. Ford Motor Company's new auto plant will last twenty years or longer. Boeing's rate of major new product launches is slightly under two products per decade, while Disney seems to aim for the release of one new children's animated movie per year. In the software industry, it's not uncommon for new upgrades to be released twice a year, if not more often. Computer operating systems, such as Windows XP, tend to have product clockspeeds of five years or longer.

Fine emphasizes that the faster an industry evolves—the faster its clockspeed—the more temporary a company's advantage. Furthermore, measuring industry clockspeeds is a complex process. First, clockspeed varies within an industry. For example, within the electronics industry, the semiconductor and the circuit-board industries have relatively fast clockspeeds. Microprocessor development, however, followed a low-variance path as predicted by Moore's law, whereas the development of circuit-boards was slow-moving until the advent of surface-mount technology.

EXHIBIT 14: Industry Clockspeeds (Selected Industries)

Industry	Product Tech	Organization (years)	Process Tech (years)
FAST CLOCKSPEED			
Personal computers	<6 months	2–4	2–4
Computer-aided software engineering	6 months	2–4	2–4
Toys and games	<1 year	5–15	5–15
Athletic footwear	<1 year	5–15	5–15
Semiconductors	1–2 years	2–3	3–10
Cosmetics	2–3 years	5–10	10–20
MEDIUM CLOCKSPEED			
Bicycles	4–6 years	10–15	20–25
Automobiles	4–6 years	4–6	10–15
Computer operating systems	5–10 years	5–10	5–10
Agriculture	3–8 years	5–10	8–10
Fast food	3–8 years	25–50	5–25
Beer brewing	4–6 years	400	2–3
Airlines	5–7 years	25 (hardware) 2–3 years (software)	<5
Machine tools	6–10 years	6–10	10–15
Pharmaceuticals	7–15 years	10–20	5–10
SLOW CLOCKSPEED			
Aircraft (commercial)	10–20 years	5–30	20–30
Tobacco	1–2 years	20–30	20–30
Steel	20–40 years	10–20	50–100
Aircraft (military)	20–30 years	5–30	2–3
Shipbuilding	25–35 years	5–30	10–30
Petrochemicals	10–20 years	20–40	20–40
Paper	10–20 years	20–40	20–40
Electricity	100 years	25–50	50–75
Diamond mining	Centuries	20–30	50–100

Source: Charles Fine, *Clockspeed.*

Second, clockspeed may not be consistent in any industry. Often there is an early burst of technological discovery that causes clockspeed to increase, but as the industry matures, clockspeed begins to slow. Alternatively, a slow-moving industry could be hit with a technological invention or innovation that drives up the clockspeed.

Fine argues that industry clockspeeds are increasing almost everywhere today and two principal reasons are technological change and competition. These two factors whip up the winds of creative destruction, he notes, especially in fast-clockspeed industries. When an industry is subjected to an important innovation, it typically experiences a significant uptick in overall clockspeed. Genomics is having this kind of impact on the pharmaceutical and life science industry. Advances in optics and wireless technology are having a similar impact on the communications sector. The migration from analog to digital power is increasing the clockspeed of the utility sector. It's possible that the transition from fossil fuels to hydrogen fuel will have a similar effect on the energy and transportation industries.

Haim Mendelson, a Stanford University Graduate School of Business professor, echoed Fine's views on the rising pace of change in industry. In his book *Survival of the Smartest,* he notes that the clockspeed of business processes is increasing dramatically today. Unlike the gradual hundred-year transition from the agricultural age to the industrial age, the information age has arrived at lightning speed, leading to dramatic changes in the competitive business landscape. Mendelson points out that most corporate executives are still unclear how business practices should change in response to the new realities. He cites a survey of 350 board-level directors and executives completed by the Economist Intelligence Unit and Andersen Consulting in 1997, in which only 4 percent of senior managers said they believed themselves to be well prepared to lead tomorrow's organization.

CAMBRIAN EXPLOSION

Michael Rothschild likens the acceleration of technological innovation today to the start, 550 million years ago, of biology's Cambrian Explosion, which was the most amazing burst of evolutionary change in earth's history. As Rothschild points out, shifting to higher levels of complexity is typical of evolution. The consequence of new forms of quantum-based technologies will be a massive pulse of economic evolution. As Rothschild notes, virtually none of the life forms that flourished before the Cambrian Explosion in that precursor era survived the explosive force of biology's big bang.

You can be sure that the most profound impact of the quantum revolution will not be on the new industries it creates, but on existing businesses. Before the industrial revolution, the most labor-intensive business on the planet was farming. Agriculture accounted for the lion's share of employment and output of preindustrial economies.

After the industrial revolution, agricultural output soared, but the sector still accounted for only a tiny small share of total employment and output in most developed countries. The industrial revolution boosted the efficiency of the agricultural sector—far beyond any farmer's wildest imagination or economist's forecast. New tools and methods of farming created during the industrial revolution allowed a smaller share of the world's population to produce ever greater amounts of food. Productivity in the agricultural sector exploded.

If past is prologue, the impact of the quantum revolution on the manufacturing and service sectors will be similar to that of the industrial revolution on agriculture. These sectors should account for a smaller share of employment, but their overall output and productivity will increase as firms find new, more efficient ways of providing goods and services.

In the twenty-first century, Schumpeter's gales of creative destruction should be as forceful as they were during the industrial revolution if not more so. Like a violently erupting volcano that spews lava and creates vast new lands eventually to be inhabited by a complex global ecosystem, the quantum revolution in technology is creating a virtual landscape that will soon be occupied by a host of new economic organisms that didn't exist before.

As the pulse of technological evolution accelerates, we should expect to see Schumpeter's waves of creative destruction coming faster and faster. Some evidence suggests this is already occurring. Many analysts note that the major waves of invention and innovation have shortened from around seventy years during the time of the industrial revolution to less than forty years today. We can see clearly the economic effects of accelerating technological change by studying the evolution of the U.S.

stock market and corporate performance during the twentieth century.

In 1896, the Dow Jones Industrial Average consisted of twelve companies, most in agricultural industries or basic industries, such as coal, iron, and leather. As Exhibit 15 shows, only one company from the original Dow Twelve is still in the index today—General Electric.

EXHIBIT 15: Creative Destruction and the Original Dow Twelve

Company	What Became of It
American Cotton Oil	Distant ancestor of Bestfoods
American Sugar	Evolved into Amstar Holdings
American Tobacco	Broken up in 1911 antitrust action
Chicago Gas	Absorbed by People's Gas in 1897
Distilling and Cattle Feeding	Evolved into Millennium Chemical
General Electric	Going strong and still in the Dow
Laclede Gas	Active, removed from the Dow in 1899
National Lead	NL Industries, removed from Dow in 1916
North American Electric	Utility combine broken up in 1940s
Tennessee Coal and Iron	Absorbed by U.S. Steel in 1907
U.S. Leather	Dissolved in 1952
U.S. Rubber	Became Uniroyal, now part of Michelin

Source: John Prestbo, *The Market's Measure.*

The evolution of the U.S. stock market in the past century mirrors the changes in the technological landscape and the way we have lived, worked, and played. In the early days of the Dow Jones Industrial Average, rope and leather figured prominently. The advent of the automobile and the rising power of the U.S. auto industry were reflected in the index during the first part of the twentieth century with the additions of General Motors (1915), Studebaker (1916), Mack Trucks (1924), Nash Motors (1926), Chrysler (1928), and Hudson Motor Car (1930). In 1928, the first aerospace company, Wright Aeronautical, was listed in the Dow.

During World War II, there was no change in the composition of the Dow industrials index. Since the mid-1950s, however, the index has evolved to reflect the rising importance of the technology, entertainment, and service industries. Recent notable additions to the Dow in the technology sector have been Hewlett-Packard (1997), Microsoft (1999), and Intel (1999). All told, more than one hundred companies have been part of the Dow Jones Industrial Average at some time during the twentieth century. Today the Dow includes thirty companies from diverse industries, many of which didn't even exist at the turn of the nineteenth century.

FAST FORWARD

Consultants at McKinsey & Company have attempted to quantify the impact of accelerating change on the composition of the U.S. stock market during the twentieth century. In their book, *Creative Destruction*, Richard Foster and Sarah Kaplan point out that ninety companies on the original Standard & Poor's (S&P's) index, created in the 1920s, stayed there for an average of sixty-five years. By the end of the century, the average anticipated tenure of a company on the expanded S&P 500 index had declined to only ten years.

As Foster and Kaplan's analysis shows, turnover in the S&P 500 increased significantly along with the pace of technological innovation. In 1926, the turnover rate of the S&P index was about 1.5 percent. Today, the rate of turnover is around 10 percent, implying that the average company life cycle in the S&P 500 index is around a decade. Foster and Kaplan's research suggests that during the next twenty-five years, no more than one-third of today's major corporations will survive in an economically important way. If they are correct in their assessment, many of the stocks in the Dow Jones Industrial Average and S&P 500 will go the way of U.S. Leather and Tennessee Coal and Iron over the next quarter century.

It is difficult to predict how the U.S. stock market will evolve in the years ahead as the quantum revolution in technology accelerates. In the past several years, several biotechnology companies have joined the S&P 500, although none have been added to the Dow Jones Industrial Average. It's quite likely that as the quantum-based life science and nanotechnology revolutions evolve, we will see a significant shift in the industrial composition of the U.S. stock market.

Glimmers of the evolution of the S&P 500 index in the past several decades can already be seen. Exhibit 16 shows the shares of the S&P 500 accounted for by each broad industry in 1964, in 1991, and at the end of 2001. One obvious shift has been the rising share of the technology sector in the stock market. In the 1960s, the tech sector accounted for roughly 5 percent of the overall market. By the end of 2001, that share had risen to 18 percent.

The other notable shifts have occurred in the financial services and health care sectors where shares have risen sharply since the 1960s. In our book, *Boomernomics* Bill Sterling and I pointed out that given recent trends in demographics and technology, these two sectors were likely to constitute a relatively large share of the stock market in the coming decade or two. The industries that dominated the economic landscape at the end of the nineteenth century have declined substantially as percentages of the S&P 500 stock index.

EXHIBIT 16: Shifting Landscape of the S&P 500
(Sector Composition of the Index for Three Years)

Industry	1964	1991	2001
Basic materials	17%	7%	3%
Capital goods	9%	10%	11%
Communications services*	—	8%	6%
Consumer cyclicals	11%	11%	12%
Consumer staples	16%	17%	8%
Energy	18%	11%	6%
Financials	0%	8%	18%
Health care	2%	13%	14%
Information technology	5%	7%	18%
Transportation	3%	2%	1%
Utilities	19%	6%	3%

Author's Item:

Noninformation technology	95%	93%	82%

*Note: Communications services were included in the utilities sector in 1964.

Source: Lehman Brothers, Banc of America Securities, IBES, and Standard & Poor's.

In the investment management industry, the S&P 500 is often referred to as a "passive" index, because in the past companies that made up the S&P 500 turned over slowly compared to the average portfolio managed by professional money managers. However, the evolution of the S&P suggests that it is anything but passive today. In the past several decades, there has been a significant amount of turnover in the index, as the work by Foster and Kaplan shows.

Given the likely acceleration in pace of creative destruction associated with the quantum revolution, it's likely to become even more difficult to characterize the S&P 500 as a passive index. To be sure, the turnover in the S&P 500 is likely to remain well below that of "active" investment managers, but as Foster and Kaplan argue, the average rate of turnover in a stock index like the S&P 500 is likely to be much greater in the twenty-first century than it was in the previous century.

Echoing this sentiment, business guru Peter Drucker claims we are entering a time when the pace of new industry formation accelerates. Citing the evolution of the biotechnology industry as a prime example, Drucker argues in "Beyond the Information Revolution" that it is likely that other new technologies will arrive unexpectedly, and they will lead to the creation of major new industries. It is impossible to even guess what the technologies will be, but it is certain they will emerge fairly soon.

The quantum revolution in science and technology has contributed to a meaningful acceleration in the pulse of business activity during the twentieth century. We have seen a marked acceleration in the speed at which new technologies penetrate the marketplace. Research by Michael Cox at the Federal Reserve Bank of Dallas shows a substantial decline in the number of years it has taken for new technologies to reach critical mass and spread to 25 percent of the U.S. population.

As Exhibit 17 shows, it took only fifteen and thirteen years, respectively, for the PC and cell phone to spread to 25 percent of the population. In the early part of the twentieth century, it would have been decades before new technologies were assimilated into the marketplace. Cox notes that it took electricity and the telephone forty-six and thirty-five years, respectively, to achieve the same status. It took the automobile fifty-five years and VCRs thirty-four years to reach 25 percent of the population.

EXHIBIT 17: Technology Adoption Rates
How Long It's Taken Various Technologies to Reach 25 Percent of the U.S. Population

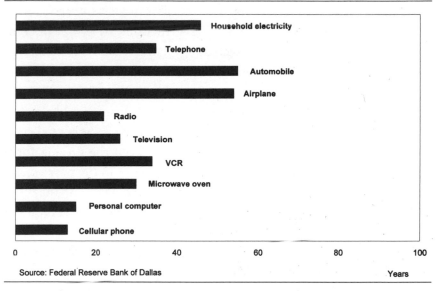

Source: Federal Reserve Bank of Dallas   Years

Cox says there is no reason to believe that the trend toward faster dispersion of new products will not continue. He argues that technological progress is coming faster today because technology is cumulative. Each invention makes the next one easier, providing the stepping-stones to future innovation. As society accumulates more know-how, it sets the stage for an acceleration of the rate of invention and more diversity in technological innovation. Cox points out that PCs developed out of technology accumulated over generations, dating back to J.M. Jacquard's binary-control system in 1801.

We know that technology is an evolutionary process, but what is it about the cumulative nature of technology that leads to an acceleration of progress over time? Raymond Kurzweil has derived what he calls the Law of Accelerating Returns to explain why an evolutionary

93

process like technology increases in speed over time. His law of accelerating returns states that as order exponentially increases, time exponentially speeds up—that is, the time interval between salient events grows shorter as time passes.

Kurzweil notes that the emergence of computation is the direct outcome of increasing order in technology. Computation, according to Kurzweil, is the essence of order. It enables a technology to respond in a variable and appropriate manner to its environment to carry out its mission. He points out that exponential growth in the power of computing is a sign that order in technology is increasing (even though sometimes it feels more like the amount of chaos is rising).

Is there any reason to expect more order as opposed to chaos in coming years? Kurzweil believes there is. It is extremely likely that the power of computers can continue to rise at an exponential pace in the future. As we know, Moore's law has been the driving force behind the evolution of computing and intelligence in the past several decades. Kurzweil reminds us that Moore's law was not the first, but the fifth paradigm that drove exponential growth in computing power.

Lately there has been much talk among scientists and in the popular press of the possibility of Moore's law petering out by 2020. This has to do with the fact that the physics of putting ever greater amounts of transistors on silicon chips eventually runs into physical limitations. At some point, scientists believe, it will be extremely difficult and prohibitively expensive for conventional chip technology to sustain the pace dictated by Moore's Law.

Whereas some analysts believe that the death of Moore's law will signal the end of exponential growth in computing, Kurzweil and others believe that the evolution of technology will start a new computing paradigm that will continue or accelerate the trend. New chip architectures, including innovative three-dimensional designs; ongoing improvements in semiconductor materials, including superconducting circuits that don't generate heat; the nanotube; optical crystalline; DNA; and other innovative computing technologies being developed in labs around the world will keep the Law of Accelerating Returns going well into the twenty-first century. The popular press is filled daily with reports of new technologies that are often indistinguishable from magic.

WHERE'S HAL?

Many scientists believe that we are on the cusp of a breakout in the acceleration of technology. Quantum-based technologies, driven by Moore's law and exponential growth, are spreading virus-like into practically every sector and industry of the global economy. And they are doing so during an era that extends beyond the thirty-second doubling in computing power. From here on out, we begin to traverse the almost vertical slope of the exponential technological growth curve. This landscape will be unfamiliar to all of us—it has to be, because we've never experienced anything similar to what we are about to encounter.

One of the most significant developments during the next two decades will be the rising intelligence of computers. Today's computers have a level of intelligence no greater than that of an ordinary earthworm, scientists tell us. But given the exponential growth in computing power, the intelligence of computers will increase rapidly in the years ahead. Scientist Hans Moravec has stated that by 2010, computers will have the intelligence of a mouse. If that does not sound impressive to you, think of it this way: PCs will have the same amount of computational power as the ASCI White supercomputer does today—over 12 teraflops. By 2020, Moravec believes that personal computers are likely to contain a level of complexity and intelligence comparable to the human brain.

From time to time, Microsoft CEO Bill Gates likes to remind his staff that today's computers are basically deaf, dumb, blind, and clueless—like The Who's pinball wizard, Tommy—who "sure plays" a mean game of pinball. Gates notes that the vast majority of Microsoft research's $5.3 billion R&D budget for fiscal year 2002 is earmarked for artificial intelligence–related projects. Microsoft's research is focused on traditional artificial intelligence areas such as decision making, learning, language, and speech recognition. Gates strongly believes these things will become realities in the future and will allow people to build far, far better software products than we have today for many hundreds of millions, if not billions, of people who will be using computers every day.

Carver Mead, the Gordon and Betty Moore Professor Emeritus of Engineering and Applied Science at Caltech, notes that scientists have had difficulty creating computers with humanlike characteristics. Researchers haven't yet been able to produce anything akin to HAL in Arthur C. Clarke's *2001: A Space Odyssey*. For example, researchers haven't yet been able to make artificial vision systems that come within orders of magnitude of that of an ordinary housefly, despite enormous advances in computational power in the last century. Mead points out in an interview in *The American Spectator* that an ordinary fly has an autonomous vision system that allows it to avoid being swatted. He and other scientists are trying to understand how flies process information and why they are effective at computation. Mead notes that insects, animals, and fish use what seems to be really slow, slimy computational material to perform computations, and yet they perform miracles with tiny amounts of power, tiny amounts of space, in real time and very fast.

Anthropologists Ian Tattersall and Jeffery Schwartz express a similar view in *Extinct Humans*. They note that scientists are handicapped by their ignorance of how human consciousness is generated in the brain. We know, for example, that there are some 10^{11} neurons in the brain and roughly 10^{15} synapses or connections among neurons. Nevertheless, scientists have no idea whatsoever about how a mass of electrical and chemical discharges within the brain is converted into what we individually and subjectively experience as consciousness. Presumably, scientists will need to achieve this knowledge if they hope to design technology with humanlike intelligence.

Grand chess master Gary Kasparov's defeat in 1997 at the hands of IBM's supercomputer Deep Blue raised a lot of eyebrows and generated much fanfare for enthusiasts of artificial intelligence. While the feat was undoubtedly a pivotal moment in the history of computing and artificial intelligence, scientists point out that speed alone will not produce humanlike intelligence. Deep Blue defeated Kasparov by leveraging a moderate amount of knowledge with a massive amount of searching power. Despite their blistering speed, supercomputers like Deep Blue still have great difficulty recognizing patterns—something that humans do quite well.

Scientists note, for example, that computers have difficulty beating a novice in the ancient Chinese game Go—a game in which pattern recognition is paramount. To play a good game of Go, a computer must be equipped with the ability to recognize subtle, complex patterns. Furthermore, computers would need to be endowed with the kind of intuitive knowledge that is the hallmark of human intelligence. In a game of chess, there are about 1.8 billion possible outcomes. In the game Go, there are 64 trillion. The inability of computers to perform complex pattern recognition is the reason why even amateur players of Go can outmatch their speedier opponents. You don't have to be a Kasparov at Go to beat a computer.

The lack of sophisticated pattern recognition also helps explain why investment managers on Wall Street who rely solely on computers have difficulty beating the stock market consistently. Pattern recognition is an essential trait for a money manager, at least a successful one. Although some analysts have managed to create very successful short-term trading models, nobody has yet built a computer that can interpret and understand the enormous complexity in the stock market.

Carver Mead notes that most work done in the past several decades in the field of artificial intelligence has failed miserably. Echoing Gates, Mead points out that machines can't see well, can't hear well, and, perhaps most important, don't learn well. He notes, however, that there have been recent successes in various biometric devices, such as face and fingerprint recognition devices.

The best results Mead has seen thus far in reverse-engineering the brain have been the auditory processors done by Caltech graduate Lloyd Watts of Audience, Inc. Watts has made remarkable progress by working with auditory neurobiologists and realizing the architecture of a much more capable hearing system in computational form. Mead believes this space is well worth watching closely in the future.

Rodney Brooks, director of the MIT Artificial Intelligence Laboratory, notes that there has been an explosion in research aimed at building robots with human forms that can interact with humans in social ways. These new robots are designed specifically for social interactions with people, says Brooks in *Flesh and Machines*. These machines have human forms and faces and their movements—from facial expressions to posture—are very humanlike, he says. The idea behind the creation of these robots is that eventually people will be able to interact with them just like they interact with other people. Still, he emphasizes that humanlike robots are unlikely to be commercially available at affordable prices for at least twenty years.

David Nolte, professor of physics at Purdue University, believes computers that use photons instead of electricity to compute will one day be so fast and efficient that they will generate a new kind of intelligence. In *Mind at Light Speed*, Nolte discusses the potential of "optical computers" with holographic storage devices in the twenty-first century that will process at light speed and access all stored information at one time. Over time, Nolte's optical computers would evolve to incorporate quantum switches.

Optical technology is primed to change how researchers go about building intelligent computing architectures. Nolte says the advantage of the optical computers over conventional electronic-based computing technology is their capacity for parallel processing, which allows computers to perform many computations simultaneously. In addition, optical computers hold the promise of abstract and associative "reasoning," based on images and symbols that exist within a language of spatial and spectral (i.e., color) relationships. As he puts it, for an optical computer, a picture may be worth *more* than a thousand words. A picture may be the program that tells the computer what functions it must perform and what concepts it must use.

Optical computers are not likely to be available at your neighborhood retailer anytime soon. A fundamental new architecture must first be designed for the next-generation machines of light. The new architecture will need a new language—an optical language in which images take the place of words and grammar—made up of visual projections and associations. That said, Nolte believes that it's just a matter of when, not if, intelligent machines appear on the economic landscape.

What are the economic implications of machines with humanlike intelligence? It's a good question, but one that few economic researchers have pondered seriously. One researcher who has thought about the economic implications of intelligent machines is Robin Hanson of George Mason University. In a research paper titled "Economic Growth Given Machine Intelligence," Hanson used standard economic tools to model a world where computers eventually become cheap and capable enough to substitute for most human labor. His models suggest that wholesale use of machine intelligence could increase economic growth rates by one order of magnitude or more. The increased growth rates stem from the two assumptions: that computer technology improves faster than general technology and that the labor population of machine intelligences could grow as fast as desired to meet labor demand. Hanson's models show that human wages can rise a great deal for a long time before eventually falling dramatically.

Hanson says his model underestimates the economic effects of machine intelligence because he assumed, probably incorrectly, that the rates of technological progress do not change when the economy grows faster; one would expect the pace of technological innovation to accelerate with faster growth. He also assumed, he says, diminishing returns even though growth theory models often favor constant or increasing returns. Hanson concludes his analysis by noting that if machine intelligences are a real prospect in the foreseeable future, their economic implications deserve closer scrutiny.

CHANGE BEYOND RECOGNITION

Despite the past difficulties associated with creating more humanlike computers and technology, many scientists believe there are enormous opportunities ahead in the field of artificial intelligence. The presence of intelligent computers, machines, and communications networks is destined to radically alter how we will live, work, and play. Some scientists believe that as the level of machine intelligence rises to, and surpasses, human intelligence, the pace of change in technology will eventually accelerate beyond the ability of the human mind to comprehend it. This view has come to be known as "the Singularity."

The Singularity is a concept most closely associated with the mathematician Vernor Vinge. In an address to the Vision-21 Symposium, sponsored by NASA's Lewis Research Center and the Ohio Aerospace Institute in 1993, Vinge noted that the acceleration of technological progress has been the central feature of the twentieth century. He asserted that we are on the edge of change comparable to the rise of human life on Earth and that the specific cause of this change is the imminent creation by technology of entities with intelligence greater than humans.

The metaphor of the Singularity comes from the field of astrophysics. Astrophysicists note that beyond a certain critical mass a star collapses to something whose mass and density are so great that its intense gravitational force prevents even light from escaping. The collapsed star becomes what astrophysicists call a *black hole*. The region where everything disappears into the black hole is called the *event horizon*. The center of the black hole is known as the Singularity. At the Singularity, laws of science and our ability to predict the future break down.

One of the consequences of the Singularity, according to Vinge, is that technological progress will become much more rapid than it is today. Another potential consequence of accelerating technical change is the potential for enormous wealth creation. Raymond Kurzweil believes the common wisdom in economic expectations is dramatically understated. He notes that the law of accelerating returns clearly implies that the rate of economic growth will continue to grow exponentially, because the rate of technical progress will continue to accelerate. On the basis of his calculations, which assume continued exponential growth in technology, the current level of the stock market in the United States should be roughly three times higher than it is today.

Scientists aren't sure exactly when the Singularity will occur. In his 1993 address, Vinge said he would be surprised if the event occurs before 2005 or after 2030. Kurzweil, however, believes that the Singularity is imminent. He believes that by 2010, computers will disappear from sight. Displays will be written directly into our retinas. Extremely high bandwidth wireless communication to the Internet will be ubiquitous by 2010. Websites will become virtual-reality shared environments, at least for the visual and auditory senses. By 2030, which is within the expected life span of many baby boomers in North America and around the world, Kurzweil foresees the nanotechnology revolution unleashing a tsunami of technological change that will alter the global economic landscape and life as we know it. There may not be a firm consensus on when the Singularity will arrive, but there is a growing number of distinguished scientists and analysts who believe that the day of hyperchange will arrive sometime within the next several decades.

THE QUICK AND THE DEAD

The Newtonian physics-inspired Industrial Revolution brought about the greatest improvement in the human condition since the invention of agriculture in the Neolithic era. The inadequacies of Newtonian physics to explain certain phenomena observed in nature sparked a revolution in science and technology during the twentieth century that appears to be gathering force today.

Science is advancing at an exponential pace. Researchers point out that the total number of articles in scientific journals throughout the world doubles every twelve to fifteen years. Meanwhile, the number of workers in science doubles every ten years in the United States. With such a furious growth rate, the contemporary generation of scientists constitutes 90 percent of all the scientists who have ever lived on Earth. The cumulative, geometric growth in science is the driving force behind technological invention and innovation today. As science evolves in the future, so will technology.

The Economist noted recently that science is an odd beast. It has its head in the clouds while at the same time manages to keep its feet firmly planted on the ground. As a result, it has revolutionized human life both intellectually and practically. Today's mental landscape is almost unrecognizable from the time of Newton. This is due almost entirely to the work of two groups of thinkers: scientists and economists. Add engineers to the mix, and you have a great explanation for why the physical, commercial, and political landscapes have changed radically in the past two hundred years.

In the past century, we have witnessed advances in science and technology that wrought massive changes in the business landscape and were mirrored in the stock market. During the twentieth century, Schumpeter's creative destruction process was the rule, not the exception. Despite the upheavals, economists tell us that during the twentieth century more wealth was created than in all previous centuries combined. Living conditions throughout the world improved substantially.

As the quantum revolution evolves, a gale of creative destruction will come faster as the pace of technological change accelerates. Scientist Neil Gershenfeld, who leads the Physics and Media Group and codirects the Things That Think research consortium at the MIT Media Laboratory, points out that we are indeed experiencing a new industrial revolution. As proof, he cites in *Things That Think,* the overwhelming number of senior executives visiting his lab who have admitted they have no idea what business they are in today.

There is consensus, too, among many senior executives on the importance of speed. Louis Gerstner, Jr. and Jack Welch have noted that the pulse of business has quickened in recent years and speed is now *the* key variable in the competitive strategy equation in many businesses. Mendelson quotes Intel Chairman Andy Grove as saying: "Today there are just two types of companies: the quick and the dead." Author Seth Godin notes that change is no longer in our control and the way companies deal with it is outmoded and ineffective. In *Survival is Not Enough,* Godin lists four significant structural changes in business over the last twenty years. These are:

- The speed with which we make decisions is now the factor that limits the speed of business.

- The Internet has made information close to free and close to ubiquitous, further fueling the need for speed.

- There's only one market; the global market.

- Metcalfe's law (that networks get more powerful as the number of people and things connected increases), has reached infinity.

All corporate strategy has been based on one fundamental assumption: We can predict the future and influence its course through our actions.

The reality, however, is that uncertainty and chaos are better bets in the twenty-first century. As a result, Godin argues that the overall corporate strategy should be to build a company that's so flexible and responsive, in both the long term and the short term that we don't care what happens in the future.

Godin believes that as change continues to create more turbulence, organizations should remember that evolution is the only way for a species to respond to change. He points out that many organizations fight hard to stop evolution because they are afraid of change. However, change is the new norm, and organizations will either embrace this notion or fade away.

The brisk pace of change in the business world has become a major threat to the very existence of even the most established companies on the planet. In this environment, firm size may no longer be regarded as an asset. In fact, large size may be a greater liability in the years ahead, particularly if it impedes organizational change. It would not be surprising to see a number of Blue Chip companies go the way of the dinosaur in coming years as the pace of creative destruction intensifies.

The great investor John Marks Templeton notes in *Is Progress Speeding Up?* that a focus on the longer term left him with a strong sense that not only is the rate of progress speeding up, but that this acceleration is apt to continue across countless areas of human endeavor in coming decades. Not every long-term trend is destined to persist indefinitely, he added. If this were true, we would be able to know the future with certainty. However, most major trends do tend to persist, often gathering speed as they go along.

In this chapter, we have seen the profound impact that technological change has had on the business landscape and the stock market in the twentieth century. In Chapter 5, we look at how the quantum revolution in technology in particular is altering the economic and business landscape, and significantly changing how wealth is created. The implications of this change are as profound as the shift from a Newtonian world to a quantum world.

Key Takeaways

- The pace of technological change is accelerating, implying that today's products will be outmoded more quickly than in the past.

- Investors need to be aware of the clockspeed of the industry they are investing in, and whether the companies they are choosing are up to the industry's speed.

- Many companies that are listed in stock market indexes (e.g., Dow Jones Industrial Average, FTSE 100, Topix) will find it increasingly difficult to adapt to accelerating technological change in coming years. Investors need to be aware of the technologies that companies should be adopting to improve their operations.

- In an environment of accelerating technical change, firm size may become a liability. Investors need to be aware of how quickly companies can change their operations, products, and development process to keep pace with competitors and consumer needs (the end market). Thus the new maxim, "the quick or the dead."

- Some scientists believe that the global economy will experience the equivalent amount of technical change in the next twenty-five years as was experienced during the entire twentieth century. Investors need to have flexible and open minds and be accepting of new theories and ideas.

- Pattern recognition will be essential for successful investors.

- Investors need to be aware that despite the limitations of computers today, some scientists believe artificial intelligence will exceed human intelligence in our lifetime.

- The concept of singularity introduces the prospect that our ability to comprehend the world around us will break down as the pace of technological change accelerates.

- According to scientist Raymond Kurzweil, the pace of technology is increasing so rapidly that the current level of stock prices in the U.S. should be roughly three times higher than they are today.

Invisible Wealth

The empires of the future are the empires of the mind.

—Winston Churchill

In 1946, on the eve of the birth of the transistor, Joseph Stalin stood before the people of the Soviet Union and boldly proclaimed that when his country produced 50 million tons of pig iron, 60 million tons of steel, 500 million tons of coal, and 60 million tons of oil, it would be *guaranteed* against any misfortune. Stalin's near-messianic belief in the power of natural resources to propel the Soviet Union to unparalleled greatness and unrivaled riches was widely shared by many political leaders of the world. Since the first industrial revolution, people's control over Mother Nature's bounty had surpassed even the most ambitious dreams of ancient pharaohs and kings.

In the mid-1900s, three hundred years after it began, the science- and technology-driven industrial revolution had evolved into the industrial age. The natural resource powered steam engine gave way to high-speed trains and heavy machinery. To generate wealth and escalate its geopolitical power, a country had to convert matter into tangible machines, equipment, and products.

Like Icarus, Stalin's vision of his empire soaring to new heights on the wings of pig iron, steel, coal, and oil was a grand illusion. Winston Churchill knew as much. Three years before Stalin's infamous proclamation, Churchill had told a distinguished audience at Harvard University that the empires of the future will be the empires of the mind.

Churchill couldn't possibly have foreseen the cornucopia of mind-leveraging technologies that swept across the global economy in the latter half of the twentieth century. Nevertheless, his brilliant command of history allowed him to peer farther into the future than his Soviet counterpart. Today, the economy of England—an island relatively poor in natural resources—has a Gross Domestic Product (GDP) far higher than that of the former Soviet Union.

What Stalin failed to see was a metamorphosis of the way wealth would be created in the future. In the twentieth century, science and technology were marching to the beat of a different drummer. Isaac Newton's physics had provided the foundation for a stunning rise in living standards and wealth in many nations, but as accurate as Newton's laws were at predicting the motions of the heavens, they could not explain certain events at the microscopic or molecular level.

The failure of Newton's mechanics at the end of the nineteenth century to describe various phenomena that scientists observed in nature gave birth to quantum theory. And new quantum-based technologies laid the foundation for the development of new industries, companies, goods, and related services—empires of the mind.

Quantum-based technologies leverage the human mind in the same way that Newtonian-based technologies leverage human muscle. For centuries, economists and accountants have viewed tangible assets as the major source of wealth in the economy and business. Wealth was gauged by the size and resourcefulness of the land and the value of labor and machinery employed on the land. Newtonian-based technology allowed producers and entrepreneurs to greatly magnify the value of land, natural resources, and human muscle.

Newtonian-based technology allowed farmers around the world to become vastly more efficient at producing crops—an economic feat that Thomas Malthus never foresaw. Steam engines and other machinery (e.g., lathes, circular saws, and conveyor belts) fueled a boom in transportation and manufacturing. Mass production was born. The father of mass production, Henry Ford, used to complain that workers came equipped with minds when all he needed were hands and muscle.

Economists, accountants, and analysts have been conditioned in the past three hundred years to measure the value of a company's stock by its tangible items, using a method developed roughly five hundred years ago by a monk called Luca Pacioli. Balance sheets today still record the book value of our companies by subtracting the value of all tangible assets from liabilities.

The wealth generated by the Newtonian revolution in science ranks among the greatest economic achievements in the history of civilization, but it is now giving way to a new form of wealth: quantum wealth, or invisible wealth. In the twenty-first century, intangible assets, not tangible ones, will drive value and wealth creation, and many people will need to re-examine their conventional notions of wealth.

NEW WEALTH OF NATIONS

In 2000, one decade after the implosion of the Soviet Union, Larry Summers, then U.S. Treasury Secretary, gave a speech to a group of investors and analysts in San Francisco titled "The New Wealth of Nations." In his speech, Summers discussed the growing importance of "knowledge capital" in the global economy. He countered everything that Stalin had believed necessary for world domination. Summers said that if there is one fundamental change in the economy today, it is the move from an economy based on the production of physical goods to one based on the production and application of knowledge.

Value used to reside in masses of wheat, ingots of iron, and barrels of oil. Today, however, the value lies in a gene sequence, a line of computer code, or a company logo. Summers observed that an information-based world is one in which more goods have the character of pharmaceuticals, or CDs, in that they involve very high fixed costs and much lower marginal costs and the bulk of their value is intangible.

The most telling empirical finding about our economy is that the return on investment in human capital has risen faster than the return on investment in physical capital, said Summers. In fact, he argued, if investments in factories were the most important investments in the industrial age, then the most important investments in an information age are investments in the human brain.

Although Summers's "New Wealth of Nations" speech was warmly received, it must have sounded dissonant and strange to many people in the audience. After all, most analysts had not been trained in the accounting of knowledge and intangible capital, let alone Schumpeterian economics.

Federal Reserve Board chairman Alan Greenspan has noted in several speeches and testimonies to Congress that innovations in IT are altering significantly how we do business and create value. Greenspan emphasizes that during the past several decades, the weight of all goods contributing to the U.S. GDP has declined precipitously. The weight of current economic output is modestly higher than it was half a century ago even though its value is three times as great. Indeed, the nation's output of goods and services probably weighs little more now than at the beginning of the twentieth century. Economic output used to consist of big, physical things—steel, huge cars, heavy machinery—but now miniaturization is pervasive.

Technological and economic changes are allowing us to produce less bulky things: tiny transistors rather than vacuum tubes, fiber-optic cables rather than copper wire, plastics rather than metals. Since 1977, government statisticians have measured the total weight of everything that goes into producing the value of goods each year. The annual tally of the weight of all raw materials, agricultural products, manufacturing goods, and the like was 1.17 trillion pounds in 1977. By 2000, the weight of the U.S. GDP had declined to 1.08 trillion pounds. In the same period, the nominal dollar value of U.S. GDP doubled, from $4.3 trillion to $8.6 trillion. As Exhibit 18 shows, U.S. GDP has soared on a value per pound basis.

Diane Coyle, former economics editor of *The Independent*, a British newspaper and managing director of Enlightenment Economics, points out that miniaturization and innovative materials have contributed greatly to a lighter weight of physical economic output. The expansion of the service sector and the shift from manufacturing, physical output, and physical capital to services, knowledge output, and human capital, have also shed pounds from America's output.

Intangible assets and knowledge capital have skyrocketed over the course of the past century. Economist John Kendrick estimates that in 1929, the mix of intangible business capital to tangible business capital in the U.S. economy was 30 percent compared to 70 percent. By 1990, the mix has shifted decidedly in favor of intangibles—63 percent to 37 percent tangible. Today, that mix is probably closer to 70 percent intangible and 30 percent tangible. As Kendrick's statistics show, wealth in the U.S. economy is increasingly related to intangible assets—not physical or tangible assets.

EXHIBIT 18: Shedding Pounds

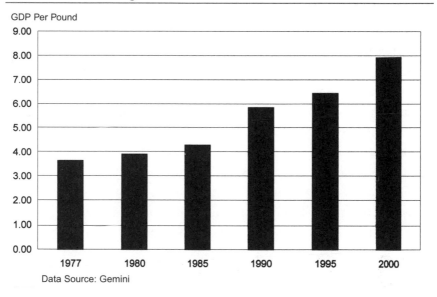

GDP Per Pound

Data Source: Gemini

VALUING UNSEEN WEALTH

Margaret Blair and Steven Wallman, researchers at The Brookings Institution, note that the large and growing discrepancy between the importance of intangible assets to economic growth and the ability to identify, measure, and account for these is a serious potential problem for business managers, for investors, and for government. In *Unseen Wealth*, Blair and Wallman point out that intangible goods and market services account for more than two-thirds of U.S. GDP today. The critical difference between an economy based on the production, trade, and consumption of physical goods and one revolving around trade in services, experiences, technology, and ideas is that the former can be readily measured.

Intangible assets are nonphysical factors that contribute to, or are used in, producing goods and providing services and are expected to generate future productive benefits. Evidence that intangibles are gaining in economic importance lies in the growth of services as a share of total economic activity; the rapid climb in the value of financial assets over the past decade and a half; relatively low growth in physical assets (such as property, plant, and equipment); and an outpouring of anecdotal evidence from firms about what is important to them and their need for new measurement and management information tools.

Leonard Nakamura, an economist at the Federal Reserve Bank of Philadelphia, estimates in "What is the U.S. Gross Investment in Intangibles" that U.S. private gross investment in intangible assets (e.g., designs, software, blueprints, and ideas) is at least $1 trillion. Most of this investment in intangibles goes uncounted by government statisticians and accountants, says Nakamura, and much of it is relatively new. He notes that the rate of investment in intangibles and its economic value have accelerated significantly since 1980.

The Bureau of Economic Analysis, the folks who collect and record U.S. investment statistics, began counting intangibles as investments in 1999. So far, the bureau has included only investment in software. Gross investment in software is already more than $230 billion, and accounting for intangible assets in U.S. GDP would raise the level of output in the economy by more than 2 percent.

Expenditures on buildings and machinery today are still treated as investments, and it is conventional for accountants to depreciate these assets over a number of years. Meanwhile, outlays for labor and R&D are typically treated as expenses. On Wall Street, analysts routinely compare the book value of a company (physical assets minus liabilities) to the price of its stock and use this ratio to make investment recommendations.

At $1 trillion per year, U.S. businesses are investing nearly as much in intangibles as they are in plant and equipment, which in 2000 totaled $1.1 trillion. Nakamura estimates that the capital stock of intangibles in the United States has an equilibrium market value of at least

$5 trillion—nearly half the market capitalization of the U.S. stock market. He argues that the enormous investment in intangible assets implies that the economics of creative destruction are rapidly becoming as important as the economics of Adam Smith's invisible hand.

Ignoring the value of intangible assets was not a problem during the early part of the twentieth century. Big machines and factories dominated the business landscape and inflation was low, so there was no question of an asset's replacement value. This changed however when inflation started accelerating in the late 1960s, and the replacement of a tangible asset was well above its book value. This became difficult for economists who, to gauge demand for investment, were accustomed to using the ratio of the market value of a company to its replacement cost. In fact, Nobel laureate James Tobin popularized this concept, which is known today as "Tobin's q."

Tobin's q was an indicator of future investment spending. For example, if q were above 1, implying that market values exceeded replacement cost, then a company would be inclined to buy new plant and equipment, financing it with stock. On the other hand, if "q" were less than 1, it would be more economical to purchase a company's existing assets in the stock market.

EXHIBIT 19: Tobin's Q: Losing Relevance

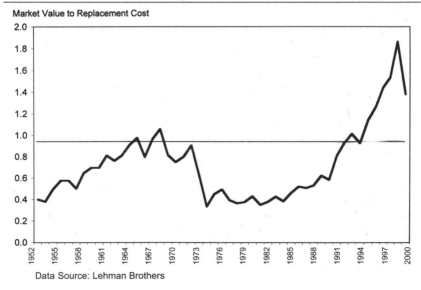

Market Value to Replacement Cost

Data Source: Lehman Brothers

•　　•　　•

In the past ten years, the value of Tobin's measurement has soared far above parity, indicating that the market values of all corporate assets greatly exceeded the replacement value of those assets (see Exhibit 19). Some economists and analysts have used the high value of Tobin's q today to argue that the U.S. stock market is substantially overvalued.

It is tempting to use q as a measure of absolute valuation in the U.S. stock market, but as Tobin himself said, the biggest problem with q today as a valuation gauge is that it excludes the valuation of intangible assets in the denominator. This suggests that conventional measures of the q ratio are overstated.

Nakamura argues that at current stock market valuations, intangibles represent one-third or more of the market value of U.S. domestic corporations. Adding this amount back into the denominator of Tobin's q ratio significantly reduces the overall value of the indicator and shows that the stock market is not wildly overestimating the value of U.S. corporations. In fact, if companies are investing $1 trillion a year in intangibles, and the obsolescence rate for intangibles is no more than 16 percent annually, the long-run equilibrium value of intangibles is in the neighborhood of $5 trillion. More and more economists are realizing today that intangibles are a serious omission, and government statisticians are seeking to rectify some of this discrepancy by including an estimate for the value of computer software in its official capital stock estimates. Yet, many forms of intellectual capital—e.g., brands, R&D, employee training, and customer acquisition—are still excluded from conventional measures of Tobin's q.

ACCOUNTING FOR UNSEEN WEALTH

Moving from the macro world of economics to the micro world of accounting, Thomas Stewart, an intellectual capital expert and author of *The Wealth of Knowledge,* observes that organizations' tangible assets—cash, land and buildings, plant and equipment, and other balance sheet items—are substantially less valuable than the intangible assets not carried on their books.

All intangibles are intellectual capital, Stewart asserts. Hard intangibles include things, such as patents, copyrights, databases, and software. Soft intangibles include employee skills, capabilities, expertise, cultures, and loyalties. Intellectual capital is simply knowledge assets that can be converted to profit.

The accounting profession is woefully behind the times, and the problem is critical, according to Baruch Lev, professor of Accounting and Finance at New York University's Stern School of Business and an expert in the field of intangible assets. In "New Math for a New Economy," by Alan Webber, Lev says it is currently acceptable practice to "mindlessly" write off all investment in knowledge or intellectual assets. Accounting, says Lev, has lost its credibility for many reasons and intangibles are one of the most obvious.

Although the actual value of companies' intangible assets has risen since 1980, the value of these assets in corporate financial reports is diminishing. Today's annual reports of intangible-rich companies do not reflect their true value. In fact, U.S. Steel did a better job of reporting its value in its 1902 annual report than many blue chip companies deliver today. Echoing Lev, Robert A. Howell, visiting professor at the Tuck School at Dartmouth and an authority on the changing role of finance and accounting notes in "Accounting Gets Radical," that modern-day financial statements—including the income statement, balance sheet, and statement of cash flows—are as useful as an eighty-year-old road map of Los Angeles.

Lev believes the failure of accounting today lies in the breakdown of its founding principle: matching. To determine a firm's earnings, you match revenues against expenses. If the matching system is good, you get a reliable income number. The primary problem, as Lev sees it, is that with intangible assets, you get a complete mismatch. As a result, the system breaks down completely.

To make his case, Lev cites the example of America Online (AOL) in the late 1990s after the Internet was commercialized. During its period of hypergrowth, AOL was forced to immediately expense all of its customer acquisition costs, so the company showed these costs as big losses without a matching income stream on the income statement. Over time, as customers were acquired, the company realized large benefits but without the matching costs, because they had already been incurred. Because the investments of one period could not be matched with resulting income in another period, AOL appeared to have magically increased its income without incurring any associated costs. Lev notes that both periods are badly misstated in AOL's financial reports. The intangible nature of most businesses today often results in a huge disconnect between reality and what a firm's balance sheet and income statement represent at a particular period of time.

Another difficulty in accounting for intangible assets is R&D. Before a product is brought to market and sold, there has been a great deal of value creation and destruction. Yet this is not recorded on a company's balance sheet until the product is sold. For example, when a drug passes all stages of clinical tests, or when software passes a beta test, huge value is created but nothing is recorded by accountants.

The treatment of many key investments as expenses can be misleading. For example, accountants in the United States treat outlays on R&D as an expense, so it is immediately written off and deducted from income. For many companies, particularly those in information and communications technology, pharmaceutical, and consumer product industries, R&D is often the largest cost on the income statement and there is no offsetting revenue at that stage.

The advantage to companies that spend large amounts of money on R&D is that they can write it off and reduce their pretax net income, dollar for dollar. The disadvantage is that it appears that these types of companies do not have high earnings and therefore may have trouble attracting investors. In contrast, firms that invest in tangible assets such as plant and equipment are allowed to depreciate these investments over a number of years, which gives them a tax advantage but only modestly reduces their stated income. The asymmetrical treatment of accounting for hard and intangible assets has the potential to drive a huge wedge between conventional valuation ratios of tangible and intangible asset-intensive companies.

Lev admits that part of the problem is that it is extremely difficult to come up with a comprehensive definition of intangible assets. He classifies them into four categories:

1. assets associated with product innovation, such as those that come from a company's R&D efforts;

2. assets associated with a company's brand, which let a company sell its products or services at a higher price than its competitors;

3. structural assets associated with solid, better, smarter, different ways of doing business that can set a company apart from its competitors;

4. the market share or "monopoly" asset, that is whether a company has a franchise or substantial sunk costs or other barriers to entry that a competitor would have to match.

Lev measures intangibles by combining historical accounting data with forward-looking consensus analyst forecasts of earnings, with which he creates an average, or "normalized earnings." From the normalized earnings, Lev subtracts an average return on physical and financial assets. The residual is knowledge earnings. Lev then calculates a firm's "Comprehensive Value" (intangible assets plus tangible assets) and compares it to the company's market or conventional book value.

Lev's method reveals that hundreds of billions of dollars in intangible assets are not being captured by conventional financial statements. In fact, when intellectual property is properly accounted for, the valuations of intangible-rich firms appear more reasonable, or less over-valued, relative to conventional valuation metrics, such as market-to-book ratios.

Exhibit 20 compares conventional market-to-book value and Lev's market-to-comprehensive value for selected companies. There is a large discrepancy between the two measures, particularly for those companies in R&D-intensive knowledge industries, such as IT (hardware and software), semiconductors, communications equipment, pharmaceuticals, and biotechnology.

EXHIBIT 20: Accounting for Intangible Assets

Company	Industry	Market Value to Book Value	Market Value to Comprehensive Value
Honeywell International	Aerospace and defense	3.3	0.7
Boeing	Aerospace and defense	3.8	1.3
AMR	Airlines	0.7	0.3
Southwest Airlines	Airlines	3.7	1.2
Amgen	Biotech	22.4	3.2
MedImmune	Biotech	24.3	3.4
DuPont	Chemicals	3.5	0.8
Dow Chemical	Chemicals	2.0	0.5
IBM	Computer hardware	12.1	1.6
Dell Computer	Computer hardware	17.5	1.3
Microsoft	Computer software	8.9	1.6
Computer Associates	Computer software	2.7	0.4
AES	Electric utilities	7.3	0.9
Duke Energy	Electric utilities	2.9	1.1
Coca-Cola	Food/beverages	14.2	1.7
H.J. Heinz	Food/beverages	8.1	0.7
Gillette	Home products	13.3	1.1
Colgate-Palmolive	Home products	17.8	1.4
United Technologies	Industrial	3.9	0.9
Illinois Tool Works	Industrial	3.3	0.8
Walt Disney	Media	3.5	1.1
Viacom	Media	2.1	1.6
Ford Motor	Motor vehicles	2.1	0.4
General Motors	Motor vehicles	1.3	0.5
Gannett	Newspapers	3.2	0.7
Dow Jones	Newspapers	1.7	0.7
Exxon Mobil	Oil	4.2	1.6
Chevron	Oil	2.9	1.3
Pfizer	Pharmaceuticals	18.2	1.9
Johnson & Johnson	Pharmaceuticals	7.1	1.4
Wal-Mart	Retail	7.5	1.9
Target	Retail	3.2	1.0
Intel	Semiconductors	13.7	2.1
Texas Instruments	Semiconductors	8.7	2.1
Verizon	Communications services	3.5	0.8
SBC Communications	Communications services	5.0	1.0
Cisco Systems	Communications equip.	18.5	2.6
Motorola	Communications equip.	3.7	1.6

Note: Data are based on market values as of August 31, 2000.

Source: *CFO Magazine* (based on analysis by Baruch Lev and Mark Bothwell).

For decades, investment managers have used the ratio of stock price-to-book value as an overall measure of corporate value that suited companies with many tangible assets. Today, however, without a measure of the value of intangibles, conventional price-to-book ratios are inadequate for stocks in knowledge industries. Even conventional income statements have lost a lot of their relevance, says Lev. His research finds an extremely low correlation between corporate earnings and stock price changes. The message is that reported earnings, like corporate balance sheets, are playing a decreasing role in the total information affecting investors' decisions in the stock market.

At the dawn of the twenty-first century, we have no formal accounting methodology for recognizing the value of investments in people and intangible assets. Commenting on the serious shortcomings of conventional analysis in an economy increasingly driven by knowledge, chartered accountant Sir Matthew Webster Jenkinson put it this way:

> *Though your balance sheet's a model of*
> *What balance-sheets should be,*
> *Typed and ruled with great precision*
> *In a type that all can see;*
> *Though the grouping of the assets is commendable and clear,*
> *And the details that are given more*
> *Than usually appear;*
> *Though investments have been valued*
> *At the sale price of the day,*
> *And the auditor's certificate shows*
> *Everything O.K.*
> *One asset is omitted—and its worth*
> *I want to know,*
> *That asset is the value of the people who run the show.*

In addition to including the value of people and knowledge capital in general, traditional accounting needs to develop new standards for the capitalization of intangible assets. Any intangible assets that can be associated with identifiable and measurable benefits (e.g., R&D expenditures and customer acquisition costs) should be treated similar to investment in physical capital.

SHIFTING FORTUNES

To understand the changing nature of wealth, compare U.S. Steel, which transformed natural resources into value-added products, to Pfizer, a company that shapes new formulas and discoveries into gene-based medicines. The contrast between these two corporations, as Paul Romer points out in "The Soft Revolution: Achieving Growth by Managing Intangibles," is really a microcosm for the transformation of the entire U.S. economy—and much of the global economy as well.

The cost structure of industrial age firms like U.S. Steel is much different from what you typically see in a knowledge age company like Pfizer. In industrial age industries, costs decline as output increases until a point of diminishing returns is reached. After this point, costs begin to rise per unit of additional output. Industrial age companies have no choice but to raise prices to cover the additional costs of expanding their operations.

Knowledge companies like Pfizer in contrast, have cost structures that exhibit increasing returns to scale. Instead of rising with each unit of additional output, average costs decline. As a result, products become cheaper to produce as the size of the market increases. Instead of relying on price increases, firms in knowledge industries often discount heavily as the incentive to price aggressively is afforded by the unique cost structure.

Today, firms can reproduce and distribute knowledge-based products such as software and electronic media for almost no marginal costs. Companies in knowledge industries typically have large fixed costs and low marginal costs. Researching, designing, and developing new products often require hundreds of millions of dollars of startup costs. Once production begins, however, putting out additional units of a product is relatively inexpensive. For example, the cost of the first new Microsoft operating system is, say, $400 million. The average cost of the next 1 million units is $400. At 100 million units, the average per unit cost is only $4. It may cost a company like Pfizer or Microsoft $300 or $400 million or more to bring a new drug or operating system to market. However, the cost of producing one additional pill or one more copy of the operating system plunges as the market expands. Products produced by companies in industries, such as software, biopharmaceuticals, IT, communications, music, movies and other media have cost structures that generate increasing returns to scale.

Knowledge-intensive physical goods, such as microprocessors and digital signal processing chips, also are becoming cheaper. Satellite imaging, for example, dramatically speeds up the process of finding mineral resources. Unlike the economics of scarcity, which have a built-in inflation bias, the economics of abundance are inherently deflationary.

As the economy transitions away from traditional manufacturing toward knowledge- and service-related activities, we see a profound shift in corporate organizational structures. An organization like U.S. Steel resembled a pyramid, with a large amount of physical capital (e.g., land, plant, and equipment) at its foundation, a good deal of working capital, and little in the way of intangible assets and knowledge capital (see Exhibit 21). Knowledge-producing firms resemble inverted pyramids. The bulk of their value is tied up in brand and knowledge capital. Relatively speaking, these companies have little in the way of physical and working capital; some even have negative working capital. Companies are increasingly substituting cyberspace and communications bandwidth for land. In addition, there is a migration away from in-house production toward outsourcing.

EXHIBIT 21: The Upside-Down Corporation

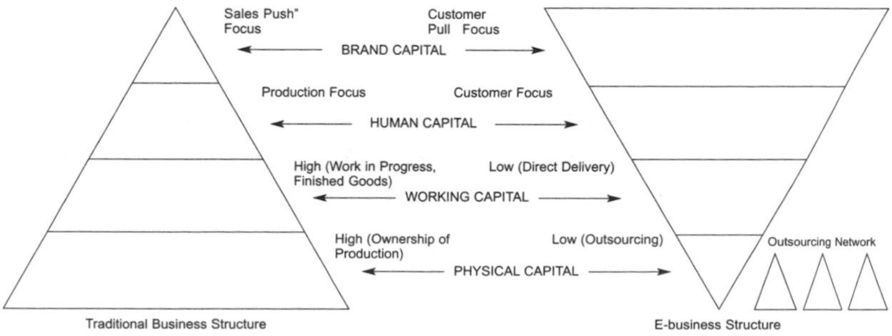

Source: Meta-Capitalism

Henry Ford's archetypal organization built on physical capital and vertical integration effectively has been turned upside down. The Ford Motor Company of the twenty-first century will become more intangible-asset intensive and driven by knowledge capital. In fact, senior executives at Ford have been investing aggressively in intangible assets in recent years. The company has spent billions of dollars acquiring prestigious brand names like Jaguar, Aston Martin, Volvo, and Land Rover. None of these marquees brought much in the way of plant and equipment, but plant and equipment are not what the new business model at Ford is all about. It's about brands and brand building and consumer relationships. The Ford of the twenty-first century is in the business of selling customer products they can touch and buying what exists only in consumers' minds.

In a knowledge economy, financial analysts find themselves asking questions like: How do we value Jack Welch's learning center at GE? How do we value Andy Grove's paranoia? How do we value Bill Gates's business acumen? In the future, we may be asking questions like, How do we value intelligent computers and communications networks? How do we value a universal replicator based on nanotechnology that is able to create any object, from a gourmet meal to a diamond? Whatever the answers, in the twenty-first century, how we value information and knowledge will be paramount.

Conventional economics and accounting no longer tell the whole story. The concepts and mental models that we associate with a Newtonian-based economy are useful, but they are not sufficient to understand a quantum physics–based knowledge economy. To fully comprehend and make sense of the economy, we will need to augment our mental models with concepts such as knowledge capital, increasing returns, nonlinear dynamics, knowledge management, and positive sum economics (see Exhibit 22).

•   •   •

EXHIBIT 22: Economic Paradigms of the Twentieth and Twenty-first Centuries

Twentieth Century	Twenty-first Century
Scarcity	Abundance
Physical capital	Knowledge capital
Tangible assets	Intangible assets
Diminishing returns	Increasing returns
Comparative statics	Nonlinear dynamics
Command and control	Networks and webs
Data processing	Knowledge management
Zero sum	Positive sum

BEYOND BRICKS AND MORTAR

The change in the composition of wealth reflects the use of quantum mechanics and physics. Henry Ford prized hands and muscle. Bill Gates wins with intellectual capital.

Former Citicorp chairman Walter Wriston notes in *The Twilight of Sovereignty* that although many people understand that computers and communications have become powerful economic forces, they do not realize that the world is changing. It is not changing because computer operators have replaced clerk typists and produce more work in less time, but because the human struggle to survive and prosper now depends on an entirely new source of wealth: information and knowledge applied to work to create value. Quantum-based information technologies have created an entirely different economy, as different from the industrial economy as the industrial economy was from the agricultural economy.

The industrial revolution changed the source of wealth, transforming natural resources such as rock and ore into riches of steel and steam. Likewise, the quantum revolution is changing atoms and molecules into chips and gene-based medicines. The pursuit of wealth today involves invisible or, at least, very tiny products and intellectual capital. As a result, outlays on IT in the United States have risen fourteenfold in the past twenty-five years (Exhibit 23).

•   •   •

EXHIBIT 23: The Rising Value of Knowledge

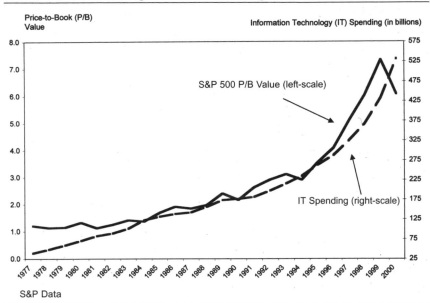

Price-to-Book (P/B) Value

Information Technology (IT) Spending (in billions)

S&P 500 P/B Value (left-scale)

IT Spending (right-scale)

S&P Data

Given the ability of quantum-based technologies to leverage the human mind, it is not surprising that intangible assets, intellectual capital, and knowledge management have drawn the attention of business executives around the world. Many business leaders readily acknowledge that knowledge is the most important factor of production and intangible assets are the most powerful producers of wealth in their firms. The management at General Electric, the only surviving member of the original Dow Jones Industrial Average, have incorporated intellectual capital into the company's core values.

Business guru Peter Drucker emphasizes the radical change in the global economy as the industries that have moved into the center of the economy in the last forty years have as their main business the production and distribution of knowledge and information, rather than consumer or industrial goods. Drucker says IT (e.g., computers, semiconductors, and software), communications, media (e.g., movies and advertising), financial services, management consulting, and health care and education are "knowledge industries." Together, they comprise roughly 60 percent of the S&P 500.

In 1958, knowledge industries accounted for around 29 percent of current dollar gross national product. By 1980, that share had risen to over 34 percent of U.S. GNP. Today, the share of GNP accounted for by knowledge industries is probably closer to 40 percent. More than one-third of all employment growth during the past decade was in knowledge sectors.

Drucker points out that we do not yet fully understand how knowledge behaves as an economic resource, because we don't have enough experience to formulate a theory and test it empirically. An economic theory that puts knowledge into the center of the wealth-producing process, says Drucker, would be able to explain economic growth, market share dynamics, and innovation in the twenty-first century.

Economic studies by Romer and others go even further and suggest that current thinking in economics has gone beyond the 1970s concept of investing in human capital. What economists recognize today is that the essence of economic growth goes beyond either physical or human capital, and now hinges on the ideas and formulas that we use to increase the value of raw material. Furthermore, scarcity, the concept on which conventional economics is founded, does not exist in knowledge industries, according to Romer.

There is no scarcity in Romer's economics because there are an infinite number of instructions, formulas, recipes, and ideas that can be discovered. There is unlimited scope for discovering new ideas, new chip architectures, new pieces of software, new drugs, new types of financial services, and new media. In fact, in complete opposition to the industrial age economy, in a knowledge economy, driven by intangible assets, economics becomes the study of the allocation of abundant resources—not scarce ones.

Knowledge assets are easily replicated because an infinite number of people can use an idea, recipe, software, or formula. Compare for example a piece of music, say a Beethoven sonata, to a barrel of oil. Once a piece of music is recorded, it can be copied over and over by millions of people and never lose its original form. Everybody could conceivably listen to Beethoven's piano sonata #8 in C Minor at the same time. This is dramatically different from the economics of oil. One barrel of oil can be used only by a handful of car owners and once it is consumed, it's gone. A similar type of economics applies to land and buildings.

Instead of a zero-sum society, we can create, through replication of knowledge, a win-win economy. Rather than having to divide up a pie of scarce resources, we can create and share ever larger pieces of knowledge-intensive wealth. As Romer states, this new perspective on value and wealth is much more optimistic than the one based on scarce physical resources, which gave economics its nickname "the dismal science."

The traditional view of wealth based on scarce resources is outmoded for the twenty-first century. Future increases in living standards in America and the rest of the world will be driven by the accumulation of knowledge and intellectual capital. In the past two hundred years, U.S. GDP growth per capita (a measure of the standard of living) has gone from from 0.6 percent per year from 1800 to 1840 to 2.3 percent from 1960 to 1999 (see Exhibit 24). Going forward, the pace of technical change will lay the groundwork for faster growth—in the 2.5 to 3 percent range.

EXHIBIT 24: Rising Tide:
Growth in the U.S. Gross Domestic Product Per Capita

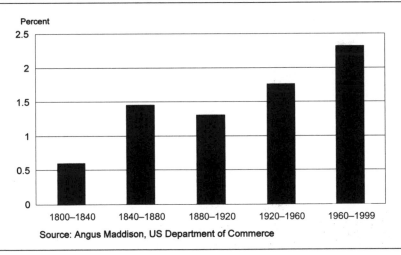

Source: Angus Maddison, US Department of Commerce

FUTURE WEALTH

The seismic shift from an economy based on resources and scarcity to one based on knowledge and abundance is equivalent to a ten on the economic Richter scale. Many people are undoubtedly aware of the transformation underway in the global economy from tangible assets and scarcity toward intangible assets and abundance. Still, there is confusion on the part of economists and business people about exactly how to characterize these changes.

Ancient pharaohs, medieval priests, and the great industrialists displayed their knowledge and wealth in giant pyramids, magnificent cathedrals, and sprawling factories. These monuments of wealth were plainly visible to the naked eye—some could be seen from miles away. Today, knowledge and wealth are displayed in almost invisible objects—microchips as small as a fingernail, fiber-optic cables as thin as a hair, and capsules as small as a grain of sand.

The real wealth embedded in the circuitry of a microchip is not detectable by the human eye. The more than 40 million transistors etched onto a silicon wafer are seen only by a powerful microscope. A cutting edge computer chip contains as much as seven miles of wire, while a Pentium microprocessor has wire stretching about a quarter mile. In the not too distant future, microchips will contain a level of complexity equivalent to putting a street map of the entire planet on a chip the size of a fingernail.

In the communications industry, researchers are harnessing the power of quantum physics to expand the amount of information that can be carried by a single strand of fiberoptic cable. A technology known as wavelength division multiplexing enables many colors of light to travel at light speed down a single fiber thread. State-of-the-art fiber technology permits more than 2,000 wavelengths, or lambdas (think of these as lanes on a highway), on a single fiber thread no thicker than a strand of human hair. In the past year, the capacity supported by optical fiber transmission systems has grown a thousandfold—a pace well in excess of Moore's law.

In coming years, the number of wavelengths permitted on a single strand of fiber-optic cable will soar amid a wave of innovation in laser and communication networking technology. Indeed, as George Gilder points out in *Telecosm*, in the late 1990s researchers learned how to inscribe dense arrays of optical stripes, each with a different refractive index, within the very core of a fiber-optic cable. Optical communications technology is at a stage of evolution similar to where integrated chips were in the 1960s.

In the biopharmaceutical sector, scientists are finding new ways of developing drugs. Researchers are creating fully human monoclonal antibodies in mice. These "transgenic mice" are capable of producing antibodies that can be used safely by physicians to treat cancer and other life-threatening diseases. The immune systems that transgenic mice possess are invisible to the naked eye, but their potential value is clear in the possibility of new drugs and antibodies to battle life-threatening diseases. The economic value of this medical research, say economists Kevin Murphy and Robert Topel, is in the tens of billions of dollars.

MIND OVER MATTER

In *Monitoring the World Economy*, economist Angus Maddison states that four main influences go a long way toward explaining long-term economic growth and the huge increases we've seen in per capita output. These are:

1. Technological progress;

2. Accumulation of physical capital (in which technical progress usually needs to be embodied);

3. Improvement in human skills, education, and organizing ability;

4. Closer integration of individual national economies through trade in goods and services.

Maddison argues that technological progress has been the most fundamental element of change. If there had been no technical progress, he notes, the accumulation of physical capital since the early part of the nineteenth century would have been relatively modest. Investment would have been devoted largely to replacing worn-out machinery and buildings with new and identical replicas, and increasing the stock to accommodate the needs of an expanding workforce. Maddison points out that the major incentive to accumulate physical capital has arisen because new technology brings new products and better ways of producing older products. This is exactly what Schumpeter's economics tell us.

The capital stock and gross domestic product in the United States and the United Kingdom have risen exponentially—as have technology and scientific knowledge—since the industrial revolution. From 1820 to 1992, Maddison estimates that the stock of machinery and equipment increased 5,400-fold—a stunning rise by any measure. Adjusted for the number of workers, Maddison's calculations show that there was a 141-fold increase in the amount of machines and equipment in the U.S. in that period.

Prior to the industrial revolution, Maddison shows growth in living standards was paltry. Measured in 1990 U.S. dollars, the world GDP rose from $565 per person in 1500 to $651 per person in 1820. That works out to an increase in wealth of roughly 27 cents per year. After the industrial revolution, living standards skyrocketed. The total world GDP grew from $695 billion in the early nineteenth century to nearly $28 trillion in 1992. At the same time, the world's population rose from just over 1 billion to nearly 5.5 billion. Adjusting for population, world output per capita jumped from $651 to a whopping $5,145 or, by $26 per year. Thus, Maddison's figures show that global wealth has been growing a hundred times faster than it did before the industrial revolution.

It may be difficult for some people to grasp the significance of these numbers. There is another way of putting the industrial revolution in perspective, one used by David Landes, doyen of economic historians at Harvard University. In his popular undergraduate economics course, Landes asks students to first look to their left and then look to their right. Once the students have done this, he points out that were it not for the industrial revolution, two out of every three students in the class would not be alive today.

In early 2002, Federal Reserve Board chairman Alan Greenspan remarked that it has been abundantly clear in recent years that advances in technology have enhanced the growth of productivity, which in turn has been essential to lifting our standards of living. Future gains in wealth and living standards, Greenspan argued, will be closely associated with not only technological progress and the accumulation of physical capital, but also improvement in human capital or knowledge capital as well as global economic integration.

Economists tell us that wealth is created when assets are moved from lower to higher valued uses. The convention in accounting and economics of associating value and wealth with tangible or hard assets has a long legacy. The inventions of the seventeenth, eighteenth, and nineteenth centuries catapulted physical assets to the fore of the global economy. The defining inventions of the industrial age were threshing machines, swing plows, cotton gins, steam engines, electric looms, and internal combustion engines (see Exhibit 25). These machines drove production and wealth creation. They turned barren land and commodities into products with higher added-value. Natural resources, however, consumed by the machines of the industrial era were scarce. As production increased, so did costs.

EXHIBIT 25: A History of Invention

Newtonian Age		Quantum Age	
Invention	*Year*	*Invention*	*Year*
Pressure cooker	1680	Radio	1906
Threshing machine	1732	Television	1926
Swing plow	1780	Radar	1934
Cotton gin	1793	Electron microscope	1939
Ball bearings	1794	Computer	1946
Lathe	1798	Transistor	1947
Steam engine	1800	Integrated circuit	1958
Conveyor belt	1804	Laser	1960
All-iron plow	1808	Microprocessor	1971
Circular saw	1810	Personal computer	1975
Hydraulic jack	1812	Fiber-optic cables	1977
Standard nuts & bolts	1825	Facsimile machine	1981
Reaper	1826	Camcorder	1982
Sewing machine	1846	Cell phone	1983
Electric loom	1846	Compact disk	1983
Bessemer steel making	1860	Carbon nanotubes	1990
Internal combustion engine	1860	World Wide Web	1991

Source: Michael Cox and Richard Alm, *Myths of Rich and Poor*.

The Newtonian-based inventions that fueled the industrial revolution have an extensive and illustrious history. In contrast, the inventions spawned by the development of quantum theory are of recent vintage. All of the important quantum physics–related inventions and innovations have occurred in the past sixty years (see Exhibit 25). The quantum revolution is now about where the Newtonian revolution was back in the mid-eighteenth century, around the time the threshing machine was invented.

From this perspective, we can see that many of the most important quantum-based inventions and innovations lie ahead of us in the twenty-first century. Given the relative newness of the quantum economy, it is not surprising that many nonconventional models and metrics have been slow to catch on. In the years ahead, they are likely to receive a great deal of attention.

Could the quantum revolution in science and technology usher in a period of wealth creation equal to or greater than the industrial revolution? Perhaps. Should the pace of knowledge creation and technological invention and innovation accelerate in the twenty-first century, as many scientists expect, it's quite possible that the amount of real wealth created could exceed that created by the industrial revolution.

The experience of the past two decades is instructive. Over 1,745 technology companies have gone public in the last twenty years, and they carried an aggregate equity market value of more than $2.3 trillion. Interestingly, there has been a noticeable concentration of wealth in the technology industry. Analysts at Morgan Stanley estimate that 5 percent of the companies that have issued stock since 1980 account for more than 100 percent of the wealth creation in the stock market.

Since the commercialization of the Internet, the number of U.S. technology companies receiving financing from venture capitalists has soared. As Exhibit 26 shows, more than 6,000 tech companies received venture financing in 2000, up from 637 in 1995 and 216 in 1980. Much of the financing activity since 1995 has been related to the build-out of the Internet sector. Companies receiving venture financing exploded after 1995. Recently, there has been a shift away from the Internet sector toward the life science and nanotechnology industries. Venture financing will intensify in these two sectors in coming years as the pace of quantum technological innovation accelerates.

EXHIBIT 26: Financing the Future:
Number of U.S. Tech Companies Receiving Venture Financing

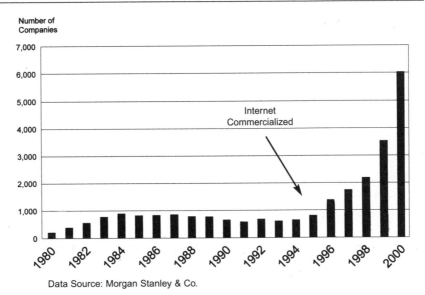

Data Source: Morgan Stanley & Co.

WAKE-UP CALL

P.J. O'Rourke has observed that there is a heartfelt and nearly universal refusal of people to understand the basic economic principles behind the creation of wealth. This peculiarity seems to defy rational explanation, especially in the face of overwhelming evidence. Stalin was not the only political leader in the twentieth century who thought that commanding the bulk of the world's natural resources would guarantee against any misfortune in the future.

The quantum revolution in science has affected the economic and accounting world in much the same way that it has jolted the physical sciences. To understand the quantum world, physicists have had to develop new models that are a radical departure from classical, Newtonian physics. Likewise, economists and accountants must embrace new models, concepts, and tools to understand the quantum economy.

In coming years, we will see more emphasis on nonconventional modes and methods of accounting and economic analysis. *The quantum economy doesn't repeal the laws of supply and demand. However, understanding this large and growing piece of the economy does require augmenting the Newtonian physics–based mindset that has dominated economic thinking for the past century.*

The collapse of the Soviet Union at the end of the twentieth century should have been a wake-up call for those who continue to believe that the rules of the industrial age still apply. The empires being built today are, as Churchill predicted, empires of the mind. As we will see in Chapters 6 and 7, scientists and researchers around the world are forging a new science to help us comprehend the increasingly complex world we live in. Those who understand and embrace this new science will become the economic, political, and cultural superpowers of the twenty-first century.

Key Takeaways

- Quantum-based technologies leverage the mind in the same way Newtonian-based technologies leveraged human muscle. Unlike in the industrial revolution, return on investment in human capital has risen faster than the return on physical assets.

- Today, "knowledge industries" comprise 60 percent of the S&P 500 and approximately 40 percent of U.S. GNP.

- Intangible assets, such as R&D, human knowledge, designs, software, ideas, and technology, have risen sharply over the past century and today many companies are investing just as much or more in intangible as tangible assets.

- Accountants and financial analysts have been slow to develop metrics designed to measure intangible assets. The centuries-old matching principle may be outmoded in the intangible-asset-intensive business world.

- Based on more comprehensive measures of value developed by Baruch Lev, the actual value of companies' intangible assets has risen, and yet it is not accounted for on the balance sheet. Therefore valuations of intangible-rich companies may be more attractive than their current and conventional price-to-book value.

- The quantum economy doesn't repeal the laws of supply and demand, but requires understanding that there is a new meaning to scarce resources. The new economy requires augmenting the Newtonian-physics-based mindset that has dominated economic and financial thinking for the past century.

- Venture capital financing will increase significantly in the next decade in the life science and nanotechnology sectors.

Pagels' Prophesy

The important thing is to observe the actual living economy out there. It's path-dependent, it's complicated, it's evolving, it's open, and it's organic.
—Brian Arthur

In 1988, after the spectacular crash in global stock markets and on the eve of the disintegration of the Soviet Union, a distinguished physicist named Heinz Pagels published a book titled *The Dreams of Reason*. He wrote that for the first time in history, scientists were liberating themselves from primitive calculating tools, and they were harnessing the power of personal computers to model and simulate Mother Nature in all of her glorious complexity.

Complex systems are everywhere. We see complexity in our own human bodies and brains, in the galaxies sprawling across the universe, in weather patterns, in the economy, and even in the stock market. Complex systems are inherently difficult to analyze with conventional tools of scientific analysis, because they are dynamic and don't behave in a predictable, linear fashion. This challenge led scientists to use new methods of computer-based analysis.

As PCs transformed how scientists did their analysis and research, networked computing brought them together. The

Internet and the World Wide Web blew away the barriers that had been separating scientific disciplines. What emerged from the quantum-based technological and communications landscape was a new interdisciplinary effort among scientists to meet the challenges of understanding the behavior of complex systems. By 1999, this multidisciplinary research effort yielded to scientists profound insights into their understanding of complex systems.

The concepts of the new "science of complexity," as Pagels pointed out, are unconventional: The importance of biological organizing principles; the computational view of mathematics and physical processes; the emphasis on parallel networks; the importance of nonlinear dynamics and selective systems; the new understanding of chaos; experimental mathematics; neural networks; and parallel distributive processing. Many of these themes were the equivalent of a foreign language to conventional thinkers.

The science of complexity heralded a new scientific synthesis that would eventually overturn our traditional way of organizing reality that dated back to Newton's time. In Pagels' view, the nations and people who mastered the new sciences of complexity would become the economic, cultural, and political superpowers of the twenty-first century—the titans of the third millennium.

COMPLEXITY AND THE MARKETS

One of the areas where complexity theory is having a major impact on thinking is in the social sciences, particularly economics and finance. For years, economists have been puzzled by the occurrence of recessions, stock market bubbles and crashes, and other oddities that we observe in the real world. Business cycle scholar Victor Zarnowitz once noted that the very occurrence of a recession is an unsolved puzzle in economics. There is no generally accepted explanation for why the normally well-functioning economy of a country with a growing population and other productive resources should repeatedly suffer overall declines in employment, production, real income, and sales. Yet recessions have been a permanent feature of the business landscape for centuries.

Stock market crashes are another unsolved mystery. In conventional economics, market participants are assumed to be omniscient and rational. Under these assumptions, stock market crashes and even extreme volatility in financial markets are anomalies that shouldn't occur. And yet, as the eminent economist Charles Kindelberger traces in his classic work *Manias, Panics, and Crashes*, stock market crashes and financial crises have a long and distinguished history. Many have occurred around the time of the invention of a major new technology. For example, one of the fiercest financial storms of the eighteenth century occurred in Britain around the time the steam engine and steam-powered trains were invented. The panic of 1837 in the United States—an event Kindelberger refers to as "one of the most disastrous panics this nation ever experienced"—occurred during the year the telegraph was invented.

Complexity theory sheds much light on why we observe major fluctuations and crashes in the stock market. Complexity theorists note that financial markets like the U.S. stock market are among the most complex systems on the planet. Per Bak, a pioneer of a branch of complexity science known as *self-organized criticality*, points out that large fluctuations in the stock market indicate a self-organized critical state where minor shocks lead to avalanches. Most of the changes that occur in self-organized critical states take place through catastrophic events. This view is in direct contrast with conventional economic models in which catastrophic events are considered anomalies and not part of the system.

Geologists who study earthquakes are intimately familiar with self-organized critical states. When analyzing earthquakes geologists often see a pattern of stability and calm, followed by minor tremors and eventually major quakes that send powerful shock waves through the earth's crust. Evolutionary biologists observe a similar pattern when studying the evolution of species. They often speak of the "punctuated equilibrium"— a period of tranquility, or stasis, followed by intermittent bursts of activity and volatility in which many new species become extinct and new ones emerge. The Cambrian explosion, which occurred about 550 million years ago, is perhaps the most celebrated punctuated equilibrium.

The earthquakelike fluctuations we observe in the stock market are part of the complex system, and thus unavoidable. Complexity theorists say they are an emergent property of the system. Given this, there is no way policymakers, such as the Federal Reserve, can fully stabilize the economy and get rid of all market fluctuations.

In *How Nature Works*, Bak uses the metaphor of a child building a sandpile on a beach to show the principles of self-organized criticality. As the child begins to build the sandpile, it is relatively flat. As more sand is added to the pile, it becomes steeper. Some sand falls to either side. Eventually, some of the sand slides may even span most or all of the pile; at that point, the system is far out of balance, and its behavior can no longer be understood in terms of the behavior of the individual grains of sand. The avalanches form a dynamic of their own, which can be understood only from a holistic description of the properties of the entire pile rather than from a reductionist description of individual grains: the sandpile is a complex system.

In Bak's "sandpile economics," conventional economic theory can be depicted as a flat sandpile that is in equilibrium. In complexity, the sandpile is constantly evolving, getter steeper and steeper, and emitting avalanches of all sizes over time. He notes that the dynamics of the nonequilibrum critical state could not be more different from the quiet dynamics of a flat beach. Such states evolve by means of catastrophic avalanches rather than gradually.

When a complex system, such as the stock market, is in a critical state, it only makes sense to look at the overall dynamics of the market, not each individual's trades. A reductionist approach is fruitless. Trying to ascertain what is going on in the stock market by studying what individual investors are doing doesn't tell us what is going on in the whole market. As Bak puts it, nothing in the grains of sand suggests the emergent properties of the pile.

Michael Mauboussin is one of the few analysts on Wall Street who has thought about complexity. Mauboussin, an investment strategist and adjunct professor at Columbia Graduate School of Business, notes in "Shift Happens," that Bak's theory and the work of other complexity theorists goes a long way toward unraveling the puzzles that plague conventional economics and finance. The booms, busts, and crashes we observe from time to time in the economy and financial markets are part and parcel of complex adaptive systems. Viewing the markets in this way helps us explain the wild fluctuations in financial markets that cannot be accounted for by conventional theory as well as the skewed (i.e., non-normal) distribution of returns we see in the marketplace.

THE DAWNING OF COMPLEXITY

In the fourteen years since the publication of *The Dreams of Reason*, we can already see Pagels' prescience. Complexity theory is shedding new light on the inner workings of Mother Nature, the global economy, and the financial markets. In the past decade, research on complexity theory has turned from a trickle to a flood.

Theoretical biologists and complexity researchers Ricard Solé and Brian Goodwin say this burst of creativity in science is transforming traditional disciplines, catalyzing movements, dissolving old boundaries, and integrating new territories. The new movement began in physics and mathematics, with complexity, chaos, and emergent order. It is now moving into the life and social sciences, revealing the underpinnings of creative processes, from the evolution of organisms to the dynamics of stock markets.

The leading center for complexity research today is the Santa Fe Institute (SFI). Located high in the foothills of the Sangre de Cristo Mountains of northern New Mexico, SFI has become the most prominent multidisciplinary scientific research and education center focused on complex systems research. Since its founding in 1984, SFI has sponsored more than two hundred interdisciplinary workshops, attended by hundreds of academic scientists and researchers from research centers, government agencies, academic institutions, and private industry around the world.

SFI has brought together a captivating range of thinkers, from Nobel laureates in physics and economics to gifted graduate students, senior corporate executives, and prominent public officials. Notable physical and social scientists who have been or are currently associated with SFI include: Philip Anderson, Kenneth Arrow, Brian Arthur, George Cowan, Manfred Eigen, Doyne Farmer, Murray Gell-Mann, Don Glaser, John Holland, Stuart Kauffman, Chris Langton, and David Pines.

One of the most distinguishing features of complexity science is the focus on multidisciplinary research. SFI has devoted itself to the creation of a new kind of scientific research community, pursuing emerging syntheses in science. Its broad mission encompasses a number of complementary views and encourages exploration of previously uncharted domains of science. SFI uses the term "transdisciplinary" to describe its unique approach to research. Topics of interest transcend any single scientific discipline and cannot be studied adequately in traditional disciplinary contexts.

Complexity is a complex subject, as scientist William Brock once put it. Since complexity, and its counterpart, simplicity, are givens at different levels of a system, there is no way to define an absolute measure of complexity. Scientists note that it is difficult to compare the complexity of a cell in a living organism with that of a galaxy in the universe. As a result of this contextual identity, many researchers believe complexity can be defined only in a relative sense.

The study of complexity differs from the study of chaos. Chaos deals with nonlinear patterns that are too complicated to be analyzed easily, even though they are deterministic systems. Chaotic systems are extremely sensitive to what scientists call "initial conditions" of the system. A classic case of chaotic behavior is the weather. Chaos theorists often speak of a "butterfly effect" with respect to weather patterns. The butterfly that flaps its wings in Asia can have an effect on weather conditions in New York City. In chaos, small errors of measurement often give rise to huge errors in prediction, making accurate prediction impossible.

In contrast, complexity scientists seek to understand the emergent and self-organizing characteristics of dynamic systems; they seek to explain phenomena that we observe in nature and our daily lives that defy all conventional categories. Complexity theorists look for patterns in dynamic processes that possess a property of universality, and chaos appears to play a role. Complexity theorist Stuart Kauffman suspects that all complex systems, from single cells to economies, evolve to a natural state that he calls "the edge of chaos." This state between order and chaos is a grand compromise between structure and surprise, as Kauffman puts it. In *Complexity: The Emerging Science at the Edge of*

Order and Chaos, Mitchell Waldrop lists some of the questions that complexity theorists are grappling with:

- Why did the Soviet Union's forty-year hegemony over Eastern Europe collapse within a few months in 1989? Why was the collapse of communism so fast and so complete?

- Why did the stock market crash more than five hundred points on a single Monday in October 1987?

- Why do ancient species and ecosystems often remain stable in the fossil record for millions of years—and then either die out or transform themselves into something new in a geological instant?

- Why do trust and cooperation not only exist but flourish?

- How can Darwinian natural selection account for such wonderfully intricate structures as the eye or the kidney?

- What is life, anyway?

- What is a mind? How does a three-pound lump of ordinary matter, the brain, give rise to such ineffable qualities as feeling, thought, purpose, and awareness?

- What accounts for the things we observe in the universe— the galaxies, stars, planets, bacteria, plants, animals, and brains?

At first glance, these questions appear to have absolutely nothing in common, except for the fact that they all have the same answer: "Nobody knows." But, closer inspection reveals a universal thread. Each question refers to a complex system, in the sense that various independent variables are interacting with each other in a variety of ways. Moreover, in every case, the outcome of the interactions produces a universal pattern that scientists refer to as *self-organization.*

Self-organization is a primary feature of all complex systems. Complexity theorists note that dynamic systems have a tendency to organize themselves into ever more complex structures, even in the presence of strong forces of dissolution. As Kauffman puts it, there is a kind of deep, inner creativity that is woven into the very fabric of nature.

Emergence is another important characteristic of complex systems and is ubiquitous. Complexity pioneer John Holland says that emergence lies at the heart of all creative activities of humans, including technological invention and innovation, business and industry development, the formation of government, and the creation of scientific theories. Researchers observe emergence when they study ant colonies, networks of neurons in the brain, the human immune system, the Internet, and the global economy. In all cases, the theorists find the behavior of the whole system is much greater than the behavior of its individual parts. Emergence is the arising of the patterns, structures, and properties that are not explained by the system's pre-existing components. Unpredictability, on the other hand, is a primary feature of emergent phenomena and plays an important role in chaos and quantum mechanics. Knowing the properties of the individual components of a complex adaptive system doesn't accurately predict the behavior of the whole system. For example, understanding the properties of hydrogen and oxygen does not allow researchers to predict the properties of H_2O. Self-organizing behavior emerges unpredictably in complex systems at different levels.

One of scientists' major tasks is to understand how the behavior of nonlinear systems changes when circumstances change. Unpredictability is a characteristic of both chaos and complexity. In chaos, the inability to predict stems from the sensitivity of a system to initial conditions. In complexity, unpredictability is associated with emergence and the inability of scientists to predict the behavior of nonlinear systems from knowing their individual parts.

Another important feature of complex systems is that they are *adaptive*. Complexity theorists often speak of *complex adaptive systems*. John Holland believes that adaptation is the sine qua non of complex adaptive systems. Adaptation is a concept often used by biologists, who define it as a process whereby an organism fits itself to its environment. Biologists note that experience is what guides change in an organism's structure. Over time, organisms make better use of their surroundings for their own needs which means they incorporate concepts related to learning.

THE HIDDEN ORDER

Complex systems are nonlinear, adaptive, and, because their behavior is more than the sum of their individual parts, difficult to understand. Unfortunately, as Holland says, scientists' most useful analytical tools, such as trend analysis, determination of equilibrium, and sample means, are not well suited to analyzing complex, adaptive systems. Therefore, complexity scientists resort to cross-disciplinary comparisons to extract common characteristics. They can then use those characteristics as building blocks to formulate a general theory about complex systems.

In *Hidden Order*, Holland identified "seven basics"—four properties and three mechanisms—of complex adaptive systems:

1. Aggregation: Complex systems have a property whereby they can be simplified into categories—trees, cars, banks—and then treated as equivalent; in addition, they possess emergent properties that stem from the aggregate interactions of less complex agents.

2. Tagging: A mechanism that consistently facilitates the formation of aggregates (e.g., a flag, banner), tags are a pervasive feature of complex adaptive systems because they facilitate selective interaction.

3. Nonlinearity: Complex adaptive systems are inherently nonlinear; the interactions of agents produce effects greater than the sum of the constituents.

4. Flows: There are two properties of flows. The first is the multiplier effect, which is akin to an amplifier; the second is the recycling effect—the effect of cycles in the networks.

5. Diversity: Perpetual novelty is the hallmark of complex adaptive systems; the diversity observed in such systems is the product of progressive adaptations—each new adaptation opens the possibility of further interactions and new niches.

6. Internal models: Complex adaptive systems use internal models as the mechanism for anticipation and prediction.

7. Building blocks: Agents in complex adaptive systems use building blocks to generate internal models.

• • •

These seven basics are common to all complex adaptive systems, and they exhibit coherence under change, via conditional action and anticipation, and they do so without central direction. At the same time, complex adaptive systems have the unique property whereby small increments of input produce large, directed changes.

UNRAVELING FINANCIAL MYSTERIES

The scholars working in the interdisciplinary network at the SFI have been studying the global economy and the stock market as complex adaptive systems. They say that the standard model taught to beginning economic and finance students is a useful starting point but is flawed in several important ways.

The standard model—what's known as the efficient market theory—states that investors will use any information about future changes to set prices of financial assets. In this model, it is assumed that investors have perfect information and homogeneous expectations; that prices adjust instantaneously to any new information in the marketplace; and that there is no information in past prices. In other words, investors or traders cannot profit from using past patterns of prices to forecast future prices. SFI economist Brian Arthur points out that although the standard theory of finance is very successful, it cannot explain everything that we observe in real-world financial markets, such as crashes and bubbles. Standard theory says these events are empirical or statistical anomalies. The standard theory also cannot account for the huge volume of trading that occurs or why technical trading is profitable. In sum, Arthur notes, the standard theory does not explain about half a dozen major statistical "anomalies" in real-world financial markets.

Complexity theory offers a richer understanding of how the global economy and financial markets function, because it allows for predictions that fit real-world situations, such as crashes and bubbles that have puzzled conventional financial theorists over the years. Complexity models do not assume perfect rationality and perfect information. Analysts do not have perfect knowledge of the underlying structure of the global economy. They do not and cannot have a perfect understanding of how complex adaptive systems like the global economy and financial markets function. Rather, what we observe in the real world are analysts with highly imperfect knowledge of the underlying economy and its complexity. These imperfections give rise to heterogeneous expectations and model uncertainty—two of the primary determinants of fluctuations we observe in the economy and financial markets.

Arthur has observed that the economic realm is nothing like that assumed in conventional textbooks. The world we live in is inherently subjective, psychological, and unpredictable. Indeterminacy percolates through the system and adaptation becomes paramount. In the case of high model uncertainty, where there are complicated problems and issues, analysts attempt to frame these situations with temporary hypotheses even if they are simplistic and crude.

Because we live in a sea of uncertainty, learning and adaptation are necessary for survival. In a complex adaptive system, such as the U.S. stock market, analysts are constantly learning which of their hypotheses work by discarding poorly performing hypotheses and replacing them with more promising ideas. In a world fraught with uncertainty, the process of learning becomes extraordinarily messy as analysts struggle to adapt to a rapidly evolving global economic landscape.

Oddly enough, conventional economic theory largely ignores the process of learning. Michael Rothschild notes that the term "learning curve" is not even mentioned in most economic textbooks, except some that include evolutionary game-theory models.

As complexity pioneer Doyne Farmer points out, what you find in these models is that with even fairly simple games, like the children's game "rock paper scissors," there are complicated dynamics in which the learning may never converge. This happens because the success or failure of an individual depends on the behavior of other people in the marketplace. Each person tries to learn what the other is doing, but the behavior of other people is changing at the same time. What I do influences what you do, and what you do influences what I do, and so on. As a result, everyone is always shooting at a moving target and the model never settles into equilibrium.

Conventional financial theory bears a strong resemblance to Newtonian or classical physics. It describes a hypothetical state where the future is known rather than uncertain. But there is no certainty in the real world. Just as it is in the quantum world of atoms and subatomic particles, uncertainty is pervasive in the investment world. Reflecting on this uncertainty, Sir Isaac Newton once remarked that he could calculate the motions of heavenly bodies, but not the madness of people.

THE HIDDEN FUTURE

The essence of investment is "the hidden future," observes investment advisor Peter Bernstein. If the road ahead were always clear, we would readily adjust to what we see and tomorrow's stock prices would always equal today's. In their calmer moments, investors recognize their inability to know what the future holds. In moments of extreme panic or enthusiasm, however, they become remarkably bold in their predictions. During such times, they act as though uncertainty has vanished and the outcome is beyond doubt. Reality is abruptly transformed into that hypothetical future where the outcome is known.

These are rare occasions, to be sure, but they are also unforgettable. A switch from doubt to certainty defines major tops and bottoms in the stock market. At such moments, convictions about the future are so strong that no force is left to extend the current price trend further in the direction from which it has come. The tipping point is at hand.

This behavior we observe on Wall Street and in all financial markets is the emergent outcome of millions of people with adaptive, heterogeneous beliefs and imperfect knowledge. The complexity models assume these characteristics and therefore can generate many of the important anomalies unaccounted for by the standard theory, including fat-tailed events (e.g., booms, busts, bubbles, and crashes), high market trading volumes, and volatility clustering.

Investors steeped in conventional finance theory cannot explain these events. They assume the distribution of price returns is a normal, bell-shaped distribution. Over long periods of time, price patterns may be normally distributed. For example, in the past decade, 80 percent of all stocks in the S&P 500 produced returns within 10 percent of the market average or mean. However, over short periods of time, price patterns can be anything but normal.

From April 2000 to April 2001, there were four large daily moves in the S&P 500 stock index. Traditional risk indicators based on conventional finance theory state that each large gyration in stock prices should have occurred once every 120 years. And yet we saw four such events in one year. Rather than normal distributions, we observe fat-tailed distributions which imply that extreme fluctuations in financial asset prices are more frequent than those assumed in a textbook, normal distribution.

Complexity theorists have discovered that diversifying the investment horizons of various market participants typically results in a more stable market environment. The stability in the marketplace comes from diversifying the knowledge base of the market participants. Complexity theorists have also discovered that wild fluctuations and extreme volatility in financial markets—things that cannot be explained by mainstream models—can be easily produced in nonconventional economic models by assuming that heterogeneous expectations and beliefs suddenly become homogeneous. When expectations and beliefs switch from heterogeneous to homogeneous, the result is extreme volatility. These are exactly the same salient points that seasoned investment professional Peter Bernstein has made in the past.

BOUNDED THINKING

Many complexity theorists in economics and finance are fond of the concept of bounded rationality. The pioneer of bounded rationality was Nobel laureate Herbert Simon, considered by many to be the father of behavioral finance and economics. He was noted for the extent of his cross-disciplinary contributions in science—from economic theory to psychology to behavioral science to computer science.

Simon challenged the assumptions of conventional economics and finance. He believed that Rational Economic Man, the hallmark of conventional theory, did not exist in the real world. Simon argued that people's ability to recognize alternatives and calculate optimal solutions to problems is quite limited. He replaced the assumption of rationality with the more realistic assumption of bounded rationality. Bounded rationality asserts that people cannot always make perfect decisions, because the computational demands of doing so are beyond their capability. Instead of always making the best choice, people resort to making choices that appear good enough at the time.

Simon noted that bounded rationality is procedural, not substantive rationality. Human behavior, he argued, cannot be predicted from the optimal behavior in a given environment. People's behavior depends on how they perceive and represent their environment, how they define their goals and methods for assessing goal attainment, what facts they know or assume, and what strategies they have for problem solving. Simon notes that individuals are likely to be greatly influenced by contemporary social beliefs that in turn undergo gradual change with the course of historical events.

Simon points out that there is a tremendous amount of evidence in support of behavioral economics and finance and the assumption of bounded rationality. Behavioral rationality explains how people make decisions and solve problems in the real world far better than the theory of perfect rationality. Moreover, as Simon notes, it explains why people stay alive and even thrive despite having modest computational abilities compared to the complexity of the world that surrounds them.

Complexity theorists note that much of the instability we observe in the marketplace stems from the nature of investor psychology. Investor psychology is a subject that falls into the field of behavioral finance. Behavioral financial theorists note that investors have a number of psychological traits, such as loss aversion, overconfidence, and anchoring that can cause prices to depart from fundamental values, which in turn can produce bubbles and crashes.

Analysts often use rules of thumb that behavioral psychologists refer to as "heuristics." These heuristics are often the product of trial and error and sometimes formed from stereotypes or a small sample of information. Many times analysts stay attached to their views even when presented with new information that conflicts with their opinions.

People are also prone to prefer the familiar to the unfamiliar and more often than not are overconfident in their predictions.

Behavioral finance pioneer Daniel Kahneman notes that the failure of the rational model in economics and finance is not in its logic, but in the human brain it requires. Our brains are not designed to perform the way the rational model mandates. Every person would have to know and understand everything completely and at once. The human brain is composed of several parts that have evolved over millions of years. One of the most primitive parts is the limbic system, which creates strong emotions and convictions that make humans act impulsively. The neocortex is the more evolved part of the brain, and it performs logical and rational analysis. The limbic system functions faster than the neocortex. This helps explains why, when in danger, people often run first and reason later. Clinical studies have shown that the limbic and neocortex parts of the brain can function independently of each other.

As a result of our neural wiring, we often overhype the short run and underestimate the long-term impact of technological change. This behavior—which seems eminently rational from a biological or cognitive psychology perspective—helps explain why we see periodic cycles of panic and exuberance in financial markets. Put simply, analysts and investors frequently are blindsided by the future.

Theorists in behavioral finance note that people often look at problems in pieces rather than in the aggregate. They point out that even academic scholars writing for prestigious journals reach incorrect conclusions by failing to recognize that the whole is the product of interaction among its parts, rather than just a collection of discrete pieces. This interaction effect is exactly the same kind of effect that complexity theorists describe when discussing complex adaptive systems. The outcome we observe is often more than the sum of the individual parts.

Researchers in behavioral finance spend a lot of time analyzing how investors make decisions in the marketplace. They note that investors and analysts often mix rational thinking with emotional impulses that produce deviations from an asset's intrinsic value. Humans, they point out, at times have a great propensity to panic, especially over imaginary dangers. Panic has been a permanent feature of the financial market landscape. Consider the panics of 1825 and 1857 in Great Britain and the great panics of 1837, 1929, and 1987 in the United States. Clearly, as these instances show, there are times when cool-headed thinking rushes for the exits and emotional impulses take over.

ENDOGENOUS RISK

A concept that is related to and is as important as bounded rationality is endogenous risk. Endogenous risk arises in situations when a significant number of investors sharing common expectations about the future all discover they are wrong at once. They respond to this error by shifting their portfolio holdings in the same way and at the same time.

Conventional finance assumes that risk is exogenous. Exogenous risk in a given market refers to unexpected news or changes in fundamentals that cause financial asset prices to fluctuate. However, depending on the particular asset class under examination, somewhere between 65 and 95 percent of price movements cannot be explained by the standard model.

Endogenous risk is the extra volatility that arises in financial markets as a result of market participants having inadequate information. Edogenous risk is the centerpiece of Stanford University economics professor Mordecai Kurz's theory known as rational beliefs. In Kurz's model, people are assumed not to know the underlying or true state of the economy; rather they form rational beliefs about what they think it is.

Kurz demonstrates theoretically that the presence of what he calls "correlated belief structures" explains much of the volatility we observe in the real world. When many investors have the same expectations about the future—that is, when their belief structures are correlated—and these expectations are disappointed, a large amount of trading (i.e., buying and selling) will take place in a short period of time. When this occurs, prices will overshoot either on the upside or downside.

Kurz observes that the use of leverage in financial markets can amplify the dynamics of price movements. In his model, if a significant number of leveraged investors possess correlated expectations and if their views turn out to be mistaken, a huge amount of trading will occur and prices will adjust rapidly. Investment strategist Woody Brock notes that this is precisely what happened during the bond market crash of 1994, the emerging market currency crisis of 1998, and the collapse in the Nasdaq index in 2000.

Kurz observes that the origins of endogenous risk lie in the interplay of the prior beliefs of investors and the actual course of events that unfold in the economy and in financial markets. Correlated belief structures and leverage are the primary source of market volatility. Another source of endogenous risk is what he calls "trend following" behavior. "The trend is your friend" is a phrase heard frequently on Wall Street. Often, traders and investors sell or take short positions or buy and take long positions in various securities if they detect a change in trend. Kurz's theory tells us that the more technical a market becomes—that is, the more trend-following there is—the greater the endogenous risk in the marketplace.

The difference between exogenous and endogenous risk may seem academic, but it is not. A market that has a higher level of endogenous risk should, Brock says, command a higher risk premium. The risk premium of any financial asset is a function not only of the total amount of risk but also of the proportion of total risk that is exogenous/endogenous. The intuitive reason why a unit of endogenous risk is "worse" than one of exogenous risk is that endogenous risk is inexplicable. When the source of price movements is exogenous—that is, when it is based on changes of the fundamentals—it is easier to understand.

Bounded rationality, rational beliefs, and other important concepts embraced by complexity theory are shedding a great deal of light on the real-world financial market dynamics. Using computers, complexity theorists at the SFI have developed "artificial agent-based" models using computers to better understand the complex interactions we see in financial markets. In one simple model, developed by Brian Arthur, John Holland, physicist Richard Palmer, and financial theorist Blake LeBaron, investors in a single security are represented by adaptive agents dealing with one another through a central clearinghouse. The artificial agents buy and sell securities from one another. The computer displays the stock's price and dividend, who is buying and selling, who is making money and who is not, who is in the market and who is out, and so on. The model assumes that agents form their expectations not deductively, but rather inductively, as cognitive theory suggests.

What emerges from the model are price fluctuations that resemble those we observe in real-world financial markets. The model generates speculative booms and busts amid slowly changing fundamental values. That is, prices gyrate frequently above and below a security's intrinsic or fundamental value. Doyne Farmer, currently McKinsey Professor at the SFI, is developing a number of promising artificial agent-based computer models in the hopes of providing researchers with a better understanding of how complex, real-world financial markets behave.

Complexity researcher John Casti notes in *Would-Be Worlds* that scientific work using computer-based simulations to model complex systems is in its infancy today. He likens the position that complexity theorists are in now the same position that physicists were in at the time of Galileo. Galileo is the scientist credited with ushering in the idea of such experimentation on simple systems. It was his efforts that paved the way for Newton's development of a theory of such processes, which in turn paved the way for the industrial revolution.

According to Casti, complex systems are still awaiting their Newton. But with our newfound ability to create worlds for all occasions inside the computer, we can play myriad what-if games with genuine complex systems. No longer do researchers have to break the system into simpler subsystems or avoid experimentation completely because the experiments are too costly, too impractical, or just plain too dangerous.

BACK TO THE FUTURE

Until recently, the lack of sophisticated mathematical tools and computational devices (e.g., high-speed computers) was an impediment in economics and finance. During much of the twentieth century, economic theorists spent their time analyzing static worlds of micro-equilibrium and general equilibrium. Differential calculus—a calculus invented by Newton and others—was an extremely useful mathematical tool for analyzing such systems. The study of dynamic systems did not receive a lot of attention from researchers mainly because of difficulties associated with analyzing nonlinear systems.

The elegant general equilibrium analysis, which still reigns supreme in economics, can be defined only with the structure of the economy given and unchanging. Economist Walt Rostow points out in his preface to Robert Allen's *Opening Doors* that unlike conventional static systems, dynamic systems are rarely in equilibrium. Dynamic systems are often characterized by increasing returns, positive feedback loops, and other nonlinear processes that are difficult to analyze with conventional mathematical tools.

In *Investigations,* Stuart Kauffman argues that general competitive equilibrium theory is indeed elegant and mathematically beautiful. However, it does not account for the persistent secular explosion of diversity of goods, services, and ways of making a living we observe in the global economy. Kauffman believes that future economic research needs to construct a theory of the persistent coming into existence of new goods and services and extinction of old goods and services, similar to the emergence and extinction of species in an ecosystem, or Schumpeter's theory of creative destruction.

Kauffman and researcher Vince Darley are developing models to explain this emergence of diversity of goods and services in the global economy. As the complexity of those theories increases however, they become more fragile. The models developed by Kauffman and Darley never settle down to an equilibrium point.

Despite their focus on static analysis and equilibrium, mainstream economists have long recognized the existence of complex systems. Alfred Marshall, the mathematically gifted and exceptional nineteenth-century neoclassical economist, judged economics to be essentially a biological subject rather than an offshoot of Newtonian physics. Schumpeter argued that the introduction of a succession of major technological innovations renders economic growth a profoundly nonlinear process. These innovations create passages of bounded creative-destructive turbulence that could well generate chaotic and complex outcomes. Schumpeter argued that equilibrium analysis could not deal with the complexities of organic growth—the type of growth he argued was the driving force of a capitalist system. Now, complexity theorists around the world are redirecting the study of economics and finance to the dynamic systems that are so pervasive in the real world.

Few Wall Street analysts and investment professionals currently are well versed in complexity theory. Moreover, only a handful of researchers and policymakers at the Federal Reserve Board or other central banks around the world appear to have embraced complexity theory. The same can be said for the highest levels of governments in the developed and developing countries. Nevertheless, it is extremely likely that economic and financial academics and practitioners all over the world will embrace many of the key insights of complexity in coming years.

Many analysts and policymakers view the global economy as a machine. This mindset is an outgrowth of Newtonian thinking. As we shall see in Chapter 7, complexity scientists are discovering that economies and financial markets have much in common with patterns observed in biological systems. In the coming century, analysts and policymakers are likely to view the quantum economy as an evolving ecosystem, with rhythms that are in harmony with nature.

Key Takeaways

- The quantum revolution in technology has given birth to a new science—the science of complexity, which is the discipline of studying complex, adaptive, nonlinear systems.

- Complexity theory is having a major impact on economics and finance because the stock market and our economic system are complex, adaptive systems. Complexity helps explain stock market crashes, economic booms, and extreme financial market volatility.

- It has been observed that many booms and busts of the stock market follow the invention of a General Purpose Technology. From this perspective, the volatility associated with Internet investments is not surprising.

- Investors and analysts often mix rational thinking with emotional impulses that produce deviations from an asset's intrinsic value. Bounded thinking tells us that investors make decisions that seem right at the time.

- In the future, computer-based agent models are likely to help researchers better understand how complex, real-world financial markets behave. These models simulate the real world and can generate stock market booms and busts.

- Investors should focus on the endogenous risk of particular asset class (what investors in that asset class collectively think of the asset's risk) because endogenous risk explains between 65 and 95 percent of the price movement in financial markets. The standard, efficient market model based on exogenous or, market risk, does not fully explain price movement.

- Investors and analysts who embrace many of the key insights of complexity theory are likely to outperform those who do not.

Nature's Patterns

What is the weave? No one yet knows. But the tapestry of life is richer than we have imagined.
—Stuart Kauffman

Amid the chaos and complexity, there is a hidden order in the ways of Mother Nature. Back in the mid-1970s, an IBM scientist named Benoit Mandelbrot wrote about his discovery that nature exhibits not simply a higher degree, but an altogether different level of complexity. Paying homage to Mandelbrot, Ian Stewart, mathematics professor, wrote that although we can learn about nature from mathematics, what is more important is that mathematics has learned from nature.

In *What Is a Snowflake?*, Stewart honored Mandelbrot for his study of apparently disconnected problems—the stock market, the amount of water in rivers, and the interference in electronic circuits. Mandelbrot was the first to uncover that there is a common thread to all of nature's structures at all scales of magnification. He recognized that these patterns also were reflected in the stock market, and named them "fractals," or geometric shapes that are self-similar.

Carrying on in Mandelbrot's spirit, transdisciplinary researchers at the Santa Fe Institute have made a number of general empirical observations across the individual sciences that cannot be understood within the set of references developed with the specific scientific domains. These phenomena are the occurrence of large catastrophic events (e.g., major earthquakes and stock market crashes), one-over-f noise (i.e., $1/f$ noise), Zipf's law, and fractals.

A fractal is a geometric shape that can be separated into parts, each of which is a smaller-scale version of the whole. They are objects in which the parts are in some way related to the whole. Fractal patterns appear in the price changes of securities, as well as in the distribution of galaxies in the cosmos, in the shape of coastlines, and in the decorative designs generated by various computer programs. Fractals have found applications in the most diverse and surprising areas of both the physical and social sciences, from geology and physiology to botany and financial markets.

The movements of stock prices look alike when a market chart is enlarged or reduced. It's difficult to tell which of the data concern prices that change from week to week, and which concern prices that change day to day or hour to hour. This property is known as "self-affinity." Self-affinity is related to self-similarity, in which every feature of a picture is reduced or blown up using the same ratio (as discussed later in this section).

Fractals and multifractals do not predict the future with certainty, but they create a more realistic picture of risks in financial markets than conventional theory. The beauty of fractal geometry is that it describes a model general enough to reproduce the patterns that characterize modern portfolio theory's placid markets as well as tumultuous trading conditions that occur from time to time.

Nature, it appears, has a great affinity for fractal structures. In geology, fractal geometry has been used to describe the topography of our planet's surface. Fractal structures can also be found in human anatomy: the network of blood vessels in our bodies, from the main aorta to capillaries, has a fractal nature. Scientists note that accelerating technological change follows a fractal process, over multiple substrates (e.g., galactic-atomic, stellar, planetary-molecular, cellular-genetic) and all known time scales. Fractals, it appears, are the language of nature.

Mathematicians note that fractal objects and chaos are intertwined.

"Strange attractors" associated with chaotic systems exhibit a fractal-like pattern of repetitions that is invariant to scale. The father of fractals, Mandelbrot, discovered a set of patterns now known as the Mandelbrot set. The Mandelbrot set is a fractal structure whose pattern repeats itself ad infinitum at any magnification scale. The patterns produced by a Mandelbrot set are complex and strangely beautiful. Some resemble sea horse tails, spirals found on seashells, and curlicues. James Gleick's superb book *Chaos* contains several beautiful color illustrations of Mandelbrot sets.

One-over-f noise is ubiquitous in nature. Complexity theorists see $1/f$ noise in a variety of systems, from traffic patterns on the highway to the flow of the Nile. One-over-f noise differs from random noise or white noise. In $1/f$ noise, there are no correlations between the values of the signal from one moment to the next.

Zipf's law, named after the Harvard University linguistics professor George Kingsley Zipf, refers to regularities in systems of human origin. Zipf showed that systems of human origin, things like the number of cities in the world with a given number of inhabitants, how often a given word is used in a piece of literature, or the income or revenue of a company, can be expressed by a straight line in a logarithmic plot of rank versus frequency.

Exhibit 27 shows an application of Zipf's law in the real world— the breakdown of website popularity on the Internet. The horizontal axis shows the number of ranked websites as determined by the number of unique users and the vertical axis shows a plot of page views using data from MediaMetrix for the top five hundred domains in April 2000. The data tell us that the top 5 percent, or twenty-five websites, account for nearly one-third of the total volume of traffic on the Internet. A small share of all websites get large, and very few websites get a lot of user traffic (notice the clustering of data points as you follow the line from upper left hand part of the graph to the bottom right hand side). Thus, activity on the Web is highly concentrated.

Complexity theorist Per Bak notes that all of these phenomena— fractals, $1/f$ noise, and Zipf's law—have one thing in common: they are emergent. It's also been observed that many complex systems exhibit catastrophic behavior. The dynamic associated with this behavior is like a domino effect, whereby a minor disturbance in one part of the system has a major effect on the whole system. Geologists note that cracks in the earth's crust propagate in this fashion to produce earthquakes—at times, earthquakes with a huge amount of energy.

EXHIBIT 27: Power Laws
Top 500 Websites in April 2000

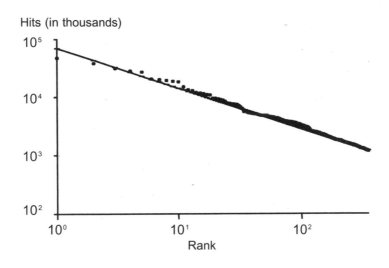

Source: MediaMetrix and CSFB analysis.

Geologists who have studied the pattern of earthquakes over time have discovered a remarkable pattern. For every one thousand earthquakes of, say, magnitude 4 on the Richter scale, there are one hundred earthquakes of magnitude 5, 10 of magnitude 6, and so on. This simple distribution is known as the Gutenberg-Richter law. What we find when plotting the number and magnitude of earthquakes over time using a logarithmic scale is a downward-sloping straight line. The importance of this law, Bak says, is that its simplicity motivates researchers to understand it.

Mandelbrot has observed an empirical pattern similar to the Gutenberg-Richter law in economics and financial markets. Plotting historical data on the prices of stocks, cotton, and other commodities, he counted how many months there were with a given price variation. What Mandelbrot discovered was a very simple pattern known as a Levy distribution. The distribution of price changes, when plotted over time on a logarithmic scale, follows approximately a straight line, or what is known as a "power law."

Power laws abound in nature. Simple power laws explain a range of complex phenomena, from the floods of the Nile to the distribution of galaxies in space. Newton's universal law of gravitational attraction is a homogeneous power law. Power laws possess a unique property that mathematicians call *self-similarity*: If an input is rescaled (i.e., multiplied by a constant), the output is still proportional to input, although the constant of proportionality differs. Think of a set of Russian dolls that look exactly alike but get progressively smaller. Scientists find examples of self-similarity deeply hidden in the behavior of physical and biological systems.

Power laws reproduce themselves upon rescaling. This "scaling invariance" sheds light on the behavior of a wide variety of complex systems studied by physicists, biologists, and other physical and social scientists. The invariance of scaling associated with power laws is due to the fact that they do not have natural scales. That is, power laws do not possess a characteristic unit (e.g., length, mass, or period of time). As a result, mathematicians refer to power laws as scale free or, "true on all scales." That is, systems driven by power laws happen on all scales. Newton's law of gravitational attraction is true on all scales, from the wavelength of light to light-years—it has no inherent scale of its own.

Manfred Schroeder points out that Johann Sebastian Bach composed his famous Brandenburg Concertos (unwittingly, no doubt) using homogeneous power functions in the selection of his notes. He also notes that quantum pioneer Werner Heisenberg's uncertainty principle is a consequence of a well-known reciprocal scaling relationship in mathematics.

Economists have largely ignored Mandelbrot's analysis, primarily because it doesn't fit with the efficient-markets hypothesis. Conventional finance theory assumes that prices in financial markets follow a random-walk process. In a random-walk process, prices change randomly and each change is statistically independent of all past ones. Complexity theorists have shown convincingly that the chance process or random-walk idea is not correct. Mandelbrot's work on stock price fluctuations show a pattern of regularity such that it is possible to make money from them, at least in principle.

Stock market crashes and wild swings in the prices of financial assets and commodities can be easily explained when they are viewed as following a power law. Extreme events fall within the pattern traced out by a power law. In fact, there is nothing special about crashes and large gyrations in financial markets. Large events follow the same law as small events, even though the consequences can be quite different.

FILL AND KILL

Evolutionary biologists note that similar patterns exist in the distributions of speciation and extinction events in the geological record. The distribution of extinction events follows a smooth line whereby large events, such as the Cretaceous extinction of dinosaurs and the Cambrian explosion, occur with fairly well-defined probability and regularity (see Exhibit 28). It appears from the study of earthquakes, stock markets, and fossils, that speciation and extinction or alternatively, booms and busts, are emergent properties of biological and economic evolution.

EXHIBIT 28: Speciation and Extinction

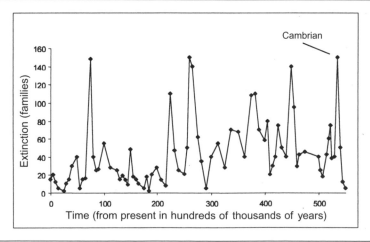

Source: Sole & Newman "Patterns of Extinction and Biodiversity in the Fossil Record," Santa Fe Institute

Stuart Kauffman believes that Schumpeterian gales of creative destruction also follow a power law distribution, with many small bursts of invention and innovation followed by large ones, including new general purpose technologies. Moreover, he reckons that if species and genera have a power law distribution of lifetimes, firms might also.

Indeed, there is evidence that firms show a power law distribution of lifetimes. Kauffman observes that most firms die young and only a few last a long time. Michael Mauboussin analyzed forty-six sectors from eighteen different industries for possible power law trends. He found that nine of the forty-six sectors showed strong power law characteristics. In every industry he studied, he found that the largest companies follow a power law (see Exhibit 29).

EXHIBIT 29: Power Laws in Industry

Industry	Percentage of Companies following Power Law	Market Share Held by Companies in Top 5%	Root Mean Square of Residuals in Power Law Fit
Internet	47%	64%	0.152
Biotech	46%	64%	0.094
Savings and Loan	45%	66%	0.091
Telecom equipment	39%	86%	0.209
Specialty chemicals	35%	40%	0.121
Semiconductors	28%	64%	0.137
Restaurants	19%	85%	0.214
Software	17%	85%	0.126
Apparel	16%	67%	0.127

Source: CSFB Research

Complexity theorists tell us that the natural history of life for the past 550 million years since the Cambrian explosion has echoes of small and large avalanches. These occur at all levels in nature, from biological ecosystems punctuated by a burst of speciation that eventually leads to widespread extinction to global economic systems undergoing technological evolution, in which avalanches of innovative technologies and goods emerge and cause older ones to become extinct.

Mauboussin notes that speciation and extinction are natural occurrences in the business world. The histories of the automobile and television industries, as well as the more recent history of the computer and disk drive industry, show similar patterns. As Exhibit 30 shows, the pattern is a sharp increase in the number of firms in a new industry followed by a dramatic decline in the number of active competitors. The dynamic often occurs over very short periods of time. As Mauboussin's analysis shows, fill and kill is a recurring process in business, just as complexity theorists tell us it is in biological systems.

EXHIBIT 30: The Rise and Decline of Firms in the Automobile and Television Industries

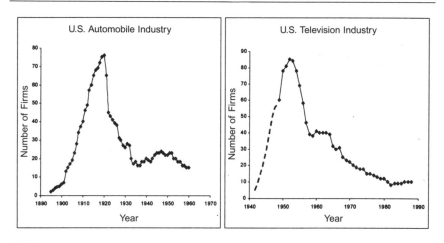

Source: James M. Utterback, *Mastering the Dynamics of Innovation.*

Many commentators appeared to be shocked by the rapid rise and decline of the dotcoms after the commercialization of the Internet. But complexity theorists note that there is nothing significant or special about the evolution of dotcoms. The pattern of speciation and extinction observed in the dotcom sector is normal. Indeed, as Mauboussin points out, the pattern of births and deaths in Exhibit 31, the dotcom sector bears a striking resemblance to what we saw in the automobile and television industries. The companies that are able to survive major industry shakeouts often post good returns for investors—even in industries with enormous ongoing competitive pressures.

EXHIBIT 31: Dotcom Creative Destruction

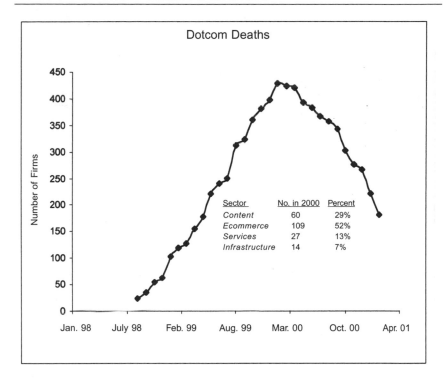

Sector	No. in 2000	Percent
Content	60	29%
Ecommerce	109	52%
Services	27	13%
Infrastructure	14	7%

Source: Michael Mauboussin, Fill and Kill, CSFB Equity Research

LESSONS FROM THE HIVE

Biologists tell us that what makes complex systems robust and adaptable is they contain a unique structure—one that balances dynamic change with static forces. Diversity in both the size and speed of interactions (e.g., fast, slow, and moderate) within a system are what make a complex system resilient. As Stewart Brand puts it in *Clock of the Long Now*, "fast learns and slow remembers. Fast proposes, slow disposes. Fast is discontinuous, slow is continuous. Fast and small instruct slow and big by accrued innovation and occasional revolution. Slow and big control small and fast by constraint and constancy. Fast gets all our attention, slow has all the power."

Those who fret about accelerating technological change in the future should not fear that the whole complex ecosystem we call the global economy will come crashing down. The total effect of the layers of different paces in the economy is that they provide many-leveled, corrective, stabilizing negative feedback throughout the system. As Brand notes, it is precisely in the apparent contradictions of pace that civilization finds its surest health.

Robustness is a subject that is beginning to receive much attention from complexity researchers at the Santa Fe Institute. Robustness is important to all complex systems. Researchers note that robustness is critical to self-assembling or self-repairing systems that may be subject to external fluctuations and noise. Think, for example, of the human body and how it responds to cuts and abrasions. Robustness will be important for the development of nanotechnology, as many types will be self-assembled rather than manufactured.

Robustness is also important in biological and social systems, especially in regard to how much diversity is required to sustain an ecosystem, or a stock market; the responses of cellular processes to fluctuations in their environments; and the stability of social organizations in the face of war, famine or, perhaps even changes in social policy. Complexity theorists believe that understanding robustness, in both systems that occur in nature and systems that are engineered, will be critical to gauging a system's sustainability.

Swarm intelligence is also receiving a great deal of attention by complexity researchers. In the past twenty years, scientists have developed mathematical models to describe the behavior of social insects, such as ants and bees. The collective intelligence of an ant colony or beehive is far greater than the sum of the intelligence of each ant or bee. So theorists are now applying these techniques to various fields, including the business world.

A recurring theme in swarm intelligence (and in complexity science in general) is that even if individuals follow simple rules, the group behavior can be complex and effective. To understand the power of swarm intelligence, consider how certain species of ants are able to find the shortest path to a food source merely by laying and following chemical trails. Individual ants emit a chemical substance—a pheromone—that attracts other ants. In a simple case, two ants leave the nest at the same time and take different paths to a food source, marking their trails with pheromone. The ant that took the shorter path will return first, and this trail will now be marked with twice as much pheromone (deposited during the trip from the nest to the food and during the return trip) as the path taken by the second ant, which has yet to return. Their nest mates are attracted to the shorter path because of its higher concentration of pheromone. As more and more ants take that route, they too lay pheromone, further amplifying the attractiveness of the shorter trail. The colony's efficient behavior emerges from the collective activity of individuals following the two very basic rules: Lay pheromone and follow the trails of others.

Researchers believe that the success and sustainability of social insects are due to a number of properties, such as flexibility and robustness. For example, colonies of ants can adapt to a changing environment, and the failure of one or more members of a group or colony does not impair the functioning of the entire system. A third key property is self-organization. Many evolutionary success stories have activities that are neither centrally controlled nor locally supervised.

A honeybee colony, for example, with some twenty thousand worker bees, several hundred drones, and one queen bee operates as a thoroughly integrated unit in gathering its food. Thomas Seeley, professor of biology at Cornell University and a leading authority on bee colonies, notes that honeybee colonies are extremely sophisticated. They are endowed with exquisite powers of adaptive response, both to internal changes and to external contingencies.

Seeley's extensive work with bee colonies in the past fifteen years shows that there is a large degree of cooperation in bee colonies but no central authority. There is no evidence whatsoever of a control hierarchy in colonies of bees, with certain individuals acquiring information, deciding what needs to be done, and issuing instructions to other individuals that then perform the necessary tasks. As Seeley notes, the queen bee does not supervise the activities of the worker bees. She does not and cannot provide comprehensive instructions to the thousands of bees in a hive. Coherence in honeybee colonies depends on mechanisms of decentralized control.

The absence of a central planning authority in bee colonies, Seeley believes, is the core of the problem a colony must solve in allocating its foragers among food sources: adaptation to countless changes in the particular circumstances of time and place. Some of these changes occur inside the hive as a colony's resource needs vary from hour to hour, but most occur outside the hive as the colony's many, widely scattered food sources vary in "profitability" from minute to minute, hour to hour, and day to day.

Norman Johnson, a researcher at Los Alamos National Laboratory, has been involved in a range of studies that demonstrate how groups can solve problems better than individual experts. His analysis shows how diversity, robustness, and self-organization play important roles in a variety of decentralized systems, including ant colonies, ecosystems, social groups, large organizations, political systems, free-market economies, the stock market, our society—any system in which individuals or groups make decisions or solve problems without total centralized control or planning.

Researchers cite five elements as necessary ingredients for assembling a collective learning machine, or what author Howard Blooms calls "a global brain." The five elements are conformity enforcers, diversity generators, inner judges, resource shifters, and intergroup tournaments. Conformity enforcers are the glue of the learning machine. Diversity generators generate variety. Inner judges dish out rewards and punishment. Resource shifters make sure that the members of the learning machine are used efficiently. Intergroup tournaments produce competition that drives the learning machine's evolution.

Collective learning machines provide a fresh way of thinking about organization structures inside a company. Most CEOs don't think about collective learning machines. They are still stuck in the command-and-control era of the industrial age. However, senior executives in a wide variety of industries, including investment management, could profit handsomely from studying the learning machine model.

In "The Future of Distributed Generation: Musing on Boundaries, Criticality, and Emergence," Judith Warrick, senior advisor at Morgan Stanley, wrote that the science of complexity holds the key to building a vastly more efficient and productive utility sector. She argues that swarm intelligence, complex adaptive systems, emergence, and self-organized criticality are concepts that could profoundly transform the electricity industry in the twenty-first century. Warrick points out that higher reliability in the electric power grid could result from bundled networks of small, localized power plants that "learn" and grow more intelligent over time. She notes that the use of complexity science could help solve the transmission bottleneck issue prevalent in the electricity industry today.

Complexity theory may also become the foundation for understanding computing in the future. Larry Smarr, a leading computer scientist, is helping to design a new architecture that could fundamentally change the way we think about—and use—computing. The grid Smarr and other scientists are developing will connect multiple regional and national computational grids to create a universal source of computing power.

Smarr believes that computational grids are going to have similar revolutionary effects on the global economy that power grids had on railroad networks. However, instead of waiting thirty or forty years to see the changes brought about by this infrastructure, we are going to see the changes much sooner.

Computational grids are becoming economically feasible in the twenty-first century because of greater provisioning of communications bandwidth, increasing computer processing power, and cheap storage. Smarr argues that the emergence of more powerful communications networks and computers provides the foundation for building grids that will turn a network of personal computers into supercomputers—computers so powerful that someday they could become self-aware.

Smarr believes that the emerging computational grid is going to be far more pervasive than the electric power grid is today. His new institute, the California Institute for Telecommunications and Information Technology, will bring together more than two hundred

Ph.D.s and other highly trained professionals to reinvent the Internet using technologies like fiber-optic cables, digital wireless networks, and microelectromechanical systems.

Smarr notes that the grid is about collaboration—about working together. He believes that as the new grid technologies come into widespread use, we will shift our social patterns of interaction and our reward structure to realize the potential gains from the nonlinear advancements that collaboration will create. Collaboration, he points out, can be a magic amplifier for human work. The success of the grid will both enable and depend on this amplification.

REAL WORLD APPLICATIONS

The science of complexity sheds a great deal of light on why the Soviet Union disintegrated. No central planning authority in the early part of the twentieth century could have forecast the emergence of quantum technology—transistors, integrated circuits, microprocessors, and the cornucopia of goods and related services they spawned. Yet these technologies emerged as the driving force of growth, wealth creation, abundance, and scarcities in the later part of the century.

The emergence of new quantum-based technologies in the global economy will continue to fundamentally alter the equations of abundance and scarcity in coming years. As they do, adaptation will become paramount. As we saw during the past century, big, bureaucratic, centrally planned economies and companies are extremely limited in the ways they evolve. Adaptation is the key for survival. Without it, economies, companies, and their leaders eventually perish.

If China wants to become an economic, political, and cultural superpower in the twenty-first century, it will have to shed its communist skin, discard central planning, and evolve into something that resembles a honeybee colony. The same goes for companies. Former General Electric chairman and CEO Jack Welch instinctively understood the need for adaptation in the business world. Adaptation helps explain the extraordinary success GE has enjoyed in the past two decades. Welch, unwittingly, is a complexity theorist at heart.

Complexity researchers Eric Bonabeau and Chris Meyer note that despite its fascinating insight and higher degree of applicability to the business world, the field of swarm intelligence faces several obstacles. First, many senior executives have difficulty understanding how swarm intelligence can work, because they are familiar with the science of complexity. Second, understanding how group behavior that emerges (often, it seems, by magic) from the collective interactions of individuals goes against the grain of those accustomed to command-and-control organizational structures. Business consultants have often found it difficult to convince managers to deploy swarm-intelligence solutions even after much education and hard data that quantify the benefits.

In the future, it's quite conceivable that many companies in a wide array of industries around the world will grow or restructure their organizations from the ground up using the principles of complexity. Business organizations that firmly embrace concepts such as swarm intelligence, robustness, emergence, and self-organization will be far better equipped to adapt to fast-changing markets in coming years than will their command-and-control peers. Just as quantum physics required a significant change in how physicists viewed nature, putting complexity to work in business will require a change in mindset—something that is easier said than done.

QUANTUM COMPLEXITY

One of the great unresolved problems in science is the interference pattern observed by quantum physicists. Is light a particle or a wave? The interference pattern produced by sending light through a slit suggests that light travels in waves. However, the theories of Max Planck and Albert Einstein, which assume discrete units called quanta and photons, precisely explain phenomena we observe in nature. Might there be an emergent property associated with the interaction of trillions of atoms that accounts for the interference pattern scientists detect in their experiments?

In *Collective Electrodynamics*, physicist Carver Mead treats the photon as an interaction rather than a particle. Treating the photon as an electromagnetic interaction of atoms removes the duality problem that has puzzled physicists for decades, Mead says. This approach was first identified in 1926 by Gilbert Lewis, a chemistry professor at the University of California at Berkeley in his treatise, *The Anatomy of Science*. Lewis makes the assumption that an atom never emits light except to another atom. In this process of exchange, the two atoms play quite coordinate roles, so that we can no longer regard one as an active agent and the other as an accidental, passive recipient.

Murray Gell-Mann notes that chaos gives rise to effective indeterminacy at the classical level over and above the indeterminacy in principles of quantum mechanics. The interaction between these two kinds of unpredictability is a fascinating and still poorly studied aspect of contemporary physics. Ongoing work by theoretical physicists seems to confirm that for many purposes it is useful to regard chaos as a mechanism that can amplify to macroscopic levels the indeterminacy inherent in quantum mechanics.

Phenomena such as superconductivity and lasers are quantum systems that cannot be understood by the behavior of their individual parts. Quantum states can become entangled—that is, the positions of atoms become highly or "super" correlated with one another—in ways that make a description of separate components and their local causal interactions impossible. The occurrence of emergent properties in quantum systems does not necessarily mean that these properties also occur in macroscopic systems. However, emergent phenomena like superconductivity are macroscopic, so emergence is not restricted to micro states.

Unlike conventional theorists, complexity theorists believe that progress in understanding natural phenomena requires more than a study of parts in interaction. It often involves grasping relevant aspects of whole systems and finding appropriate mathematical descriptors that capture these properties. Once an emergent property is observed in a complex adaptive system, scientists first try to find the appropriate descriptors that capture the essence of the dynamic pattern and then show how it is consistent with lower level properties of the system.

The science of complexity has revealed much about the patterns hidden in nature. Clearly, there is much work to be done. One area that is receiving a great deal of attention today by researchers is *cellular automata*.

Cellular automata were originally conceived by Stanislaw Ulam and Konrad Zuse and later developed by the great mathematician John von Neumann. The study of cellular automata involves examining self-replicating patterns and structures. Mathematicians have discovered they can take extremely simple equations, specify a few rules, and produce marvelous patterns that bear a striking resemblance to objects in nature. Cellular automata are capable of producing patterns for everything from quasars to bumblebees, hurricanes, stock markets, and rose petals.

In "God, Stephen Wolfram and Everything Else," Michael Malone wrote that scientist Stephen Wolfram believes that cellular automata represent the basis for a whole new science. He notes that biologists have never been able to really explain how things get made, how they evolve, and where complicated forms come from. Wolfram thinks organisms run what he calls "biological software programs." The programs appear to be very complex, but he has discovered that they are actually very simple. Simplicity, it seems, can produce infinite amounts of complexity.

Wolfram believes that cellular automata can help explain a host of questions that have vexed scientists since time immemorial: Why does time go only one way? Why does the stock market behaves as it does? How do complex systems, from thunderstorms to galaxies, exhibit intelligence? Why leaves, trees, seashells, and snowflakes take the shapes that they do? Cellular automata will give scientists profound insights into the quantum world and show them new ways to design and build integrated circuits and computers from the atomic level on up, according to Wolfram. He predicts that by the middle of the twenty-first century, more pieces of technology will be created on the basis of cellular automata than on the basis of traditional science.

Einstein said that quantum mechanics is an imposing science, but he rejected the uncertainty associated with it. God, said Einstein, does not play dice with the universe. The complexity of the natural world is the longest-standing mystery in all of science. Nature appears to be far messier and more unpredictable than any single mathematical equation can capture. It is difficult to describe nonlinear patterns of nature with classical mathematics. Mathematics, as the language of physics, enables science to describe the movement of bodies in space and the workings of atomic and subatomic particles, but it hasn't yet described the full complexity of flowers, plants, organisms, economies, and markets.

THE EDGE OF CHAOS

The quantum revolution in computing has sparked a revolution in science that is gathering momentum at the beginning of the twenty-first century. Complexity theory, by encouraging cross-disciplinary research and focusing on dynamic forms of analysis, is yielding profound insights into the inner workings of the economy, financial markets, and Mother Nature herself. The evolutionary biologist Charles Darwin, quantum physicist Richard Feynman, and economist Joseph Schumpeter would all feel right at home at the Santa Fe Institute were they alive today.

In *At Home in the Universe*, Stuart Kauffman suspects that the fate of all complex adaptive systems, from single cells to economies, is to evolve to a natural state that he calls "the edge of chaos." The edge of chaos is the state between order and chaos—a grand compromise between structure and surprise. In Kauffman's view, life evolves toward a regime that is poised between order and chaos. In a world evolving toward the edge of chaos, avalanches, big and small, are a permanent feature of the landscape.

Tragically, Pagels died in a mountain climbing accident several years ago. His prophesy about the sciences of complexity lives on. It remains to be seen whether those who master the sciences of complexity will become the economic, cultural, and political superpowers of the twenty-first century. What seems clear today is that future discoveries associated with the sciences of complexity will cause a profound shift in how we think about nature and the world around us. They may also help scientists unravel the mysteries of the quantum world and forge a path toward a unified scientific theory of nature in coming years.

Oscar Wilde once remarked that it is because humanity has never known where it was going that it has been able to find its way. Looking back at the broad sweep of history, we can see just how far we have come. Consider that in 1450, you would have flunked geography class if you didn't believe the world was flat. In 1600, you would have burned at the stake for believing the Earth revolves around the Sun. One hundred years ago, you would have flunked Physics 101 if your equations suggested it was possible to make machines that fly. In 1980, you would have been ridiculed at a physics convention for believing that superconductors were possible at temperatures as warm as liquid nitrogen.

Scientists note that at no time in the ten thousand years or so since the last Ice Age has the human race been in a state of constant knowledge and fixed technology. There have been a few setbacks, to be sure, like the Dark Ages after the fall of the Roman Empire. But they have been temporary, as knowledge and technology have found a way to march on. As Stephen Hawking notes, there is no sign that scientific and technological development will slow down and stop in the near future. Quantum-based technology may usher in an era of accelerated knowledge creation driven by minds that are not biological in nature.

In *The Universe in a Nutshell*, Hawking argues that the human race needs to improve its mental and physical qualities if it is to thrive in the years ahead. Hawking believes that humans need to increase their complexity if biological systems are to keep ahead of electronic ones. Hawking believes neural implants may allow a much faster interface between the brain and computers, dissolving the distance between biological and electronic intelligence. He also notes that within a decade, many of us may even choose to live a virtual existence on the Internet.

The universe has evolved over the course of billions and billions of years. In the past four billion years, the entities that constitute functionally organized units of life in our galaxy have increased their range of complexity through a nested series of stable units: replicating molecules, prokaryotic cells, eukaryotic cells, and multicellular organisms (e.g., human beings). The complexity we observe around us is the cumulative effect of billions of years of evolution, but its origins appear firmly rooted in simplicity. Scientists have yet to fully understand how, out of the union of sperm and egg, a human brain grows into the most complex thing in the universe, with billions and billions of nerve cells making trillions of connections. The complexity of the brain and the nervous system are almost overwhelming.

In coming years, complexity scientists hope to reveal the true source of Mother Nature's beauty and genius. Nobody yet knows the weave, Kauffman points out, but the tapestry of life is richer than we have imagined. It is a tapestry with threads of accidental gold, mined quixotically by the random whimsy of quantum events acting on bits of nucleotides and crafted by selection sifting. But the tapestry has an overall design, an architecture, a woven cadence and rhythm that reflect underlying laws—principles of self-organization.

Reflecting on the complexity of the universe and scientists' search for an explanation, physicist John Archibald Wheeler stated in *Geons, Black Holes and Quantum Foam: A Life in Physics,* that behind it all is surely an idea so simple, so beautiful, so compelling that when—in a decade, a century, or a millennium—we grasp the idea, we will say to each other, how could it have been otherwise? How could we have been so blind for so long?

The quantum revolution in science and technology has given birth to a new science—the science of complexity. What will emerge from the future advances in quantum technology and complexity theory? No one knows for sure. The coming quantum-based revolutions in the life sciences and nanotechnology are a vast unexplored frontier, just as the microelectronics revolution was in the twentieth century.

Like its predecessor, the quantum technology revolution will empower scientists and researchers with new tools in coming years to map this uncharted territory. And like Columbus, the world we eventually discover is likely to be far richer, and perhaps even stranger, than anybody could have possibly imagined at the beginning of the twenty-first century.

Key Takeaways

- There are numerous patterns, called fractals or self-similar geometric shapes, found in nature that resemble price movements in the stock market.

- Stock market crashes and wild swings in financial asset prices follow power law patterns. Power laws tell us that booms and busts are infrequent but they do occur and should not be ignored.

- Some complexity theorists believe that Schumpeterian gales of creative destruction follow a power law distribution. This helps explain the clustering of technology development over the course of economic history.

- Just as in nature, speciation and extinction are natural occurrences in the business world. The dotcom phenomenon of the late 1990s may seem unique, but the pattern is similar to others we have experienced in the past.

- Swarm intelligence tells us that the collective intelligence of a group of people is far greater than the individual intelligence of each person. Investment processes based on swarm intelligence are likely to outperform conventional investment processes.

- Researchers cite that collective learning machines are composed of conformity enforcers, diversity generators, inner judges, resource shifters, and intergroup tournaments. Companies that organize their people as collective learning machines will learn more effectively and adapt to change.

- Investors who take a transdisciplinary approach to research are likely to outperform those who do not.

Quantum Future

> You cannot resist technical change. You have to learn
> to adjust to it.
>
> —Lawrence Klein

At the dawn of the twenty-first century, a time of great economic and financial market turmoil, the well-known futurists Alvin and Heidi Toffler proclaimed in a *Wall Street Journal* editorial that the economic turbulence had only just begun. The Tofflers argued that something new is arising on the planet that doesn't fit the assumptions, models, and paradigms left over from the industrial age. A new economic and social system, they said, is taking shape that will profoundly transform us, from our financial systems to our family life, from work to war, from resource use to religion.

In the late twentieth century, many analysts and commentators spoke of the emergence of a New Economy, often in the context of some hot dotcom. Talk of the New Economy subsided greatly however, when many of the dotcoms went out of business. To imagine that the New Economy is over because dozens of dotcoms went bust, said the Tofflers, is the equivalent of thinking in the early 1800s, that the industrial revolution was over because textile manufacturers were going broke in Manchester. The debate over the existence of a New Economy still rages on.

A NEW CIVILIZATION

The evolution of technology points to an emergence of something far deeper than a new economy. The Tofflers argue that we are moving into a new level of civilization. One scientist who has pondered the long sweep of technological invention and considered its implications for civilization is Douglas Robertson. In *The New Renaissance*, Robertson notes that history has never seen a revolution on the scale of the one being sparked by computers today. He believes that the invention of the digital computer is one of the pivotal events in the history of civilization.

Robertson argues that the digital computer is changing civilization to a degree not seen since the Renaissance of the fifteenth and sixteenth centuries—the time of the last great revolution in information handling. He points out that the computer revolution is being buffeted by another scientific milestone: the quantitative theory of information. Pioneered by Claude Shannon, the theory of information is one of the great triumphs of twentieth-century science. Together, information theory and quantum theory will fundamentally transform science, mathematics, education, language, the arts, and everyday life in the twenty-first century.

The revolution in computing presages nothing less than the dawn of a new level of civilization, a new renaissance comparable in scope to the changes in civilization that occurred after the invention of language, writing, and printing. As Robertson notes, the invention and widespread adoption of language, writing, and printing created a fundamentally new form of human society. The invention of language is associated with the very beginning of the human race, the invention of writing with the beginning of civilization, and the invention of printing with the beginning of modern civilization.

The common thread is that an information explosion accompanied them. Robertson defines five broad categories of civilization that differ principally in how they store and handle information. He also identifies the approximate quantitative limits on information available at each level of civilization. The categories are:

- Level 0—Prelanguage: 10^7 bits
- Level 1—Language: 10^9 bits
- Level 2—Writing: 10^{11} bits
- Level 3—Printing: 10^{17} bits
- Level 4—Computers: 10^{25} bits

These are estimates and may be off by orders of magnitude, but they are accurate enough to allow us to begin assessing the information limitations of the different levels of civilization. Great literature was the product of Level 1 civilization. A democratic system of government on a continental scale is beyond the scope of Level 2 civilization, and sending humans into space is a task that exceeds the information capacity of Level 3 civilization. Robertson points out that Level 3 civilization includes technologies such as internal combustion engines, telephones, and telegraphs.

Speculating about Level 4 civilization, Robertson believes that an explosion of information on the order of 10^{25} bits (that is, 10,000,000,000,000,000,000,000,000 zeros or ones of information) could allow civilization to overcome such things as famine, pestilence, poverty, war, illiteracy, and intolerance. He notes that the full range of what is possible in Level 4 civilization is as far beyond our present imagination as our present civilization is beyond medieval times. Information and quantum theories are altering the course of information generation around the globe. Analysts point out that since 1994, traffic on the Internet has increased 5,500-fold.

Last year, Hal Varian and Peter Lyman, two researchers at the University of California at Berkeley, estimated that we currently produce an amount of information that exceeds Robertson's estimate of the Level 3 quantitative limit on information availability. They estimate that the total digital storage requirement of all information being produced today (including music, film, and data CDs and

DVDs, as well as information associated with paper and magnetic storage devices such as camcorder tapes and disk drives) exceeds 10 exabytes (that is, 10 to the 18th power).

To put these numbers in perspective, consider that 5 exabytes of storage could hold all the words *ever* spoken by human beings since the invention of language. While 10 exabytes of digital storage may sound like an extremely large number, it's small compared to what it will likely be a few years hence. Varian and Lyman note that the growth rate of information in the digital economy today is around 50 percent. Fueling this growth are activities in the physical sciences and the revolution underway in the life science industry.

Consider the huge volume of information that will be generated by particle physicists in coming years. The Large Hadron Collider, which scientists are using to probe the deep mysteries of the universe, will generate a data stream of 10 million gigabytes every year when it becomes operational in 2006. The experiments at European Organization for Nuclear Research's (CERN's) Large Electron Positron collider currently generate only a few terabytes per year. According to Princeton University physicist David Strickland, the new experiments at CERN associated with the LHC will create one thousand times more data than what is being generated by the LEP collider.

Information generation in the life science industry will explode in coming years. There is a vast amount of information associated with the Human Genome Project, as well as a number of other genome mapping projects. Looking beyond the next several years, scientists tell us that in the not too distant future they will be able to scan the human brain in new ways with quantum-based-brain scanning technology. One human brain scan may rival all the information produced during Level 3 civilization, which encompassed the commercialization of Gutenberg's printing press. Hans Moravec, founder of the world's largest robotics program at Carnegie Mellon University, notes that a human brain equivalent could be encoded in less than 100 million megabytes. Storing such a massive amount of bits will require new innovations in storage technologies that will in all likelihood be based on nanotechnology.

It appears that we have indeed gone beyond Robertson's Level 3 and moved into a new level of civilization. Quantum-based computer and communications technology has set off an information explosion that has changed civilization beyond recognition. By 2010, it's likely that our children will have the equivalent of the ASCI White supercomputer on their desktops. It's also likely that they will have access to high-speed communications networks that will make today's networks look like the Model T.

Considering the vast amount of information and knowledge that will be generated in coming years, as well as the distinct possibility of ever more intelligent technology, it is clear we are entering an era that has no precedence in the history of civilization. In coming years, talk of a New Economy may well be overwhelmed by discussion of a new level of civilization.

HYPER SHOCK

Signs of future shock are everywhere. To paraphrase the quantum theorist Niels Bohr, anybody who isn't shocked by quantum-based technology doesn't understand it. It is clear that the quantum technology revolution is still in an early stage. You could even say the true quantum revolution in technology hasn't even arrived. On the economic horizon lies the commercialization of astonishing new types of superconductors, quantum energy sources, nanotechnology, DNA, quantum computers, and much more. As remarkable as the technological advances of the twentieth century have been, they are just a small evolutionary step in quantum technology. This appears to be the view of a number of distinguished scientists and analysts such as Stephen Hawking, Michio Kaku, Raymond Kurzweil, and Arthur Clarke.

Recently, Clarke published his predictions for the twenty-first century (see Exhibit 32). While examining Clarke's predictions, keep in mind that long-term predictions about technical developments have frequently fallen short of reality.

• • •

EXHIBIT 32: Arthur Clarke's Predictions for the Twenty-First Century

2003 The automobile industry is given five years to replace fossil fuels.

2004 First publicly admitted human clone is announced.

2006 Last coal mine is closed.

2009 A city in a third world country is devastated by an atomic bomb explosion.

2009 All nuclear weapons are destroyed.

2010 A new form of space-based energy is adopted.

2010 Despite protests against "big brother," ubiquitous monitoring eliminates many forms of criminal activity.

2011 Space flights become available to the public.

2013 Prince Harry flies in space.

2015 Complete control of matter at the atomic level is achieved.

2016 All existing currencies are abolished. A universal currency is adopted based on the "megawatt hour."

2017 Arthur C. Clarke, on his one-hundredth birthday, is a guest on the space orbiter.

2019 There is a meteorite impact on Earth.

2020 Artificial Intelligence reaches human levels. There are now two intelligent species on Earth, one biological and one nonbiological.

2021 The first human landing on Mars is achieved. There is an unpleasant surprise.

2023 Dinosaurs are cloned from fragments of DNA. A dinosaur zoo opens in Florida.

2025 Brain research leads to an understanding of all human senses. Full-immersion virtual reality becomes available. The user puts on a metal helmet and is then able to enter "new universes."

2040 A universal replicator based on nanotechnology is now able to create any object from gourmet meals to diamonds. The only thing that has value is information.

2040 The concept of human "work" is phased out.

2061 Hunter-gatherer societies are recreated.

2061 The return of Haley's comet is visited by humans.

2090 Large-scale burning of fossil fuels is resumed to replace carbon dioxide.

2095 A true "space drive" is developed. The first humans are sent out to nearby star systems already visited by robots.

2100 History begins.

Source: http://www.kurzweilai.net.

As we can see from Clarke's predictions, the twenty-first century is not likely to look anything like the twentieth. Although some, or even many of Clarke's predictions, are likely to be ill timed, or even wrong, it is interesting to note that the evolution of quantum-based technologies plays a prominent role in his vision of the future: a new, cold-fusion energy source, complete control over matter at the atomic level, and the invention of a universal replicator based on nanotechnology.

It is also intriguing that Clarke predicts that artificial intelligence will reach human levels by 2020. Scientists tell us that the human brain is the most complex thing in the universe. Intelligence is not just the result of the raw number of neurons composing the gray matter in a human brain, rather it has much more to do with the number of interconnections among neurons. A fully developed human brain has an estimated 100 trillion neuronal connections. Complexity theory tells us that emergence is a fundamental property of all complex systems.

Some scientists believe that before long, it will be possible to reverse-engineer the brain. Researchers at the Institute of Psychology, King's College London, recently developed a system called Vivid that noninvasively detects patterns of nerve connections inside the brains of living people. By reprogramming magnetic resonance imaging scanners, Vivid tracks the random oscillation of water molecules, which can move more easily along a bundle of nerve fibers. A program makes it possible to construct a 3-D representation of the nerve connections. The researchers hope doctors will be able to use the system for routine diagnosis of schizophrenia and other brain illnesses. This research also may suggest a future method for reverse-engineering the brain.

Although the concept of reverse engineering the brain is promising, the fact that emergence plays a vital role in the human mind suggests that reverse engineering alone will not be sufficient to create technology with human intelligence. That said, advances in quantum-based scanning and imaging technology are likely to give researchers extremely powerful new tools to better understand how intelligence emerges out of trillions of neuronal connections in the brain.

Throughout history, there has been a strong relationship between intelligence and technology. Author Howard Bloom notes that the emergence of new technologies is closely associated with an increase in brain size. *Homo habilis* began to crank out crude implements roughly 2.7 million years ago. A million years later, *Homo erectus,* with a 56 percent larger brain, developed two new technologies: shape blades and the hand ax. *Homo sapiens*, our close cousin, required a 20 percent boost in brain size to accelerate the pace of technical change even more.

Around thirty-five thousand years ago, our brains allowed us to create technologies far beyond any species in the animal kingdom. Full-fledged language emerged at the very latest around 30,000 B.C. The printing press, which arguably launched the scientific revolution and the period of Enlightenment, was commercialized in the middle of the fifteenth century.

No futurist in his or her right mind (including Arthur Clarke) would ever claim perfect foresight, but there is still an emerging view that sometime within the next thirty years, the pace of technology change will accelerate beyond our comprehension. As the mathematician and computer scientist Vernor Vinge points out, we are on the verge of a "Singularity" (see Chapter 4) by several means:

- Computers that are "awake" and superhumanly intelligent may be developed.

- Large computer networks and their associated users may "wake up" as superhumanly intelligent entities.

- Computer/human interfaces may become so intimate that users may reasonably be considered superhumanly intelligent.

- Biological science may provide the means to improve natural human intellect.

The first three possibilities depend on improvements in computer hardware. Progress in hardware has followed an amazingly steady upward curve in the last few decades. Given this trend, Vinge believes that the creation of greater than human intelligence will occur sometime before 2030—a time when many baby boomers (people born between 1946 and 1964) will be in retirement.

The consequences of the Singularity are likely to be intense. Technical progress will be much faster than at any time in the history of civilization. Vinge sees no reason why progress itself will not involve the creation of still more intelligent entities—on a still shorter time scale. Developments that were thought possible in "a million years," says Vinge, will likely happen in the twenty-first century.

Once the Singularity is reached, Vinge believes our old models will have to be discarded because of the emergence of a new reality. The pace of technological change will become so rapid and so profound that it will rupture the basic fabric of human history.

Raymond Kurzweil, who embraces Vinge's Singularity thesis, adds that as the exponential growth of technology continues to accelerate into the first half of the twenty-first century, it will appear to explode into infinity, at least from the limited, linear perspective of contemporary humans. The progress of technical change will ultimately become so fast that it will leave behind our ability to follow it.

The Singularity will transform every aspect of human life: social, sexual, and economic. In Kurzweil's view, the emergence early in the twenty-first century of a new form of intelligence on Earth that can compete with, and ultimately significantly exceed, human intelligence will be a development of greater import than any of the events that have shaped human history.

Some analysts believe that computers with human-level intelligence will be a threat to humankind. In the 1950s, many analysts expressed a similar concern. Clarke addressed this issue head-on in *Profiles of the Future*. He said the notion that intelligent machines must be malevolent entities hostile to human is "so absurd that it is hardly worth wasting energy to refute it." Clarke asserted that those who worried about hostile intelligence machines were merely projecting their own aggressive instinct, inherited from the jungle, into a world where such aggressive instincts do not exist. In Clarke's view, the higher the intelligence, the greater the degree of cooperativeness. If there is ever a war between humans and machines, he noted, it is easy to guess who will start it.

QUANTUM COMPUTING

Signs of the Singularity are detectable in the information technology sector. Recent advances in scientific labs around the United States and elsewhere indicate that we are approaching the twilight of one computing paradigm and the dawn of another. The binary computing paradigm that has powered the revolution in microelectronics for more than half a century appears to be giving way to a far more powerful computing revolution—quantum computing. The commercialization of quantum computers could be the technological event that triggers the Singularity that Vinge, Kurzweil, and others foresee happening.

Quantum computing, a field closely associated with nanotechnology, is in its infancy today. Nevertheless, the past few years have witnessed astonishing breakthroughs that many distinguished scientists and researchers had thought impossible. In 2001, scientists at the IBM Almaden Research Center, in San Jose, California, announced an important milestone toward making powerful quantum computers. By manipulating single atoms simultaneously using the principles of quantum mechanics, researchers were able to factor the number 15. This marked the first time scientists factored a number using a quantum computer.

Unlike conventional computers, quantum computers are not based on binary arithmetic (zeros and ones). Instead, quantum computers use the properties of quantum mechanics that allow a single atom to point both up and down simultaneously. Thus a single atom, or what's known as a "qubit" in the quantum computing world, can represent one and zero at the same time. Two atoms can simultaneously register four quantities: 00, 01, 10, and 11. Three atoms can hold eight numbers, four can hold sixteen numbers, and so on. A seven-qubit quantum computer, such as the one created by scientists at IBM, has the capability of simultaneously registering 128 different numbers. At much higher levels of qubits—say, in the hundreds or thousands—the power of quantum computers becomes almost incomprehensible to the ordinary human mind.

Isaac Chuang, who led the team of researchers from IBM and Stanford University, originally thought that quantum computing was not going to be a viable enterprise. However, during the announcement of the milestone, he stated that he now believes that quantum computing is going to be a fact of nature. To be sure, there is still a long road ahead before commercially useful quantum computers are developed.

Some scientists believe that quantum computers will never replace digital computers for the same reasons that quantum physics does not replace classical physics. As physicist Andrew Steane of Oxford University was quoted in *The Quest for the Quantum Computer*, "No one ever consulted Heisenberg in order to design a house, and no one takes their car to be mended by a quantum mechanic."

In Steane's view, if large quantum computers are ever made, they will be used to address just those special tasks that benefit from quantum information processing. He believes that a more lasting reason to be excited about quantum computing is that it is a new and insightful way to think about the fundamental laws of physics.

Steane may be correct in his assessment of the future of quantum computing, but as Julian Brown notes in *The Quest for the Quantum Computer*, there is a wider aspect of the quantum computing revolution that could bring about enormous change not only in the way we think about the world but in the way we live. This aspect concerns developments in nanotechnology, a parallel quantum-based revolution that is likely to be instrumental in the development of quantum computation.

As Oxford University scientist David Deutsch told Brown in private conversations, the milestones of nanotechnology are closely linked with the milestones of quantum computers. Deutsch believes that a fully fledged quantum computer will involve the same sort of technology as self-replicating nanomachines. It's quite conceivable that we will see one of those two things within months of each other. According to Deutsch, once this occurs, the quantum revolution takes off and revolutionizes the whole of human life.

A closely related development to quantum computing is DNA computing. Those looking for proof of the power of quantum technology to revolutionize the world need look no further than their own bodies. As Brown notes, life on Earth depends on its extraordinary collection of nanomachines. These include, in particular, the DNA molecules and protein molecules that coordinate and mediate processes necessary for survival and self-replication.

Brown points out that in recent years computer scientists and mathematicians have become interested in the information-processing aspects of biological systems such as the human body. In 1994, the mathematician Len Adleman published a fascinating paper on DNA computing that launched the field of molecular computation.

The idea of using DNA for computational purposes is brilliant and powerful. As we have seen, molecules are very small, and a tiny test-tube solution of DNA containing trillions and trillions of molecules could represent an astronomical number of potential processors. Adleman calculated that a DNA computer could perform up to 10^{18} operations per second. This is millions of times faster than the fastest supercomputer on the planet today.

While DNA computing certainly has promise, Brown notes that unlike quantum computing, it doesn't offer the promise of unlimited exponential resources. Still, DNA computing opens up interesting possibilities in the field of computation that will undoubtedly be the source of ongoing research in laboratories around the world in coming years.

QUANTUM PROPERTIES

Complexity theory tells us that life is a dynamic, evolutionary process that contains emergent properties. So, too, is the quantum revolution in science and technology. Quantum theory was born in 1900, when Max Planck explained black-box radiation. During the next thirty years, quantum theory grew into a remarkable body of science. In the following seventy years, scientists, researchers, and entrepreneurs around the world have been inspired by and use quantum theory to create some of the most astonishing technology humans have ever known.

Looking back over the past century, we can glean several key dynamics associated with the quantum revolution:

- Quantum theory enables new technologies that differ fundamentally in almost every conceivable way from industrial age technologies.

- The development and convergence of quantum-based technologies are a major source of creative destruction in the global economy.

- Quantum technologies produce medium and long waves of economic activity.

- The power and speed of quantum-based technologies grow exponentially, or in some cases, superexponentially over time, while the cost/performance ratio of these technologies declines.

- Quantum-based technologies leverage the human mind in the way Newtonian-based technologies leverage human muscle.

- The complexity of quantum-based technologies grows over time.

These features of the quantum revolution support the Tofflers' assertion that there is something new arising on the planet that doesn't fit the assumptions, models, and paradigms left over from the industrial age. It is only a matter of time before analysts and commentators let go of the past and embrace the new assumptions, models, and paradigms of the quantum age. After all, scientists in the twentieth century had to give up many of their most cherished Newtonian views about how nature works in order to begin to grasp the implications of quantum science.

As we can see in this book, the quantum world isn't anything like the Newtonian world. Certainty, which is central to basic economic theory, doesn't have a place in quantum theory, nor in the quantum economy. Uncertainty and imperfect knowledge are part and parcel of the quantum economic landscape. Future shock is a reality today.

INTO THE QUANTUM FUTURE

Winston Churchill once stated that the farther back you look, the farther forward you can see. We have taken a long journey back in time and traced the evolution of quantum theory and quantum-based technological inventions and innovations. The trend in quantum technology is clear: it is accelerating. Amid the accelerating pace of quantum technology, the future appears to be coming faster than ever.

Scientists, who boldly look beyond the next decade, speak of a time when the pace of technical change becomes too great for human minds to comprehend and short-term prediction becomes impossible. The world becomes, in the words of marketing guru Regis McKenna, one of "continuous discontinuous change." Some scientists believe the coming century promises to be a *hypershock* future—a time unlike anything we are used to or have grown to expect.

Mr. Future Shock himself, Alvin Toffler, notes that it is now clear that the entire digital revolution—a revolution with its roots firmly planted in quantum theory—is only the first phase of an even larger, longer process. In the first phase, information technology revolutionizes biology. In the next phase, biology will revolutionize information technology. And that will in turn totally revolutionize the global economic landscape.

In Toffler's view, the revolution in information technology and biology represents a turning point not just in economics, but also in human history. Stephen Hawking makes a similar point in *The Universe in a Nutshell*, noting that neural implants may someday allow a much faster interface between the human brain and computers, thereby dissolving the distance between biological and electronic intelligence.

When historians of the future look back on the twentieth century, they will note it was a time when science and technology radically transformed the way we lived, worked, and played. As physicist Edward Witten noted, it is stunning to think how our understanding of physics has changed in the last hundred years. The great insights of the early part of the century were Einstein's relativity theory and quantum mechanics. Quantum mechanics taught us that fact is far more wondrous than fiction in the atomic world.

The twentieth century was a time of remarkable change, when the birth of a new science inspired a generation of men and women to venture where no person had ever gone before. Their prodigious efforts spawned new technologies that created entire new industries, companies, products, and related services that inhabited the global economy and became the driving force of economic evolution. The industrial and financial market landscapes of the late nineteenth century were remade and recast in the image of the science that wrought the tumultuous change.

In the future, historians may note that science-related developments in the twentieth century—notably, the birth and development of quantum theory—had laid the foundation for a technology revolution equal to or greater than the industrial revolution. They may also note that the quantum-based technology revolution gave birth to a new science in the twenty-first century—a science that few people could have foreseen at the dawn of the third millennium. It's even quite conceivable that future historians will come to regard the past seventy years of theoretical science as the Dark Ages.

The weirdness of the quantum world is real, whether we like it or not. Whatever future historians write about, nothing we have ever experienced in our lifetimes can prepare us for the enormous changes that new quantum-based technologies will bring in the twenty-first century.

Investing in the Twenty-First Century

In Vernor Vinge's book *True Names*, technology visionary Danny Hillis wrote that we are alive at a special and important moment in history. We are becoming something else. The twentieth century was a rare time when humanity was transformed from one type of human society to another. Technology was, and still is, the catalyst of this change—a self-amplifying agent—because each improvement tends to increase its capacity to improve. Better machines now enable us to build even better machines. Faster computers let us design faster computers, even faster. This accelerating change is actually compressing time.

Change was not always like this. For most of history, Hillis notes, parents could expect their grandchildren to grow up in a world like their own. Parents knew what they needed to teach their children. Planning for the future was easier. Architects designed cathedrals that would take centuries to complete. Farmers planted acorns to shade their descendants with oaks.

In an essay in *Foreign Affairs*, U.S. Secretary of Defense, Donald Rumsfeld, said our challenge in the twenty-first century is a difficult one: "To defend against the unknown, the uncertain, the unseen, and the unexpected. This may seem like an impossible task, but it is not. To accomplish it, we must put aside the comfortable ways of thinking and planning, take risks and try new things so we can deter and defeat adversaries that have not yet emerged to challenge us." Clearly, Secretary Rumsfeld was speaking from a military perspective, but the same approach applies to investing in the twenty-first century.

Our problem, says Hillis, is that we cannot imagine the future. The pace of technological change is so great that we cannot know what type of world we are leaving for our children. If we plant acorns, we cannot reasonably expect that our children will sit under the oak trees—or that they will even want this. The world is changing too fast for that. People are moving. Needs are changing. Much of our generation is employed in jobs our parents never imagined. Entire industries, indeed entire nations, can wither in the blink of an eye.

Any business plan that stretches beyond a year is "long term," according to Hillis. Investors will have to redefine the duration of a long-term holding. It used to be three to five years, if not longer. In a world of accelerating technological change, time is compressing: fifty years ago, two years was equivalent to one year today. In 2020, one year will roughly equate to four years. Many folks are having difficulty adjusting their intuitive linear view of change to the real world of accelerating, exponential change. Hillis believes that many people have become shortsighted. Yet all of this confusion is understandable, even expected, if we accept the premise that we are in a time of transition from one type of society to another. All we can really expect to understand is the good in what we leave behind.

Quantum science and technology are powerful forces of creative destruction in the global economy whose evolution will continue to alter the economic landscape. In the past fifty years, the composition of the U.S. stock market has changed beyond recognition. Investors who held blue chip stocks in 1900 did so at their own peril as many of the companies went bankrupt or were acquired.

Investors who bought and held a basket of stocks that tracked the broad stock market indexes in the past one hundred years, however, were handsomely rewarded. Equities outperformed all other conventional asset classes, and, in the years ahead, equity investors should continue to do relatively well. Given, however, the amount of creative destruction that will accompany the quantum revolution, investors should stay diversified. No industry or company will be immune from advances in quantum science and technology in the twenty-first century.

A "core-satellite" approach to investing, which involves apportioning your portfolio into many different baskets, should work well in the twenty-first century. An investor with a moderate aversion to risk, for example, might parcel his or her portfolio so that 70 to 80 percent (that is, the core) is invested in a mutual fund or index fund that tracks the broader stock market (such funds might also include an allocation toward fixed-income assets as well—these are known as "balanced funds"). The remaining 20 to 30 percent of the portfolio—the satellite portion—would be invested in individual stocks or mutual funds with specific mandates, such as focused funds or sector funds that include biopharamceutical, software, information technology, communications, and energy technology.

Many analysts on Wall Street will have difficulty comprehending the investment implications of accelerating change. The only certainty going forward, however, is change: change in the markets, changes in products, changes in accounting methodologies, and changes in life-spans. The models, mindsets, and metrics investors use to analyze companies must be updated for the twenty-first century. Would-be critics of new technologies, perhaps those caught long in the dotcom crash, should not be wary of the future. After all, it has been observed that many booms and busts of the stock market have taken place at the same time as the introduction of a major new technology—a technology that ultimately sticks.

Quantum-based technologies have created something more than a new economy: they have brought us to the brink of a new level of civilization, a new level of history. Yet, as remarkable as quantum-based technological advances have been until now, they will be superceded by more advanced technologies in the future.

Quantum Science and Technology Milestones

Year: 1900

Event: Max Planck solved the problem concerning the distribution of radiant heat energy emitted by hot bodies. He showed that this could be explained only by supposing that the electromagnetic radiation (i.e., light) was emitted from the body in discrete packets or bundles, which he called "quanta." The equation Planck derived to explain the "black-body radiation" effect was used in 1990 by astrophysicists to calculate the average temperature of the universe. This was found to be 2.73° above absolute zero; absolute zero is equivalent to approximately -273.16° Celsius or -459.69° Fahrenheit. The data sent back by the COBE satellite, which was of unprecedented precision, fit the Planck formula for black-body radiation exactly.

Year: 1905

Event: Albert Einstein successfully explained the "photoelectric effect" in which light energy is observed to displace electrons from the surfaces of metals. To account for the particular way this happens, Einstein came up with the idea that a beam of light is made up of discrete particles (later termed "photons").

Year: 1911
Event: Superconductivity—the ability of some materials to allow an electric current to flow through them with no detectable resistance—was discovered.

Year: 1913
Event: Niels Bohr proposed a theory of atomic spectra that states electrons are "quantized." His theory implies that atoms behave without loss of energy in certain fixed energy levels. When electrons jump between levels or states, electromagnetic energy is released or absorbed in discrete quantities. The packets of energy are Einstein's photons.

Year: 1924
Event: Louis de Broglie suggested that all material particles, such as electrons, can also be described in terms of waves. The wave-particle duality lies at the heart of quantum physics.

Year: 1925
Event: Wolfgang Pauli discovered the exclusion principle. This states that two electrons with the same quantum numbers cannot occupy the same atom. The exclusion principle accounts for the chemical properties of the natural elements found in nature, and it revolutionized the field of chemistry.

Year: 1925
Event: Werner Heisenberg formulated a theory known today as matrix mechanics. This theory, which Heisenberg produced in collaboration with scientists Max Born and Pascual Jordan, was the first complete, self-consistent theory of quantum physics, and it became spectacularly successful. It helps scientists explain the structure of atoms, radioactivity, chemical bonding, and the details of atomic spectra (including the effects of electric and magnetic fields). At the same time, physicist Paul Dirac propounded his own version of quantum theory, known as quantum algebra or operator theory.

Year: 1926

Event: Erwin Schrödinger published a paper in which he developed wave mechanics to describe the motion of quantum objects. Like Heisenberg's theory, Schrödinger's work was a complete, self-consistent theory of quantum physics. Before publication of Schrödinger's theory, the existence of matter waves had not been experimentally established. Today, the observation of wavelike behavior for particles is common and forms the basis for new ways of understanding the quantum world.

Year: 1926

Event: Max Born developed the idea that probability plays a key role in the quantum world. His idea suggests that the outcome of a quantum experiment depends on chance, in the same way the number that comes up on a roulette wheel depends on chance. Paul Dirac showed that Heisenberg's matrix mechanics and Schrödinger's wave mechanics are exactly equivalent to one another.

Year: 1926

Event: Scientist Gilbert Lewis introduced the term "photon" for the particle of light.

Year: 1927

Event: Heisenberg put forth his "uncertainty principle," which states that we cannot attempt to measure the position and motion of a quantum object simultaneously. If scientists try to locate the position of an electron, they must forgo information about its momentum. Despite the fact that uncertainty is woven into the very fabric of quantum theory, it churns out predictions that are accurate to eleven decimal places.

Year: 1927

Event: Bohr presented what's known today as the "Copenhagen interpretation" of quantum physics to a conference in Tomo, Italy. This event marked the completion of the consistent theory of quantum mechanics in a form that physicists can use to solve problems involving atoms and molecules.

Year: 1932
Event: James Chadwick discovered the neutron, a particle with no electric charge and almost the same mass as the proton. The nucleus of an atom was subsequently explained as a collection of protons and neutrons held together by a strong nuclear interaction, or what's known as the "strong force."

Year: 1940
Event: The first electron microscope was demonstrated. The electron microscope is now probably the most widely used device that exploits the dual particle and wave nature of matter.

Year: 1943
Event: The first electronic computer was built.

Year: Middle-to-late 1940s
Event: Physicists Julian Schwinger, Sin-itiro Tomonga, and Richard Feynman independently developed theories of quantum electrodynamics (QED). QED describes the way electrically charged particles interact with one another and with magnetic fields through the exchange of photons. In 1949, Freeman Dyson showed that all three theories were equivalent.

Year: 1947
Event: The transistor was born on December 23, when Bell Labs researchers William Shockley, Walter Brattain, and John Bardeen successfully tested a point-contract transistor. Inspired by quantum theory, their invention launched one of the biggest technology revolutions in history.

Year: 1951
Event: Remington Rand began selling the first commercial electronic computer.

Year: 1951
Event: Charles Townes invented the maser, a device that produces an intense beam of microwaves from the stimulated emission of radiation by excited atoms.

Year: 1953
Event: Francis Crick and James Watson published their discovery of the structure of DNA. The field of molecular biology was born.

Year: 1953
Event: IBM shipped its first electronic computer, the 701.

Year: 1954
Event: A silicon-based junction transistor was perfected by Gordon Teal of Texas Instruments Inc. A news release from the company on May 10 read, "Electronic 'brains' approaching the human brain in scope and reliability came much closer to reality today with the announcement by Texas Instruments Incorporated of the first commercial production of silicon transistors kernel-sized substitutes for vacuum tubes." Texas Instrument's transistor was used in the first commercial transistor radio. Brought to market by Regency Electronics, the radio cost $50. The world began to change into a global village of instant news and pop music.

Year: 1955
Event: AT&T Bell Laboratories announced the first fully transistorized computer—the TRADIC. Instead of vacuum tubes, the TRADIC contained nearly eight hundred transistors which enabled the machine to run on energy less than 100 watts, or one-twentieth the power required by comparable vacuum tube computers. The TRADIC paved the way for future generations of transistorized computers.

Year: 1956
Event: The first transatlantic telephone cable was deployed.

Year: 1957
Event: The first artificial Earth satellite (Sputnik 1) was launched.

Year: 1957
Event: Hugh Everett published the "Many Worlds" interpretation of quantum mechanics.

Year: 1957
Event: John Bardeen, Leon Cooper, and Robert Schrieffer explained superconductivity as a quantum phenomenon.

Year: 1957
Event: Mathematician John Nash's attempt to resolve the contradictions in quantum theory, which he later called "possibly overreaching and psychologically destabilizing," triggered his mental illness.

Year: 1958
Event: Jack Kilby of Texas Instruments created the first integrated circuit, or microchip. For the first time, resistors and capacitors existed on the same piece of semiconductor material. In the years ahead, the integrated circuit would explode into a multibillion-dollar market.

Year: 1959
Event: The first commercial photocopier was marketed.

Year: 1959
Event: Richard Feynman suggested that nanotechnology is a real possibility in a talk at Caltech titled "There's Plenty of Room at the Bottom."

Year: 1960
Event: The laser was discovered. It produced a powerful beam of monochromatic light from the stimulated emission of radiation.

Year: 1961
Event: Robert Noyce of Fairchild Camera and Instrument Corp. invented the resistor-transistor logic (RTL) chip. The RTL incorporated a set/reset flipflop mechanism and was the first integrated circuit available as a monolithic chip. Noyce later joined forces with Gordon Moore and others and formed Intel Corporation.

Year: 1964

Event: Online transaction processing debuted in IBM's SABRE reservation system, set up for American Airlines.

Year: 1965

Event: The first communications satellite was launched.

Year: 1965

Event: Digital Equipment Corporation introduced the PDP-8, the first commercially successful minicomputer.

Year: 1966

Event: John Bell established that John von Neumann's proof that no "hidden variables" theory could ever properly describe the workings of the quantum world is fundamentally flawed. Bell's work opened the way for further investigations into forms of the hidden-variables theory, which by the 1990s would become one of the most exciting areas of the development of models of the quantum world.

Year: 1967

Event: Fairchild Camera and Instrument Corporation built the first standard metal oxide semiconductor (MOS) product for data-processing applications. The chip is an eight-bit arithmetic unit and accumulator.

Year: 1969

Event: Americans were the first humans to land on the Moon. This historic event occurs twenty-two years after invention of the transistor.

Year: 1970

Event: Corning Glass Works developed the first low-loss fiberoptic cables.

Year: 1970

Event: Citizens and Southern National Bank in Valdosta, Georgia, installed the country's first automatic teller machine.

Year: 1971

Event: Federico Faggin, Ted Hoff, and others at Intel produced the first microprocessor, the Intel 4004. It had 2,250 transistors, handled data in four-bit chunks, and performed sixty thousand operations per second.

Year: 1971

Event: Texas Instruments began selling pocket electronic calculators.

Year: 1972

Event: Intel debuted its 8008 microprocessor. A huge improvement over its predecessor (the 4004), its eight-bit word afforded 256 unique arrangements of ones and zeros. For the first time, a microprocessor could handle both uppercase and lowercase letters, all ten numerals, punctuation marks, and a host of other symbols.

Year: 1973

Event: The magnetic resonance imaging machine made its debut.

Year: 1973

Event: Genetic engineering techniques were developed.

Year: 1973

Event: Robert Metcalfe devised the Ethernet method of network connection at the Xerox Palo Alto Research Center.

Year: 1975

Event: The first monoclonal antibodies were produced.

Year: 1975

Event: The first PCs became available in the United States.

Year: 1977

Event: The Apple II PC was launched.

Year: 1978

Event: Scientists at Genentech cloned human insulin, the first recombinant DNA drug.

Year: 1979

Event: California Institute of Technology professor Carver Mead and Xerox computer scientist Lynn Conway published a manual of chip design titled "Introduction to VLSI Systems." The manual demystified the planning of very large scale integrated (VLSI) systems, thereby expanding the ranks of engineers capable of creating such chips. Mead and Conway had observed that computer architects seldom participated in the specification of the standard integrated circuits with which they worked. They intended their book to fill an important gap in the chip literature and introduce all electrical engineering and computer science students to integrated system architecture.

Year: 1979

Event: Motorola began producing the 68000 microprocessor, with processing speeds far greater than its contemporaries. The processor was used to power high-performance work stations intended for the graphics-intensive programs commonly used in engineering.

Year: 1980

Event: Intel launched the 8087, the first math coprocessor.

Year: 1980

Event: Philips developed the first optical data storage disk. It had sixty times the capacity of a conventional 5 1/4-inch floppy disk and stored data as indelible marks burned by a laser. Because the disk could not be overwritten, it was useful for storing large quantities of information that never need revision.

Year: 1982

Event: Philips created an erasable optical disk using special material, a laser, and magnetism to combine the capacity of an optical disk with the convenience of an option to erase and rewrite.

Year: 1982

Event: Richard Palmiter of the University of Washington Department of Biochemistry, in collaboration with Ralph Brinster of the University of Pennsylvania, created the first "transgenic animal." They transferred a gene from one animal to the embryo of another—a mouse—in such a way that the gene would be expressed in the mouse and its future offspring. First in the world to accomplish this feat, the researchers were honored with the Charles Leopold Mayer prize in 1994, the highest honor bestowed by the French Academy of Sciences.

Year: 1983

Event: Apple Computer introduces Lisa, the first PC with a graphical user interface (GUI). The GUI revolutionized the PC industry.

Year: 1984

Event: Apple Computer launched the Macintosh, the first successful mouse-driven computer with a graphical user interface.

Year: 1985

Event: The modern Internet gained critical support when the National Science Foundation formed the NSFNET, linking five supercomputer centers at Princeton University, the University of Pittsburgh, the University of California at San Diego, the University of Illinois at Champaign-Urbana, and Cornell University.

Year: 1986

Event: David Miller of AT&T Bell Labs patented the optical transistor, a component central to digital optical computing. Within a decade, research on the optical transistor led to successful work on the first all-optical processor and the first general purpose, all-optical computer.

Year: 1987

Event: A research team at the University of Alabama-Huntsville created a material that superconducts at temperatures warmer than liquid nitrogen—a commonly available coolant.

Year: 1988
Event: The first transatlantic fiber-optic cable was laid connecting Europe with North America.

Year: 1988
Event: Congress approved funding for the Human Genome Project.

Year: 1989
Event: Intel launched a technological milestone: the i486 microprocessor—a chip that features 1.2 million transistors.

Year: 1990
Event: The World Wide Web was born when CERN (European Organization for Nuclear Research) researcher Tim Berners-Lee developed HyperText Markup Language (HTML).

Year: 1991
Event: Sumio Iijima, a scientist at NEC Corporation in Japan, invented the first carbon nanotubes. These ultra-strong (e.g., one hundred times stronger than steel), lightweight tubes have potential uses ranging from wiring in integrated circuits to components in nanoscale motors.

Year: 1993
Event: Intel launched the Pentium processor.

Year: 1993
Event: Researchers at the University of Colorado unveiled the first all-optical computer capable of being programmed and of manipulating instructions internally.

Year: 1995
Event: The Internet began to grow explosively, linking more than 7 million computers and tens of millions of users worldwide.

Year: 1997

Event: An IBM supercomputer known as Deep Blue defeated world chess champion Gary Kasparov. Deep Blue can evaluate 200 million chess positions per second versus Kasparov's ability to evaluate approximately 3 positions per second.

Year: 1997

Event: The Food and Drug Administration approved the first monoclonal antibody for cancer, Rituxan.

Year: 1997

Event: The first animal clone was created.

Year: 2000

Event: The Human Genome was mapped. Scientists view this historic event as equal or greater in significance to landing men on the moon.

Year: 2001

Event: IBM installed a new supercomputer, dubbed ASCI White, at Lawrence Livermore National Laboratory in California. ASCI White consists of 8,192 microprocessors and can perform more than 10 trillion calculations per second. ASCI White is one thousand times faster than its predecessor, Deep Blue.

Year: 2001

Event: Intel launched the Pentium 4 microprocessor. This chip contains 43 million transistors, handles data in thirty-two-bit chunks, and performs more than one billion calculations per second.

Source: IBM, Intel Corp., *Q is for Quantum*, *The Quantum Universe*, *The Timetables of Science*, *A Beautiful Mind*, and *http://www.computerhistory.org*.

Glossary

This glossary presents definitions of terms frequently used by quantum physicists, complexity theorists, and economists. If you are interested in a more comprehensive discussion of quantum terminology and the history of quantum physics, you may want to read John Gribbin's excellent book *Q Is for Quantum*.

absolute zero: The lowest temperature that could ever be attained. At absolute zero, atoms and molecules would have the minimum amount of energy allowed by quantum theory. This amount of energy is defined as zero on the Kelvin scale of temperature. Zero degrees Kelvin is equivalent to -237° Celsius, and -459.69° Fahrenheit.

amplitude: The amplitude of a wave is half the height from the peak of the wave to the trough. In quantum mechanics, the amplitude of a process is a number that reflects the probability that the process will occur.

ängström: A unit of wavelength defined as one hundred millionth (10^{-8}) of a centimeter that is equal to one-tenth of a nanometer.

atomic number: The number of protons in the nucleus of a single atom of a particular element. This is equal to the number of electrons associated with a particular atom, which determines the chemical properties of the element.

black body: A hypothetical object that absorbs all electromagnetic radiation that falls on it.

black-body radiation: The radiation emitted by a hot black body. Physicist Max Planck explained black-body radiation by assuming that the energy of light was not continuous but rather came in discrete packets he called *quanta*. Plank stated that the size of the quanta became larger at shorter wavelengths. Planck's quanta theory works because for the same total amount of energy, more waves are excited at long wavelengths; since the permitted energy packets are small, there can be more of them. At short wavelengths, fewer waves are excited, since the size of the permitted energy packets are large.

cambrian explosion: The Cambrian Period is an important point in the history of life on Earth. Beginning 550 million years ago, life took on radically new forms. Nearly all the major groups (i.e., phyla) of animals we see today arose at that time. Evolutionary innovation was rapid in as little as 5 million years. This event is called the "Cambrian Explosion" because of the relatively short time in which this diversity of forms appears.

carbon: An element with atomic number six. The most common isotope of carbon has six protons and six neutrons in its nucleus. Its mass is defined as twelve atomic mass units. This sets the standard against which all atomic and molecular weights are measured.

cathode-ray tube: A cathode ray tube (CRT) is a specialized vacuum tube (a sealed tube from which most of the air has been removed) in which images are produced when an electron beam strikes a phosphorescent surface. A thin piece of metal coated with a material that emits light when struck by electrons is sealed inside the tube to detect the path of the electrons. Most desktop computer displays make use of CRTs. The CRT in a computer display is similar to the "picture tube" in a television receiver.

charge: A measure of the strength with which some elementary particles interact with one another. The most common example is an electric charge, which comes in two forms: negative and positive. Two particles that have a similar charge repel each other, while two particles with opposite electric charges attract each other.

chemical bond: A link that holds atoms together to make molecules.

chemistry: The branch of science that studies how atoms combine to form molecules, and the way molecules interact with each other.

Clarke's laws: Named after the eminent futurist, Arthur C. Clarke.

Clarke's first law: When a distinguished but elderly scientist states that something is possible he is almost certainly right. When he states that something is impossible, he is very probably wrong.

Clarke's second law: The only way of discovering the limits of the possible is to venture a little way past them into the impossible.

Clarke's third law: Any sufficiently advanced technology is indistinguishable from magic.

complementarity: The quantum nature of certain pairs of variables that prevents them from having precise values at the same time. It is impossible for a quantum object to have a precise position and a precise momentum at the same time.

complexity: Scientists have difficulty defining complexity. A number of scientists acknowledge that they do not really know what the term means. The apparent vagueness of the term, however, may be what makes the word so valuable as a catalyst for thought. Santa Fe Institute (SFI) president Ellen Goldberg states that complexity involves "interacting parts with very simple rules," but she notes that the term does not reduce to a constant definition across disciplines. Former SFI president George Cowan also accepts the polysemantic nature of the word. He believes the chief value of complexity is that it embraces a number of possible systems.

decoherence: The process that untangles quantum states and makes it possible to assign probabilities to the outcome of an experiment, even though scientists cannot say which outcome will result.

diffraction: The way in which waves bend around corners or spread out, like ripples on a pond.

double-slit experiment: An experiment that demonstrates the wave nature of light in which particles are sent through two small holes or narrow slits. The double-slit experiment encapsulates the central mystery of quantum mechanics. The result of the experiment is impossible to explain using classical physics.

efficient market: An efficient market is one in which large numbers of rational, profit-maximizing agents are actively competing, with each trying to predict future market values of individual securities, and in which important current information is almost freely available to all participants. In an efficient market, competition among the many intelligent participants leads to a situation in which, at any point in time, the actual prices of individual securities already reflect the effects of information based both on events that have already occurred and on events that, as of now, the market expects to take place in the future. According to efficient-markets theory, at any point in time the actual price of a security is a good estimate of its intrinsic value.

electricity: One component of the electromagnetic force.

electromagnetic radiation: Radiation (including light) that is produced by interacting electric fields and magnetic fields moving together through space at light speed.

electron: One of the elementary particles of nature.

electron microscope: An electrical device that uses a beam of electrons instead of a beam of light to produce an image of an object.

elements: A substance that cannot be broken down into simple components by chemical means.

emergence: In the study of complex systems, the idea of emergence is used to indicate the arising of patterns, structures, or properties that do not seem adequately explained by referring only to the system's preexisting components and their interaction.

entropy: A measure of the amount of disorder in the universe, or of the availability of the energy in a system to do work.

exclusion principle: Developed by physicist Wolfgang Pauli in 1925. The exclusion principle states that no two fermions (i.e., elementary particles) can occupy the same quantum state. That is, they cannot have the same set of quantum numbers. Without quantum exclusion, there would be no chemistry.

fermions: These are the particles that make up the material world (e.g., the electron, the proton).

forces of nature: Gravity, electromagnetism, the strong force and the weak force (the strong and weak forces are nuclear interactions). Scientists are currently searching for an all-encompassing theory that unites the four forces.

frequency: The number of oscillations of a wave in one second.

fundamental constants: The parameters that have the same value everywhere in the Universe and whose sizes determine the way nature works. The fundamental constants in physics are the speed of light in a vacuum (c); the charge on an electron (e); Planck's constant (h); the constant of gravity (G); the electric constant (ϵ); and the magnetic constant (μ).

fusion: The process that releases energy when light nuclei fuse together to make one heavier nucleus.

hydrogen: The lightest element. Each hydrogen nucleus has a single proton, and each hydrogen atom has a single electron surrounding the nucleus. Hydrogen has an atomic number of one.

infrared radiation: Electromagnetic radiation with wavelengths longer than those of visible light. Heat emitted by a hot object is infrared radiation.

interference: How two or more sets of waves interact with one another to produce an overall pattern in which there are regions of high intensity and low intensity. An interference pattern is observed in the double-slit experiment (defined earlier).

ion: An atom that has either lost one or more of its electrons (thus becoming a positive ion) or gained one or more electrons (thus becoming a negative ion).

isotopes: Atoms of the same element that have different numbers of neutrons in their nuclei. Isotopes have different atomic weights but otherwise identical chemical properties. Each atom of every isotope of the same element has the same number of electrons.

kelvin scale: The temperature scale invented by Lord Kelvin (William Thomson) that contains an absolute lower limit to temperature. This temperature is -273° Celsius or 0° Kelvin. In quantum terminology, absolute zero is the temperature at which atoms and molecules would have the minimum possible energy otherwise known as zero-point energy.

laser: A quantum system known as light amplification by stimulated emission of radiation that is used to produce a powerful beam of monochromatic light, with waves from many different atoms marching in lockstep with one another.

light: The range of electromagnetic radiation that human eyes can detect and that consists of wavelengths ranging from 380 nanometers to 750 nanometers. Red light has the longest wavelength, violet the shortest. Ultraviolet light has shorter wave lengths than the color violet, and infrared light has longer wavelengths than the color red. There is no essential difference between light and other forms of electromagnetic radiation, such as x-rays and radio waves—they simply have different wavelengths.

magnetism: One component of the electromagnetic force.

maser: A device for creation, amplification, and transmission of an intense, highly focused beam of high-frequency radio waves. *Maser* is an acronym for *m*icrowave *a*mplification by *s*timulated *e*mission of *r*adiation, microwaves being radio waves of short wavelength, or high frequency.

mass number: The total number of protons and neutrons in the nucleus of a particular isotope.

maxwell's equations: Four differential equations that when combined, describe everything there is to describe about the classical (i.e., non-quantum) behavior of electricity, magnetism, electromagnetic fields, and electromagnetic radiation.

mechanics: The branch of science concerned with interactions between matter and forces.

microwaves: Electromagnetic radiation with wavelengths that range from 1 to 30 centimeters (short-wavelength radio waves).

molecular biology: The branch of quantum physics that studies the nature of life.

molecule: Two or more atoms held together by chemical bonds to form a stable unit.

nano: Prefix denoting one-billionth (10^{-9}). Derived from the Greek word *nanos*, meaning "dwarf."

nanometer: One-billionth of a meter. One nanometer is equivalent to roughly four atoms laid end to end.

nanosecond: One billionth of a second.

nanotechnology: Engineering at the level of atoms and molecules.

neutron: One of the elementary particles of the Universe.

Newtonian mechanics: A branch of science that studies the behavior of nature at the macroscopic level. Also known as classical mechanics or Newtonian physics.

nucleus: The central part of an atom. The nucleus contains most of the mass of the atom in the form of protons and neutrons and all of its positive electric charge. The nucleus is surrounded by a cloud of electrons, which carry a little mass and all of the negative charge associated with the atom. The nucleus has anywhere from 99.945 to 99.975 percent of the mass of the atom of which it is part. Despite its mass, the nucleus is tiny in size, with a diameter only one hundred-thousandth that of the atom. The nucleus must carry a positive electric charge of sufficient size to neutralize the charge of all of the electrons that are ordinarily to be found in a particular atom.

particles: The fundamental building blocks of matter.

photoelectric effect: The release of electrons from a substance as a result of the influence of light or other electromagnetic radiation.

photon: A particle of light defined by physicists as a boson with zero mass and spin 1. Coined by Gilbert Lewis, the term *photon* is derived from *phos*, the Greek word for "light." Light does not resemble the ordinary objects around us, and can't be forced into categories defined according to the same rules. When studied in certain ways, light shows interference phenomena, as ripples on a pond do. Studied in other ways, however, light shows energy transfers, as colliding billiard balls do. No observation, however, can show light acting as both a wave and a particle simultaneously. You can study light as either one or the other, but never both at once.

planck's constant: A fundamental constant (defined earlier), denoted by the letter h, which relates the energy (E) of a quantum of electromagnetic radiation, that is, a photon, to its frequency (f). Planck's constant relates the particle nature of a quantum entity to its wave nature through the equation $E = hf$.

probability: The chance or likelihood that a particular event will happen. At the quantum level, the Universe operates in accordance with the same laws of probability as an honest game of dice.

proton: One of the elementary particles.

quantum: The smallest amount of something that is possible to have. When used as an adjective, *quantum* refers to the world of the very small, where the rules of quantum physics apply.

quantum chemistry: The description, using the rules of quantum physics, of how atoms combine to form molecules and how molecules interact with one another.

quantum computers: Computers that would operate on quantum principles.

quantum electrodynamics: A theory, sometimes referred to as QED, that describes the way electrically charged particles interact with one another and with magnetic fields through the exchange of photons.

quantum mechanics: The laws of mechanics that apply to the world of the very small. The term "quantum mechanics" is essentially synonymous with "quantum physics." The great physicist Erwin Schrödinger noted that the greatest revelation of quantum theory was that features of discreteness were discovered in nature at a time when anything other than continuity seemed to be absurd.

quantum physics: The physics that describes the behavior of the world on a very, very small scale, the level of atoms and molecules and even lower levels.

quantum theory: See quantum physics and quantum mechanics.

scanning tunneling microscope: A microscope that uses quantum tunneling to probe the surfaces of materials.

schrödinger equation: The wave equation used in one version of quantum mechanics to describe the behavior of a quantum entity, such as an electron.

scientific notation: Shorthand scientists use for writing out numbers. The number 1,000 can be expressed using scientific notation as 10^3 and the number 0.0001 can be expressed as 10^{-4}.

self-similarity: One of the basic properties of fractals whereby parts of some object are similar to the entire object. Fractal objects act the same way no matter how you magnify them. You can find self-similarity in tree branches, mountains, clouds, rivers, and practically everywhere else in nature.

semiconductor: A crystalline substance with an electrical conductivity intermediate between that of conductors (e.g., copper, aluminum) and insulators (e.g., rubber, plastic).

singularity: A concept associated with scientist Vernor Vinge and embraced by others, including Raymond Kurzweil and John Smart. Vinge believes that the acceleration of technological progress has been the central feature of the twentieth century. He argues that we are on the edge of change comparable to the rise of human life on Earth—change that he calls "the Singularity." The precise cause of this change is the imminent creation by technology of entities with greater than human intelligence.

solid-state devices: Electronic devices such as transistors and diodes that are made out of crystalline semiconductor material and take advantage of quantum phenomena such as tunneling for their operation.

spectral lines: Sharply defined lines seen in the spectrum of light. The lines are associated with the transitions of electrons from one well-defined energy level to another well-defined energy level, with the absorption or emission of a precise amount of energy corresponding to a precise wavelength of light.

spectrum: Any representation of how the strength of the electromagnetic radiation from a source depends on its wavelength (e.g., the rainbow spectrum of visible light, from violet to red).

speed of light: A universal constant, denoted scientifically by the letter c. The speed of light is 299.792458×10^6 meters per second, or $186,000$ miles per second.

strong interaction: The force that operates within the nucleus of an atom and holds the nucleus together.

superconductivity: The ability of some materials to allow an electric current to flow through them with no detectable resistance.

temperature: A measure of how fast the atoms and molecules in a substance are moving.

tunneling: A result of the uncertainty principle of quantum physics, which allows particles to penetrate barriers.

uncertainty: In quantum physics, uncertainty is the state in which it is impossible to have a precisely determined value of pairs of parameters (known as conjugate variables) at the same time. The most important of these uncertain pairs are position/momentum and energy/time.

uncertainty principle: Werner Heisenberg's formal statement that the amount of quantum uncertainty in the simultaneous determination of both members of a pair of conjugate variables is never zero.

wave: An oscillating disturbance that moves through a medium or through space.

wave equation: Any equation that describes mathematically the way that a wave propagates. In quantum mechanics, the term is used to refer specifically to the wave equation discovered by Erwin Schrödinger, which describes the wave nature of a quantum entity such as an electron.

wave function: The mathematical description of a quantum system in terms of waves (see wave equation).

wavelength: The distance from peak to peak (or trough to trough) in a wave.

wave-particle duality: The idea that quantum entities behave either as waves or as particles, depending on the circumstances. This does not mean that the entities are waves, or that they are particles. Scientists have no way of knowing what they are. They can say only what quantum entities are like, not what they are.

The acclaimed science writer Isaac Asimov notes that the wave-particle duality of light may not be such a big mystery after all. Imagine, Asimov says, that you are looking at an empty ice-cream cone from the side, so that the wide part is at the top and the point is at the bottom. The outline is a triangle. Imagine next that you are looking at the cone with the wide opening facing you directly. Now the outline is a circle. If those are the only two ways in which you are allowed to view the cone, then you can see it as either a circle or a triangle, but you can never see it as both simultaneously. In the same way, whether light is a wave or a particle depends on which way you are observing it.

Asimov notes that physicists are now convinced that, indeed, everything has both a particle and a wave aspect, but not necessarily in equal measure. The more massive a particle is, the more prominent the particle aspect is and the more difficult it is to observe the wave aspect. Electromagnetic radiation is hard to observe in its particle aspect when the quanta are very small, as in radio waves. It is only when the quanta grow large and the wavelengths tiny, as in x-rays, that the particle aspect can be easily observed.

Electron waves are not electromagnetic waves, but rather "matter waves." An electron has such a small mass that its wave aspect can be easily observed with the proper experiment. Likewise, the less energetic a wave is, the more prominent is its wave aspect, and the more difficult it is to observe its particle aspect.

Asimov suggests that it is only because in the ordinary world around us, particles are so massive and waves so lacking in energy that we think of the two phenomena as mutually exclusive. In the world of the atom and of subatomic particles, this exclusivity disappears.

Physicist David Bohm notes that at the quantum level of accuracy, an object does not have any "intrinsic" properties (for instance wave or particle) belonging to itself alone. Instead, it shares all its properties mutually and indivisibly with the systems with which it interacts.

Moreover, because a given object, such as an electron, intersects at different times with different systems that bring out different potentialities, it undergoes continual transformation between various forms (e.g., waves or particles) in which it can manifest itself.

The wave-particle duality observed in experiments in which a photon or electron is sent through a slit is so offending to our common sense that we feel it is necessary to call the particle or wave an event rather than a "thing."

x-rays: Electromagnetic radiation with wavelengths in the range from 12 billionths of a meter (i.e., 12 nanometers) to 12 trillionths of a meter.

zero-point energy: The energy that is associated with a particle or system at a temperature of absolute zero (0° Kelvin).

Selected Websites

Below are listed the websites, books, and articles that I consulted for this book. The sites are categorized by chapters in the book. You will also find more references at my website: www.quantuminvesting.net.

The Ascending Quantum Economy
Visual Quantum Mechanics
   http://phys.educ.ksu.edu
Motion Mountain Physics Textbook
   http://www.dse.nl/motionmountain/contents
Richard Feynman links
   http://www.zyvex.com/nanotech/feynmanWeb
Guide to Semiconductor Physics
   http://www.britneyspears.ac/lasers.htm
John Gribbin's website
   http://www.biols.susx.ac.uk/home/John_Gribbin
Computer History Museum
   http://www.computerhistory.org

Quantum computing links
http://socrates.berkeley.edu/~dabacon/qlinks
Superconductors
http://superconductors.org
Center for Quantum Computation
http://www.qubit.org/index

The Fifth Wave
Joseph Schumpeter
http://www.utdallas.edu/~harpham/joseph
MIT *Technology Review*
http://www.technologyreview.com
Michael Cox's research
http://www.dallasfed.org
George Gilder's website
http://www.gilder.com
Institute for the Future
http://www.iftf.org
California Institute for Telecommunications and IT
http://www.calit2.net/
BT Exact Technologies: Predictions about the future
http://www.btexact.com/

Convergence Ahead
IBM Research Center
http://www.research.ibm.com/cross_disciplines/p_systems
George Washington University's Technology Forecast
http://www.gwforecast.gwu.edu
Foresight Institute
http://www.foresight.org
Nanomagazine
http://www.nanomagazine.com/aboutnanomagazine
Carbon Nanotubes: New Materials for the Twenty-first Century
http://www.rdg.ac.uk/~scsharip/tubes

Richard Smalley's Website
  http://cnst.rice.edu/smalleygroup/res
Zyvex (first molecular nanotechnology company)
  http://www.zyvex.com
BioWorld Online: Worldwide Biotechnology News and Information Source
  http://www.bioworld.com/
Hydrogen energy and fuel Cells
  http://www.h2fc.com/tech
U.S. Patent and Trademark Office
  http://www.uspto.gov
The Rothberg Institute for Childhood Diseases
  http://www.childhooddiseases.org
BioInsights website
  http://www.bioinsights.com
Hong Kong University of Science and Technology
  http://www.ust.hk

Fast Forward
Mark Anderson's *Strategic News Service*
  http://www.tapsns.com
Raymond Kurzweil's website
  http://www.kurzweilai.net
Singularity Watch: Interpreting a World of Accelerating Change
  http://www.members.home.net/marlon1
Robin Hanson's website
  http://hanson.gmu.edu/home
Seth Godin's website
  http://www.zoometry.com
Maxager's website
  http://www.maxager.com
John Smart's websites
  http://www.singularitywatch.com
  http://www.accelerating.org
Microsoft's Website
  http://www.microsoft.com

Invisible Wealth

Baruch Lev's website
  http://www.stern.nyu.edu/~blev
National Science Foundation
  http://www.nsf.gov
Global Financial Data
  http://www.globalfindata.com

Pagels' Prophesy

Santa Fe Institute
  http://www.santafe.edu
Complexity Digest
  http://www.comdig.org
University of Michigan Center for the Study of Complex Systems
  http://www.pscs.umich.edu
Cap Gemini Ernst & Young Center for Business Innovation
  http://www.cbi.cgey.com
Bios Group—Complexity science for the real world
  http://www.biosgroup.com
Michael Mauboussin's research
  http://www.capatcolumbia.com

Nature's Patterns

Geocomplexity
  http://www.geocomplexity.com
Norman Johnson's website
  http://ishi.lanl.gov
Stephen Wolfram's website
  http://www.stephenwolfram.com
Swarm Development Group
  http://www.swarm.org/index
Emergence
  http://www.emergence.org
Ilya Prigogine Center for Studies in Complex Systems
  http://order.ph.utexas.edu/index

New England Complex Systems Institute
  http://www.necsi.org
Woody Brock's Strategic Economic Decisions
  http://www.sedinc.com/index
Behavioral finance research
  http://www.undiscoveredmanagers.com/Behavioral%20Finance2.htm
Brains at Work
  http://www.mareshbrainsatwork.com

E
F
E
R
E
N
C
E
S

Print Sources

Aghion, Philippe, and Howitt, Peter. 1998. *Endogenous Growth Theory.* Cambridge, MA: MIT Press.

Allen, Robert Loring. 1994. *Opening Doors: The Life and Work of Joseph Schumpeter: Volume One.* New Brunswick, NJ: Transaction.

Andersen, Esben S. 1994. *Evolutionary Economics.* London: Pinter.

Anderson, Mark. 2001. "You Can't Drive a Router," *Strategic News Service,* March 14.

Anderson, Philip W., Arrow, Kenneth J., and Pines, David. 1988. *The Economy As an Evolving Complex System.* Reading, MA: Addison-Wesley.

Andriessen, Daniel, and Tissen, Rene. 2000. *Weightless Wealth.* London: Pearson Education.

Arrow, Kenneth J. 1984. *The Economics of Information.* Cambridge, MA: Harvard University Press.

Arthur, W. Brian, Durlauf, Steven N., and Lane, David A. 1997. *The Economy As An Evolving Complex System II.* Reading, MA: Perseus.

Arthur, W. Brian. 1997. "How Fast is Technology Evolving?" *Scientific American,* February.

Ashton, T. S. 1968. *The Industrial Revolution.* Oxford, England: Oxford University Press.

Asimov, Isaac. 1992. *Atom.* New York: Plume.

Asimov, Isaac. 1993. *Understanding Physics.* New York: Barnes & Noble Books.

Axelrod, Robert, and Cohen, Michael D. 1999. *Harnessing Complexity.* New York: Free Press.

Bailey, James. 1996. *After Thought.* New York: Basic Books.

Bak, Per. 1996. *How Nature Works.* New York: Springer-Verlag.

Ball, Philip. 2001. *Stories of the Invisible.* Oxford, England: Oxford University Press.

Belsky, Gary, and Gilovich Thomas. 1999. *Why Smart People Make Big Money Mistakes.* New York: Simon & Schuster.

Bernstein, Peter L. 1992. *Capital Ideas.* New York: Free Press.

Bernstein, Peter L. 1996. *Against the Gods.* New York: John Wiley & Sons.

Berry, Adrian. 1996. *The Next 500 Years.* New York: Gramercy Books.

Blair, Margaret M., and Wallman, Steven. 2001. *Unseen Wealth.* Washington, D.C.: Brookings Institution Press.

Bloom, Howard. 2000. *Global Brain.* New York: John Wiley & Sons.

Bonabeau, Eric, Dorigo, Marco, and Theraulaz, Guy. 1999. *Swarm Intelligence.* New York: Oxford University Press.

Bonabeau, Eric, and Meyer, Chris. 2001. "Swarm Intelligence: A Whole New Way to Think about Business." *Harvard Business Review.* May, pp. 107–114.

Brand, Stewart. 1999. *The Clock of the Long Now.* New York: Basic Books.

Bristol Myers Squibb. *2000 Annual Report to Shareholders,* New Jersey.

Brock, Woody. 1997. The Sources of Endogenous Risk. *Strategic Economic Decisions,* May.

Brock, Woody. 2001. "Resolving the Paradox of Global Stock Market

Correlation—An Application of the Theory of Endogenous Risk." *Strategic Economic Decisions.* September.

Broderick, Damien. 2001. *The Spike: How Our Lives Are Being Transformed by Rapidly Advancing Technologies.* New York: Forge.

Brooks, Rodney. 2002. *Flesh and Machines: How Robots Will Change Us.* New York: Pantheon Books.

Brown, John Seely. 1997. *Seeing Differently.* Cambridge, MA: Harvard Business School Press.

Brown, Julian. 2001. *The Quest for the Quantum Computer.* New York: Touchstone.

Brown, Shona L. and Eisenhardt, Kathleen M. 1998. *Competing on the Edge.* Cambridge, MA: Harvard Business School Press.

Buderi, Robert. 2000. *Engines of Tomorrow.* New York: Simon & Schuster.

Burton-Jones, Alan. 1999. *Knowledge Capital.* Oxford, England: Oxford University Press.

Camazine, Scott, Deneubourg, Jean-Louis, Franks, Nigel R., Sneyd, James, Theraulaz, Guy, and Bonabeau, Eric. 2001. *Self-Organization in Biological Systems.* Princeton: Princeton University Press.

Caplow, Theodore, Hicks, Louis, and Wattenberg, Ben J. 2001. *The First Measured Century.* Washington, D.C.: American Enterprise Institute Press.

Casti, John L. 1997. *Would-Be Worlds.* New York: John Wiley & Sons.

Chandler, Alfred D. Jr. 2001. *Inventing the Electronic Century.* New York: The Free Press.

Chandler, Alfred D. Jr., and Cortada, James W. 2000. *A Nation Transformed by Information.* New York: Oxford University Press.

Churchill, Winston S. 1944. *Onwards to Victory.* Boston: Little, Brown.

Clarke, Arthur C. 1962. *Profiles of the Future.* New York: Holt Rinehart and Winston.

Clarke, Arthur C. 1999. *Greetings, Carbon-Based Bipeds!* New York: St. Martin's Press.

Clippinger, John H. 1999. *The Biology of Business*. San Francisco: Jossey-Bass.

Cobb, Cathy, and Goldwhite, Harold. 1995. *Creations of Fire*. Cambridge, MA: Perseus.

Colander, David. 2000. *The Complexity Vision and the Teaching of Economics*. Northampton, MA: Edward Elgar.

Cox, W. Michael, and Alm, Richard. 1999. *Myths of Rich and Poor*. New York: Basic Books.

Cox, W. Michael, and Alm, Richard. 1999. "The New Paradigm." *Federal Reserve Bank of Dallas Annual Report*. pp. 3–23.

Coyle, Diane. 1998. *The Weightless World*. Cambridge, MA: MIT Press.

Crichton, Michael. 1999. *Timeline*. New York: Alfred Knopf.

Cropper, William. H. 2001. *Great Physicists*. Oxford, England: Oxford University Press.

Davis, Stan, and Meyer, Christopher. 1998. *Blur*. Reading, MA: Addison-Wesley.

Davis, Stan and Meyer, Christopher. 2000. *Future Wealth*. Cambridge, MA: Harvard University Press.

Denning, Peter J. 2002. *The Invisible Future*. New York: McGraw-Hill.

Dertouzous, Michael. 2001. *The Unfinished Revolution*. New York: HarperCollins.

Deutsch, David. 1997. *The Fabric of Reality*. New York: Allen Lane.

Drexler, K. Eric. 1987. *Engines of Creation*. New York: Anchor Books.

Drexler, K. Eric, Peterson, Chris, and Pergamit, Gale. 1991. *Unbounding the Future*. New York: William Morrow.

Drucker, Peter. 1992. *The Age of Discontinuity*. New York: Harper & Row.

Drucker, Peter. 1993. *Post-Capitalist Society*. New York: HarperBusiness.

Drucker, Peter. 1995. *Management in a Time of Great Change*. New York: Truman Talley Books/Dutton.

Drucker, Peter. 1999. "Beyond the Information Revolution." *Atlantic Monthly*, October.

Economic Report of the President. 2001. Washington, D.C.: U.S. Government Printing Office.

Enriquez, Juan. 2001. *As the Future Catches You*. New York: Crown Business.

Enriquez, Juan, and Goldberg, Ray A. 2000. "Transforming Life, Transforming Business: The Life-Science Revolution." *Harvard Business Review*. March/April, pp. 96–104.

Feynman, Richard P. 1965. *The Character of Physical Law*. Cambridge, MA: MIT Press.

Feynman, Richard P., Leighton, Robert B., and Sands, Matthew. 1964. *The Feynman Lectures on Physics: Volume III*. Reading, MA: Addison-Wesley.

Feynman, Richard P. 1999. *The Pleasure of Finding Things Out*. Cambridge, MA: Perseus.

Fine, Charles H. 1998. *Clockspeed*. Reading, MA: Perseus.

Fogel, David B. 2002. *Blondie24: Playing at the Edge of AI*. San Francisco: Morgan Kaufmann.

Foster, Ian, and Kesselman, Carl. 1999. *The Grid*. San Francisco: Morgan Kaufmann.

Foster, Richard, and Kaplan, Sarah. 2001. *Creative Destruction*. New York: Doubleday.

Gamow, George. 1985. *Thirty Years that Shook Physics*. New York: Dover.

Gamow, George, and Stannard, Russell. 1999. *The New World of Mr. Tompkins*. Cambridge, England: Cambridge University Press.

Gell-Mann, Murray. 1994. *The Quark and the Jaguar*. London: Little, Brown.

Gernshenfeld, Neil. 1999. *When Things Start to Think*. New York: Henry Holt.

Gernshenfeld, Neil. 2000. *The Physics of Information Technology*. Cambridge, MA: Cambridge University Press.

Gigerenzer, Gerd. 2000. *Adaptive Thinking*. Oxford, England: Oxford University Press.

Gilder, George. 1989. *Microcosm*. New York: Simon & Schuster.

Gilder, George. 2000. *Telecosm*. New York: Free Press.

Gilmore, Robert. 1995. *Alice in Quantumland*. New York: Springer-Verlag.

Gleick, James. 1987. *Chaos*. New York: Viking.

Gleick, James. 1999. *Faster: The Acceleration of Just about Everything.* New York: Pantheon.

Godin, Seth. 2002. *Survival Is Not Enough.* New York: Free Press.

Gribbin, John. 1984. *In Search of Schrödinger's Cat.* London: Black Swan.

Gribbin, John. 1985. *In Search of the Double Helix.* London: Black Swan.

Gribbin, John. 1995. *Schrödinger's Kittens and the Search for Reality.* Boston: Little, Brown.

Gribbin, John. 1998. *Q Is for Quantum.* New York: Touchstone.

Gross, Michael. 1995. *Travels to the Nanoworld.* New York: Plenum.

Grove, Andrew S. 1996. *Only the Paranoid Survive.* New York: Doubleday.

Hagstrom, Robert G. 1999. *The Warren Buffett Portfolio.* New York: John Wiley & Sons.

Hagstrom, Robert G. 2000. *Latticework.* New York: Texere.

Hall, Gregory M. 1997. *The Ingenious Mind of Nature.* New York: Plenum Trade.

Hanson, Robin. 1998. "Economic Growth Given Machine Intelligence." Working Paper. pp. 1–13.

Haseltine, William. 2001. "Perspective on the Biotech Revolution." In Woody Brock's *Strategic Economic Decisions,* pp. IV-1–IV-10.

Hawking, Stephen. 2001. *The Universe in a Nutshell.* New York: Bantam Books.

Hawking, Stephen. 2001. "A Brief History of Relativity," *Time,* December 31, 2001, pp. 67–81.

Hawn, Carleen. 2002. "The Man Who Sees Around Corners," *Forbes,* January, pp. 72–78.

Hayek, F. A. 1948. *Individualism and Economic Order.* Chicago: University of Chicago Press.

Hecht, Jeff. 1999. *City of Light.* New York: Oxford University Press.

Heilbroner, Robert L. 1992. *The Worldly Philosophers.* New York: Simon & Schuster.

Hellemans, Alexander, and Bunch, Bryan. 1988. *The Timetables of Science.* New York: Touchstone.

Helpman, Elhanan. 1998. *General Purpose Technologies and Economic Growth*. Cambridge, MA: MIT Press.

Herbold, Robert. 2002. "Inside Microsoft: Balancing Creativity and Discipline." *Harvard Business Review*. January. pp. 73–79.

Hey, Tony, and Walters, Patrick. 1987. *The Quantum Universe*. Cambridge, England: Cambridge University Press.

Holland, John H. 1995. *Hidden Order*. Reading, MA: Addison-Wesley.

Holland, John H. 1998. *Emergence: From Chaos to Order*. Reading, MA: Addison-Wesley.

Huberman, Bernardo A. 2001. *The Laws of the Web*. Cambridge, MA: MIT Press.

IBM. Annual Report to Shareholders, 2001.

Johnson, Steven. 2001. *Emergence*. New York: Charles Scribner & Sons.

Jones, Roger. 1992. *Physics for the Rest of Us*. Chicago: Contemporary Books.

Judson, Horace Freeland. 1996. *The Eighth Day of Creation*. New York: Cold Spring Harbor Laboratory Press.

Jurvetson, Steve. 2001. Transcript. *Merrill Lynch Technology Strategy*, October, pp. 1–25.

Kahneman, Daniel, and Tversky, Amos. 2000. *Choices, Values, and Frames*. Cambridge, England: Cambridge University Press.

Kahneman, Daniel, Slovic, Paul, and Tversky Amos. 1982. *Judgment under Uncertainty: Heuristics and Biases*. Cambridge, England: Cambridge University Press.

Kaku, Michio. 1997. *Visions: How Science Will Revolutionize the 21st Century*. New York: Anchor Books.

Kauffman, Stuart A. 1993. *The Origins of Order*. New York: Oxford University Press.

Kauffman, Stuart. 1995. *At Home in the Universe*. New York: Oxford University Press.

Kauffman, Stuart. 2000. *Investigations*. New York: Oxford University Press.

Kelly, Kevin. 1994. *Out of Control*. London: Fourth Estate.

Kelly, Kevin. 1998. *New Rules for the New Economy*. New York: Viking.

Kennedy, James, and Eberhart, Russell C. 2001. *Swarm Intelligence*. San Francisco: Morgan Kaufmann.

Kindleberger, Charles P. 1978. *Manias, Panics, and Crashes*. New York: Basic Books.

Kirkland, Rik, and Colvin, Geoffrey. 2001. "Jack: The Exit Interview," *Fortune*, September 17.

Krugman, Paul. 1996. *The Self-Organizing Economy*. Cambridge, MA: Blackwell.

Kumar, Manjit. 2002. "Quantum Reality," *Prometheus*. London, Issue 4.

Kurzweil, Raymond. 1999. *The Age of Spiritual Machines*. New York: Penguin Books.

Kurzweil, Raymond. 2001. The Singularity Is Near. (unpublished manuscript).

Langton, Christopher G. 1997. *Artificial Life: An Overview*. Cambridge, MA: MIT Press.

Lederman, Leon. 1993. *The God Particle*. New York: Dell.

Lev, Baruch. 2001. *Intangibles*. Washington, D.C.: Brookings Institution Press.

Levy, Steven. 1992. *Artificial Life*. New York: Vintage Books.

Lewis, Gilbert A. 1926. *The Anatomy of Science*. New Haven, CT: Yale University Press.

Loasby, Brian. 1999. *Knowledge, Institutions and Evolution in Economics*. London: Routledge.

Luger, George F. 1994. *Cognitive Science: The Science of Intelligent Systems*. San Diego: Academic Press.

Maddison, Angus. 1991. *Dynamic Forces in Capitalist Development*. Oxford, England: Oxford University Press.

Maddison, Angus. 1995. *Monitoring the World Economy: 1820–1992*. Paris: Organization for Economic Cooperation and Development.

Maddox, John. 1998. *What Remains to Be Discovered*. New York: Free Press.

Malone, Michael S. 1995. *The Microprocessor: A Biography*. New York: Springer-Verlag.

Malone, Michael S. 2000. "God, Stephen Wolfram and Everything Else," *Forbes*, November.

Mandelbrot, Benoit B. 1982. *The Fractal Geometry of Nature.* New York: W. H. Freeman.

Mandelbrot, Benoit B. 1997. *Fractals and Scaling in Finance.* New York: Springer.

Mauboussin, Michael. 1997. "Shift Happens: On a New Paradigm of the Markets as a Complex Adaptive System," *Credit Suisse First Boston,* October 24.

Mauboussin, Michael. 1999. "Absolute Power," *Credit Suisse First Boston* Equity Research, December 21.

Mauboussin, Michael. 1999. "The (Fat) Tail that Wags the Dog," *Credit Suisse First Boston* Equity Research, February 4.

Mauboussin, Michael. 2000. "Fill and Kill: Succeeding with Survivors is Nothing New," *Credit Suisse First Boston,* Equity Research, April 5.

Mauboussin, Michael. 2000. "It's the Ecology, Stupid," *Credit Suisse First Boston,* Equity Research, September 11.

Mauboussin, Michael. 2000. "Innovation and Markets," *Credit Suisse First Boston* Equity Research, December 12.

Mauboussin, Michael. 2000 "Still Powerful," *Credit Suisse First Boston* Equity Research, July 7.

Mayo, Andrew. 2001. *The Human Value of the Enterprise.* London: Nicholas Brealey.

McCrone, John. 2001. *Going Inside.* New York: Fromm International.

McEvoy, J. P., and Zarate, Oscar. 1996. *Introducing Quantum Theory.* New York: Totem Books.

McKelvey, Maureen. 2000. *Evolutionary Innovations.* Oxford, England: Oxford University Press.

Mead, Carver A. 2000. *Collective Electrodynamics.* Cambridge, MA: MIT Press.

Mead, Carver, 2001. "Twenty-First Century Physicist: A Conversation With Carver Mead," *The American Spectator,* September/October, pp. 69–75.

Means, Grady, and Schneider, David. 2000. *Meta-Capitalism.* New York: John Wiley & Sons.

Meeker, Mary, and Cascianelli Fabriizio, 2002. "The Technology IPO Yearbook: 8th Edition." *Morgan Stanley Equity Research,* March.

Mendelson, Haim, and Ziegler, Johannes. 1999. *Survival of the Smartest*. New York: John Wiley & Sons.

Metcalfe, J. Stanley. 1998. *Evolutionary Economics and Creative Destruction*. London: Routledge.

Milburn, Gerard. 1997. *Schrödinger's Machines*. New York: W. H. Freeman.

Mokyr, Joel. 1990. *The Lever of Riches*. New York: Oxford University Press.

Moore, Stephen, and Simon, Julian. 2000. *It's Getting Better All the Time*. Washington, D.C.: Cato Institute.

Moravec, Hans. 1999. *Robot: Mere Machine to Transcendent Mind*. New York: Oxford University Press.

Moschella, David C. 1997. *Waves of Power*. New York: American Management Association.

Mowery, David C., and Rosenberg, Nathan. 1989. *Technology and the Pursuit of Economic Growth*. Cambridge, England: Cambridge University Press.

Mowery, David, and Rosenberg, Nathan. 1998. *Paths of Innovation*. Cambridge, England: Cambridge University Press.

Murphy, Kevin, and Topel Robert, 2002. "Medical Research: What is it Worth?", *The Milken Institute Review*, First Quarter, pp. 23–30.

Nakamura, Leonard. 2001. "What is the U.S. Gross Investment in Intangibles?", Federal Reserve Bank of Philadelphia, April, pp. 1–42.

Nasar, Silvia. 2001. *A Beautiful Mind*. New York: Touchstone Books.

Nelson, Richard R. 1996. *The Sources of Economic Growth*. Cambridge, MA: Harvard University Press.

Nielsen, Michael A., and Chuang, Isaac L. 2000. *Quantum Computation and Quantum Information*. Cambridge, England: Cambridge University Press.

Nolte, David D. 2001. *Mind at Light Speed*. New York: Free Press.

O'Rourke, P. J. 1998. *Eat the Rich*. New York: Atlantic Monthly Press.

Osterland, Andrew. 2001. "Grey Matters: CFO's Third Annual Knowledge Capital Scoreboard," *CFO Magazine*, April.

Pagels, Heinz. 1982. *The Cosmic Code*. New York: Simon & Schuster.

Pagels, Heinz. 1988. *The Dreams of Reason: The Computer and the Rise of the Sciences of Complexity*. New York: Simon & Schuster.

Peters, Edgar E. 1991. *Chaos and Order in the Capital Markets*. New York: John Wiley & Sons.

Peters, Edgar E. 1999. *Patterns in the Dark*. New York: John Wiley & Sons.

Piel, Gerard. 2001. *The Age of Science*. New York: Basic Books.

Plous, Scott. 1993. *The Psychology of Judgment and Decision Making*. New York: McGraw-Hill.

Polanyi, Karl. 1944. *The Great Transformation*. Boston: Beacon Press.

Polkinghorne, J. C. 1984. *The Quantum World*. Princeton, NJ: Princeton University Press.

Prestbo, John A. 1999. *The Market's Measure: An Illustrated History of America Told through the Dow Jones Industrial Average*. New York: Dow Jones & Company.

Rappaport, Alfred, and Mauboussin, Michael J. 2001. *Expectations Investing*. Cambridge, MA: Harvard Business School Press.

Reagan, Michael. 1999. *The Hand of God*. Philadelphia, PA: Templeton Foundation Press.

Regis, Ed. 1995. *Nano: The Emerging Science of Nanotechnology*. Boston: Little, Brown.

Reid, T. R. 2001. *The Chip*. New York: Random House.

Robertson, Douglas S. 1998. *The New Renaissance: Computers and the Next Level of Civilization*. New York: Oxford University Press.

Rohlfs, Jeffrey H. 2001. *Bandwagon Effects in High-Technology Industries*. Cambridge, MA: MIT Press.

Romer, Paul. 1998. "The Soft Revolution: Achieving Growth by Managing Intangibles," *Journal of Applied Corporate Finance*, Summer, Volume 11 Number 2, pp. 8–14.

Rosenberg, Nathan. 1994. *Exploring the Black Box*. Cambridge, England: Cambridge University Press.

Rosenberg, Nathan. 2000. *Schumpeter and the Endogeneity of Technology*. London: Routledge.

Ross, Myron H. 1989. *A Gale of Creative Destruction*. New York: Praeger.

Roth-Robbins, Cynthia. 2000. *From Alchemy to IPO*. Cambridge, MA: Perseus.

Rothschild, Michael. 1990. *Bionomics*. New York: Henry Holt.

Rubin, Michael R., and Huber, Mary T. 1986. *The Knowledge Industry in the United States, 1960–1980*. Princeton, NJ: Princeton University Press.

Ruggles, Rudy, and Holtshouse, Dan. 1999. *The Knowledge Advantage*. Dover, NH: Capstone.

Rumsfeld, Donald H. 2002. "Transforming the Military," *Foreign Affairs*, May/June, pp. 20–32.

Sargent, Thomas J. 1993. *Bounded Rationality in Macroeconomics*. New York: Oxford University Press.

Satinover, Jeffery. 2001. *The Quantum Brain*. New York: John Wiley & Sons.

Schmookler, Jacob. 1966. *Invention and Economic Growth*. Cambridge, MA: Harvard University Press.

Schrödinger, Erwin. 1967. *What Is Life?* Cambridge, MA: Cambridge University Press.

Schroeder, Manfred. 1991. *Fractals, Chaos, Power Laws*. New York: W. H. Freeman.

Schumpeter, Joseph A. 1950. *Capitalism, Socialism and Democracy*. New York: Harper & Row.

Schumpeter, Joseph A. 1954. *History of Economic Analysis*. New York: Oxford University Press.

Schumpeter, Joseph A. 1964. *Business Cycles*. Philadelphia: Porcupine Press.

Schumpeter, Joseph A. 1997. *Essays: On Entrepreneurs, Innovations, Business Cycles, and the Evolution of Capitalism*. New Brunswick, NJ: Transaction.

Seeley, Thomas D. 1995. *The Wisdom of the Hive*. Cambridge, MA: Harvard University Press.

Shapiro, Carl, and Varian, Hal R. 1999. *Information Rules*. Cambridge, MA: Harvard Business School Press.

Shefrin, Hersh. 2000. *Beyond Greed and Fear*. Cambridge, MA: Harvard Business School Press.

Shleifer, Andrei. 2000. *Inefficient Markets: An Introduction to Behavioral Finance*. New York: Oxford University Press.

Siegel, Jeremy J. 1998. *Stocks for the Long Run*. New York: McGraw-Hill.

Silver, Brian L. 1998. *The Ascent of Science*. Oxford, England: Oxford University Press.

Simon, Herbert A. 1997. *Models of Bounded Rationality: Volume 3*. Cambridge, MA: MIT Press.

Simon, Herbert A. 1983. *Reason in Human Affairs*. Stanford, CA: Stanford University Press.

Simon, Herbert A. 1996. *The Sciences of the Artificial*. Cambridge, MA: MIT Press.

Simon, Julian L. 2000. *The Great Breakthrough and Its Cause*. Ann Arbor: University of Michigan Press.

Smarr, Larry. 2002. "Planet Internet," *Technology Review*, March, pp. 80–84.

Snowdon, Brian, and Vane, Howard R. 1999. *Conversations with Leading Economists*. Northampton, MA: Edward Elgar.

Solé, Ricard, and Goodwin, Brian. 2000. *Signs of Life: How Complexity Pervades Biology*. New York: Basic Books.

Sowell, Thomas. 1996. *Knowledge and Decisions*. New York: Basic Books.

Smith, Gordon V., and Parr, Russell L. 2000. *Valuation of Intellectual Property and Intangible Assets*. New York: John Wiley & Sons.

Stewart, Ian. 1989. *Does God Play Dice?* Cambridge, MA: Blackwell.

Stewart, Ian. 2001. *What Shape Is a Snowflake?* New York: W.H. Freeman.

Stewart, Thomas A. 1997. *Intellectual Capital*. New York: Doubleday.

Stewart, Thomas A. 2001. *The Wealth of Knowledge*. New York: Doubleday.

Stewart, Thomas A. 2001. "Accounting Gets Radical," *Fortune*, April 16.

Stork, David G. 2000. *Hal's Legacy*. Cambridge, MA:MIT Press.

Strogatz, Steven H. 1994. *Nonlinear Dynamics and Chaos*. Cambridge, MA: Perseus.

Sveiby, Karl Erick. 1997. *The New Organizational Wealth*. San Francisco: Berrett-Koehler.

Tattersall, Ian, and Schwartz, Jeffery. 2000. *Extinct Humans*. New York: Westview Press.

Taylor, Nick. 2000. *Laser*. New York: Simon & Schuster.

Tegmark, Max, and Wheeler, John Archibald. 2001. "100 Years of Quantum Mysteries," *Scientific American,* February, pp. 68–75.

Templeton, John Marks. 1997. *Is Progress Speeding Up?* Radnor, PA: Templeton Foundation Press.

Thuan, Trinh Xuan. 2001. *Chaos and Harmony.* New York: Oxford University Press.

Toffler, Alvin. 1990. *Power Shift.* New York: Bantam Books.

Toffler, Alvin, and Heidi. 2001. "New Economy? You Ain't Seen Nothin' Yet," *Wall Street Journal,* March 29.

Tvede, Lars. 1999. *The Psychology of Finance.* New York: John Wiley & Sons.

Varian, Hal, and Lyman, Peter. 2000. "How Much Information?" University of California at Berkeley.

Vinge, Vernor. 1993. "Technological Singularity." Address to the Vision-21 Symposium, sponsored by NASA Lewis Research Center and the Ohio Aerospace Institute. March.

Vinge, Vernor. 2001. *True Names.* New York: Tor Books.

Waite, Stephen, and Sterling, William. 1998. *Boomernomics.* New York: Ballantine.

Waldrop, M. Mitchell. 1992. *Complexity.* New York: Simon & Schuster.

Warrick, Judith B. 2001. "The Future of Distributed Generation: Musing on Boundaries, Criticality, and Emergence," *Global Electricity Strategy, Morgan Stanley Dean Witter Equity Research,* March.

Warwick, Kevin. 1998. *In the Mind of the Machine.* London: Arrow Books.

Webber, Alan M. 2000. "New Math for a New Economy," *Fast Company,* January–February, pp. 214–224.

Wheeler, John Archibald. 2000 *Geons, Black Holes, and Quantum Foam: A Life in Physics.* New York: W. W. Norton.

Wheeler, John, and William, Garnett P. 1997. *Chaos Theory Tamed.* Washington, D.C.: Joseph Henry Press.

Whitehead, Alfred North. 1925. *Science and the Modern World.* New York: Free Press.

Williams, Trevor I. 2000. *A History of Invention*. New York: Checkmark Books.

Wolfe, Tom. 2000. *Hooking Up*. New York: Farrar Straus & Giroux.

Wriston, Walter B. 1992. *The Twilight of Sovereignty*. New York: Charles Scribner & Sons.

Index

Page numbers of illustrations and charts appear in italics.

About TEXERE

Texere, a progressive and authoritative voice in business publishing, brings to the global business community the expertise and insights of leading thinkers. Our books educate, enlighten, and entertain, and provide an intersection where our authors and our readers share cutting edge ideas, practices, and innovative solutions. Texere seeks to cultivate, enhance, and disseminate information that illuminates the global business landscape.

www.thomson.com/learning/texere

About the typeface

This book was set in 10.5/15pt Sabon.